# Medieval Sieges & Siegecraft

# Medieval Sieges & Siegecraft

**Geoffrey Hindley**

SKYHORSE PUBLISHING

Skyhorse Publishing books may be purchased in bulk at special discounts for sales promotion, corporate gifts, fund-raising, or educational purposes. Special editions can also be created to specifications. For details, contact the Special Sales Department, Skyhorse Publishing, 555 Eighth Avenue, Suite 903, New York, NY 10018 or info@skyhorsepublishing.com.

www.skyhorsepublishing.com

10 9 8 7 6 5 4 3 2 1

Library of Congress Cataloging-in-Publication Data

Hindley, Geoffrey.
Medieval sieges and siegecraft / Geoffrey Hindley.
p. cm.
Originally published: Barnsley : Pen & Sword Military, 2009.
ISBN 978-1-60239-633-3
1. Siege warfare--Europe--History--To 1500. 2. Sieges--Europe--History--To 1500.
3. Military art and science--History--Medieval, 500-1500. 4. Fortification--Europe--History--To 1500. 5. Castles--Europe--History--To 1500. 6. Europe--History, Military. I. Title.
UG444.H56 2009
355.4'40940902--dc22
2009008554

Printed in the United States of America

# Contents

# Acknowledgments

The various narrative accounts of sieges which make up the bulk of the text have been drawn largely from the books on my shelves, with the occasional visit to the Cambridge University Library, whose staff, as always, I would like to thank for their helpfulness. I would also like to thank here my editor, Rupert Harding of Pen & Sword Books, and my copy-editor, Elizabeth Stone, for their useful comments and encouragement. My special thanks are due to Mr. Gordon Monaghan for the line drawings credited to him in the captions.

Many authors and their works are acknowledged in the text, while details of publication will be found in the bibliography. I thought it might also be useful to bring together, chapter by chapter, some of the principal sources that contributed to the story: these will be found at the end of the text, in the Notes on the Sources.

# List of Plates

# Introduction

## Siegecraft: The Basis of Medieval Warfare

*"A siege being one of the most arduous undertakings in which an army may be employed—one in which the greatest fatigue, hardship and personal risk are encountered, and in which the prize can only be won by complete victory—it is obvious that upon the success or failure of such an enterprise may depend the fate of a campaign or of an army and perhaps the existence of a state."*
*Encyclopedia Britannica*, 9th edition (1879)

For anyone interested in the history of war and armed conflict, the concept and practice of siege warfare might be expected to be a topic of special interest. The quotation above would seem to justify the assertion. Nevertheless, that nineteenth-century edition of the famous work of reference did not have a separate headword for "siege"; instead, the topic was treated in the main article on "fortification"—and that article, extending over some fifty double format pages with a wealth of diagrams and engravings, has nothing to say about the subject of this book, medieval siege warfare. The co-authors of the article, both senior officers in the British Army, were clearly practical men for whom medieval operations would probably seem irrelevant as a subject of highly topical interest. In their experience, the siege was still an integral part of warfare and the mathematical principles of fortifications and land defenses of all kinds an essential part of the professional military commander's repertoire of expertise. But today, compared with the libraries of books devoted to battlefield engagements, grand strategy or tactical maneuvers, the siege as a theme of specialized interest seems to be comparatively underwritten. Perhaps this is because it is now felt to be not only long out of date, but also lacking the excitements of warfare, let us say, of the Napoleonic era or the civil war periods in England or the United States.

It is certainly true that, before siege practice was transformed by the geometrical precision of fortification building achieved by Louis XIV's great military engineer, Sébastien Le Prestre de Vauban (d. 1707)—more or less the starting point for the generals' discussion of fortification in the *Encyclopaedia Britannica* article—and the systematized theories that Vauban designed for attacking them, the world of siege warfare can seem somewhat "medieval" in the derogatory sense of the word. But if we turn to the military theory presently preferred by the strategists of the world's hyper-power, what do we find? We find a gargantuan defensive strategy known as "Star Wars," futuristic in nomenclature but conceptually grounded in an essentially medieval siege mentality. The range of the weaponry and scope of the fortifications would be beyond the imagination of a medieval commander; yet the thinking would not, based as it is on a defensive mind-set quite familiar to him.

It is true, of course, that siege operations are essentially static, and hence can be thought to be less exciting than other forms of warfare—after all, the very word comes, via the French, from the same root as the Latin *sedere*, "to sit down." But then, Book I of the fifteenth-century prose masterpiece of the Arthurian cycle, *Le Morte d'Arthur*, opens with a siege with which Arthur's father, King Uther Pendragon, "wonderly wroth," vows to "fetch" the Duke of Cornwall "out of the biggest castle that he hath." He warned the duke "to stuff him and garnish him" (i.e., according to the rather prosaic footnote in my edition of the book, to "provision himself against a siege") and then "in all haste [went] with a great host, and laid a siege about the Castle Terrabil . . . [where] he pitched many pavilions."

In fact, the duke had cunningly lodged his wife, Igraine (the real objective of Uther's expedition) in the castle of Tintagel. It did him no good. Helped by Merlin, Pendragon heads for Tintagel, and the duke, seeing their drift, "issued out at a postern [gate] for to have distressed the king's host." He was slain in the "medley" (i.e., a mêlée): three hours later (the time delay is critical to what follows) Pendragon, magicked by Merlin into the form of the duke, lay with Igraine and "begat Arthur upon her." Fortunately, her husband being dead (though only just) it could be claimed that Arthur was not really a bastard.

There is no space to pursue the story further here, but it will be clear that a siege did not have to be a boring affair; and it is worth taking note of those "pavilions." The encampment of many a medieval siege was enriched with the banners and elaborate "tentage" of the great men of the army and their entourages, and many a time they would arrange jousting matches to pass the time while the experts, artillery men and sappers, worked to open a breach for the fighting men to assault. Often, too, participants would present themselves as members of Arthur's legendary Round Table. In passing, one notes that, paradoxically, the most dramatic and hazardous place at that Round Table was the "siege perilous," the seat of danger. The knight who occupied it was committed to the quest to find and bring back the Holy Grail. He who took that seat and failed in that most adventurous of destinies was fated to die. In any case, as will appear from the chapters that follow, the muddy and bloody business of siege history offers many instances of dramatic encounters and heroic deeds.

One of the great practitioners of the "art" (if such it may be called) Charles the Bold, Count of Charolais and Duke of Burgundy, seemed never happier than when directing or fighting this type of warfare. Richard Vaughan, the duke's most distinguished twentieth-century biographer, notes that Charles loved camp life and campaigning, spending up to fourteen hours at a stretch in full armor riding the siege lines to check his troops' readiness or his own gun placements or working on other such details at his campaign table. Johanne Pietro Panigarola, the Milanese ambassador to the court of Burgundy, recalled how, once when on mission, he had to follow the duke and his courtiers to the west bank of the Rhine opposite Düsseldorf, where Charles was "in his siege" before the walls of the city of Neuss, and make his presentation in the duke's pavilion even "as [Duke Charles] armed himself from the head to the feet laughing and joking with me the while."

In what follows I have not attempted a chronological survey of the material. It would hardly be possible because many of the techniques and weapons date back to early times, and where evolutionary developments do occur—as in castle design or artillery—they do not march, so to speak, in step. Instead, I have dealt with what I see as the essential elements of the subject in successive chapters, first treating fortification and its practitioners, then weaponry, then methods of attack and defense, followed by the chapter on logistics and how they are brought into play, and finally a group of chapters on the conventions and realities of the practice of this type of military engagement. But first, here are some comments as to the central position of the siege in medieval warfare and hence in the world of the international and national politics of the period.

## Warfare in a political context

Chapter 1 argues that siege warfare was a specialized type of conflict that originated in city culture; here I aim to show that, for most of the period we call the Middle Ages, in Europe it was the defining activity of warfare between rival power centers aiming at expansion and conquest—what at a later period we would term inter-state rivalry. But between those two stages, when territorial princes were aiming to assert their supremacy within their own territories as they saw them, siege was deployed as a tool of punitive action often against the much smaller but also concentrated and wealthy power centers of commercial as opposed to territorial power, the towns.

In the early twelfth century, Europe's dominant polity was what we commonly call the Holy Roman Empire, which comprised the German-speaking lands of the continent and was subject to monarchs who claimed to derive universal authority from the long defunct Roman Empire. As such, they asserted authority in Italy and above all in the commercial power center of Western Europe at that time, the merchant cities of the north Italian plain of the Po valley. Chief among these was Milan.

We have just left the city's ambassador on active service, in conference with the Duke of Burgundy in the 1470s. But Milan, a giant among its neighbors, had been a major power in northern Italian politics three centuries before and was not submissive before the emperors from beyond the Alps. She bullied those neighbors, her trading rivals, and expected submission from them, in the last resort destroying them in the most literal sense. In 1158, for example, the town of Lodi was razed to the ground. In that year, too, Emperor Frederick I, known to the Italians at the time and to history as Barbarossa ("Red Beard"), prepared to descend into Lombardy to demonstrate and make good his imperial claims. He ordered Milan to desist from her attacks on her neighbor and to make voluntary submission to his imperial authority. Instead, she demurred and sent ambassadors to the emperor, also, with his court, on active service at his army base near Lake Garda. With the assent of the German princes of the empire and the approval of several anti-Milanese cities, Frederick put the city "to the ban of the empire." It was a proclamation that Milan was at the mercy of imperial discipline, effectively an imposition of outlawry.

The city authorities took fright. They destroyed bridges carrying roads into their territory. They sent a second deputation to beg terms. It was refused. On the last day of July, Frederick and his army were encamped on the River Lambro, very near the place where Lodi had recently stood. Its citizens, now refugees, petitioned the emperor for redress against their enemy and permission to rebuild their town. This was readily granted. Frederick himself showed lively interest in the rebuilding plans; it seems clear he intended to site an imperial citadel there.

On August 6 the imperial force was seen approaching Milan and deploying to encircle the place. That afternoon a sortie from the garrison fell on the main body of the enemy making camp between the Porta Orientale and the Porta Nuova near the monastery of San Dionisio. There was heavy fighting, but the sortie re-entered the city without making serious impact on the situation. In fact, this first siege of Milan ended with the city coming to terms and accepting the overlordship of the emperor in exchange for clemency. But anti-imperial elements soon overturned the settlement, and in April 1159 the city was again in rebellion. This time the ban proclaimed against it at Bologna decreed that its property all be looted and its citizens sold into slavery. (The existence of slavery in Christian Europe is a study in itself.)

As a prelude to the second siege of Milan, the imperial army laid waste the lands surrounding the city in more than a month of systematic destruction. At the same time Milan's ally, the small town of Crema, was forced to submit, in January 1160, after a five-month siege in which technological ingenuity was outdone only by extreme cruelty. Confronted by wheeled siege-towers that could be moved at will against selected sections of the walls, the defenders devised an ingenious rolling bridged platform that could be maneuvered back and forth along the wall to "capture" the approaching machine. To protect the apparatus from attack by stone-throwing artillery, Frederick ordered that Cremese prisoners be suspended from its beams to deter their fellow citizens— at night the unfortunates were illuminated with giant candles. Many were in fact killed by "friendly fire" from their fellow citizens, who hardened their hearts rather than allow the enemy war machine to do its work. This brings to mind the scene in the classic British war film *The Cruel Sea* where the captain of the destroyer, played by Jack Hawkins, orders the engine-room full steam ahead, although this means certain death to British sailors in the water, rather than miss the chance of destroying the German U-boat that had sunk their ship.

Once Crema had capitulated, Frederick turned his attention to Milan. Through the summer and autumn the city held out, and when winter came the army fell back to prepared defensive positions from which it harassed the convoys struggling to bring in supplies. With the return of spring, the pattern was repeated—unable to force the place by assault, the imperialists tightened their stranglehold. Early in 1162, the strategy at last yielded results. The city prepared for a humiliating gesture of submission.

On March 1, the consuls of Milan came before the emperor, enthroned at his court in the rebuilt town of Lodi, whose destruction their council had ordered only a few years earlier, their naked swords hung about their necks. They prostrated themselves, confessed to high treason against the empire, made unconditional surrender and pledged themselves to obedience to the imperial will. Three days later, 300 of the city's knights followed the same ritual, prostrating themselves and begging mercy; in addition the *gonfalonieri* (flag bearers) surrendered the ceremonial banners of the city sections. There was one more ceremony of abasement extorted from the hapless city: on March 6 it surrendered its *caroccio*, or war wagon.

Every commune had such a vehicle, a talisman or mascot in time of war and a rallying point on the battlefield; it was bulky enough even to afford some protection for troops regrouping. From it rose a ship's mast topped by a cross and carrying the city's flag or emblem, in Milan's case a banner bearing the image of Ambrose, the patron saint. It was brought to the emperor by an escort of 1,000 foot-soldiers carrying crosses as symbols of petition. Two trumpeters sounded the call that customarily accompanied the proclamation of a city ordinance and then surrendered their trumpets. The mast was unstepped and the emperor himself detached the banner. The soldiers fell to their knees, imploring mercy. They and the city deputations were ordered to return the next day to hear their fate. Rainald von Dassel, now Archbishop of Cologne, close councilor to Frederick and sworn enemy of Milan, had already made it clear that their surrender was unconditional. As the Milanese cleared the field their way lay by the lodgings of the empress—they threw their crosses down as they passed, as if to petition her sympathy.

It was to no avail. In his biography of the emperor, on which this account of the siege is based, Peter Munz argued that Frederick intended mercy, but, on March 13, 1162, at a council of delegates from the Italian cities that had remained loyal to the imperial cause and were sworn enemies of Milan, he changed his mind. On March 19 the population was ordered to leave and the following day the place was handed over to demolition on the emperor's order. The work was divided between Milan's jubilant neighbors—each town being allocated its own zone of destruction. Everything, even churches, fell to the ram and the maul. Imperial officials (and on one occasion the emperor himself) had to intervene to save the sacred relics in the city's churches. The most treasured, the bones of the Three Magi who came from the East at Christ's birth, were assigned to Archbishop Rainald, who bore them in triumph back to Cologne. A maverick and ruthless figure, who, according to gossip, boasted himself "the ruin of the world," Rainald had urged the case of Milan's enemies. Thanks to him, as well as them, Frederick celebrated Palm Sunday that year amidst the ruins of the city of St. Ambrose.

Frederick was to lead other expeditions against the cities of Lombardy, but, thanks to the Lombard League under a resurgent Milan, was ultimately to be frustrated.

This summary has touched on various aspects to be developed in the following chapters. Among these are high politics; calculating strategy; technological expertise; and the formalities of challenge and submission. But above all is the fact that, despite the sometimes dire consequences for failure and despite the mobilization of often huge resources, a siege was a conflict where, unlike the hazards of battlefield encounters, the outcome was felt to be open to reasonable calculation.

### Battles are risky things: Bouvines, 1214

On Sunday, July 27, 1214, two great armies clashed on the marshy plains in French Flanders at Bouvines near Tournai. It was an epic engagement. The two armies were numerous and well equipped. On the one side were Otto of Brunswick, who styled himself Emperor Otto IV, and his imperial allies; on the other King Philip Augustus II of France, a statesman of stature, a wily politician and a capable if not brilliant military tactician though an essentially timorous man on the battlefield. He was definitely not in the heroic warrior mold, but he was a man of strong will and capable of the bold decision. Battle on that day could not be avoided, even though it was a Sunday and the religious conventions forbade fighting on the Lord's Day. The imperial forces had launched an assault weeks in the planning; away to the south-west, in Poitou, the army of King John of England, the second arm of a pincer movement designed to crush the royal French army, had suffered a major setback. King Philip had to face the odds. He ended the day with a crushing victory.

One of the decisive battles of European history, Bouvines ended the imperial ambitions of Otto and finally put to rest the pretensions of John of England whose Angevin Norman lands had divided monarchical rule in France for some fifty years. There was a long way to go before the last vestiges of the English lordship in France would be expelled, but the fight on that summer Sunday in 1214 secured beyond question the historic destiny of the French monarchy. The news was celebrated throughout the lands admitting allegiance to the French king, and the students at the university of Paris on the left bank of the Seine kept up the celebrations, "singing, leaping and dancing," for seven days.

### A siege easier to calculate: Pons, 1177

This was the first major battle the kings of France had fought in a century. Given the stakes involved, such set pieces were very much the exception in medieval Europe. Warfare was endemic but the classic mode was the *chevauchée*, the protracted campaign of raid and pillage, calculated to intimidate the population of the enemy, waste his resources and force him to sue for peace on one's own terms. In this type of warfare the decisive encounter came not on the battlefield but in the lines of encampment surrounding town or castle under siege. A successful siege, then, could deliver dramatic rewards, economically as well as militarily. A successful siege commander was considered a serious master in battlefield skills.

Before he became king of England, 21-year-old Richard, Count of Poitou and son of King Henry II, "formed" the siege of Pons held by a recalcitrant Poitevin vassal, Geoffrey de Rancogne. For the next three months he lay before the town. Enemies sneered that he would give up out of boredom or that his freelance mercenaries, his "routiers," would desert because of the arrears in their pay. However, thanks to a charisma that could inspire loyalty even in mercenaries—and thanks also to ruthless taxation in his lands of Poitou, which kept the arrears to a minimum—Richard was able to keep them in line, while his knights "did their [feudal] duty" because of his example. Even so, Pons held out.

Richard accordingly moved his army against the supposedly impregnable Taillebourg. The castle was built on a steep rock above a deep ravine, so that the siege-engines could not be brought to close quarters. Richard set his men to fill the ravine, and within three weeks his siege-towers were engaged with the wall.

The castle surrendered, and with it the leaders of the revolt. The town of Pons submitted. Richard had simultaneously demonstrated his technical skills as a soldier and won his reputation as a commander—at the time, it was more important to be skillful at taking castles than to be a dashing leader of cavalry. Richard had seen at a glance that, despite its apparent impregnability, the castle could be taken by just one method, a method just within his power. He had the force of character to keep his men hard at work day and night. A young prince who could bring an "impregnable" fortress to submission was a soldier to be reckoned with, while a prince who could lead a dashing charge did no more than was expected of a young knight and still had to prove himself in the political arena. Nevertheless, Richard the Lionheart was no slouch when it came to leading a charge.

### Castles and counter-castles: Parma, 1247–8

So, apart from murderous peripatetic mayhem for profit such as the *chevauchée*, siege warfare was the dominant military activity of the medieval period. Castles mattered. Often a campaign hinged on them. In his raid against the England of Henry II in the autumn of 1173, King William the Lion of Scotland came down by way of the border town of Berwick-upon-Tweed and invested first Wark, then Alnwick, then Warkworth castles. In each case, as soon as the castellan defied his summons to surrender, the Scot moved on in search of easier prey. Under King Henry, the castles that studded the English border with Scotland were always in good repair and well provisioned in time of peace so as to be effective in time of war.

The main objective of any sustained campaign was to deprive the opponent of his fortified positions, usually castles, sometimes walled towns, and so win control of the countryside. It is hard to think of a case in which the principle was more fully demonstrated in practice than in the siege that Emperor Frederick II of the house of Hohenstauffen, heir to the Italian policies of his grandfather Barbarossa, laid to the city of Parma in the Po valley in 1247. Crowned emperor by the pope twenty-seven years before, Frederick was soon at odds with the pontiff and spent much of his reign aiming to consolidate his unified rule of the German lands of the empire with the territories it claimed in Italy. By the 1240s the focus of the policy was his campaign against the papal power and the cities of the Lombard plain, led as always by Milan. At the siege of Parma, he proclaimed his grandiose titles to lordship by building an astonishing counter-castle which was in effect a city in itself.

The principle of a counter-fortress was not new. Within six weeks of their arrival before the intimidating walls of Antioch (Antakya, in modern Turkey) in the autumn of 1097, the crusading army had constructed a barbican tower or counter-castle, giving it the name Malregard, to obstruct the Turkish raiding parties' attacks on their camp. By giving the besiegers as firm and defensible a camp as the besieged it was intended to secure them against concerted sallies by the garrison and to provide a base for operations over months, possibly a year or more. In March the following year, thanks to the arrival of an English fleet in Antioch's port of St. Symeon with supplies, they were able to build a counter-fort opposite the city's Bridge Gate to block forays from the garrison. A month later they were able to establish another such containing fort in a fortified monastery opposite Antioch's Gate of St. George. All these were workmanlike examples of the counter-fortress principle, unpretentious but effective.

Frederick's base or siege city with which he confronted the citizens of Parma was, by contrast, a startling statement of imperial propaganda to which he gave the name "Victoria." Oriented according to directives from the court astrologers (procedures reminiscent of modern Chinese practice) it was planned to cover an area about 4,000 square meters. It rose rapidly to accommodate the royal chancery and courts of law; Frederick's notorious imperial harem; his menagerie of exotic animals from elephants to dromedaries; and the mews, to house his goshawks and gerfalcons. Foundations were planned for a cathedral in honor of St. Victor, and outside the walls mansions and villas, vineyards and orchards were laid out. Contemporary accounts suggest that many of these structures were actually built. The place had a thriving population in addition to the imperial court with all its hangers-on. Even though many of the buildings would have been of timber-frame construction, this was siege warfare on a truly imperial scale. But the day-to-day life of a court had to go on, which of course, in Frederick's case, meant the pursuit of the hunt and his passion for hawking and falconry. Early in 1248, leaving the Margrave of Lancia in command, Frederick left his new city of Victoria for a day at the chase.

A sortie by the garrison at Parma, clearly well informed about enemy intentions, lured the margrave and his forces into a pursuit so that a second body of troops from the city, accompanied by a throng of citizens with their wives and families, sallied out against the ill-guarded siege city bent on vengeance on the rival at their gates. The emperor returned at the end of that disastrous day to find his "Victoria" in flames from end to end, its streets littered with corpses and treasures of every kind looted. Vestments for his new cathedral clergy, the imperial crown, and an exquisite manuscript of his famous treatise on falconry were among the losses. Writing to officials in Palermo, Frederick admitted that the royal seal itself was missing, "destroyed in the burning of the camp."

The extended account of this catastrophe is recorded by a native of Parma, so there may be exaggerations. A few days later, having regrouped his scattered forces, Frederick returned, perhaps to renew the siege. But following a council of war, he abandoned the project. The people of Parma had delivered a severe setback to his policy. In far-away England, the monastic historian Matthew Paris heard that the emperor "groaned openly as if deeply wounded."

### Decisive moments

The chroniclers of the medieval period record many grand sieges, though few as elaborate as the siege described above, in which the prestige of the participants was as important as any military objective in prospect. Time and again an immense army was concentrated to besiege some fortress or walled city even though, as the twentieth-century military analyst Alfred Burne observed, "only a limited number of troops could play an effective part in the siege of a town." For him, such overkill, as we might term it, breached the principle of "economy of force"—a principle that evidently played little part in the plans of the emperor Frederick before Parma.

It was his mastery of siegecraft that enabled that more pragmatic monarch, Henry II Plantagenet, King of England and lord of large parts of France, to remain master of his vast domains. In 1161, for example, he took the stronghold of Castillon in Gascony in a matter of days and thoroughly intimidated the local lords so that they dared not take the field against him.

A master of siegecraft had to be able to tell, merely by riding around outside the walls of a hostile fortress, whether he could capture it, and, if so, whether the expense of the siege would be worthwhile. In the normal run of things several hostile castles would bar his campaign, and he could attack only one at a time. The defender, by contrast, had to be able to judge to a nicety how long the castle he commanded could hold out against any form of attack, so as to arrange his surrender on terms after the longest possible delay.

The Battle of Hastings and Saladin's victory at Hattin (1187) were, beyond question, key events which (not to labor the metaphor) unlocked developments that can be said to have redirected the course of history in those regions. But there is equally little doubt that the crusaders' capture of the city of Antioch was as decisive in securing victory in their campaign for Jerusalem as even their brilliant set-piece victory against the odds at Dorylaeum the year before when, in July 1097, they crushed the Turkish army bent on their destruction; while the French capture of Château Gaillard (1204) was epoch-making in a way that even Agincourt could not match. And, in any case, both Hastings and Hattin, being engagements determined by the defense and capture of a hilltop, though both completed within the day and fought in open terrain, displayed the characteristic feature of the siege, the defense of a strong point. And even at Dorylaeum the action was more in the nature of a siege defense than a battle of maneuver: the crusading army, stranded in open desert terrain rather than defending a strong prepared position, it is true, survived only by holding out over a daylong remorseless attack from the Turkish army, rather than by counterattack. Indeed, it seems that the army's commanders, having been alerted to the enemy's presence in the vicinity by their vanguard scouting on ahead, had deliberately taken up something approaching a siege position by pitching camp on a site protected on one flank by marshy ground.

### A miracle morale boost: Antioch, 1098

Siege warfare could be a complex and subtle business or it might be a hard steady slog demanding little more than endurance. Either way, in all but a small minority of cases, the morale of the participants, attackers as much as defenders, would be a determining factor. To return to the First Crusade, we find a dramatic instance of boosted morale for a besieging army, outside the walls of Antioch's citadel in the summer of 1098 but within the walls of the city itself. In June the army had won a great triumph with the capture of the city, but during the slaughter and sack that followed the Turkish defenders had withdrawn into the citadel to hold out in the expectation that a Muslim relief force, already on the march, would come to their aid. As a consequence the crusaders, well aware that a substantial Turkish army was indeed on the march, and war-weary after their fatiguing route march from Europe and across Anatolia, were desperate to complete the job and take the citadel. Otherwise, they would find themselves withstanding attack on two fronts. But there were divisions within the army.

Thus, when the Turkish relieving army did appear before the walls of the now Christian city, while they saw it was too late to save the place, there seemed every likelihood that they might recover it for Islam from an exhausted and depleted enemy. With the citadel garrison still in place and the bulk of the local population hostile to the invading foreign army, the Christians, thousands of miles from home, and in the torrid conditions of a Levantine summer, were in a death trap. Many deserted, many others looked about them for a chance to escape. Hope seemed to have died; God seemed to have abandoned his faithful; there were rumors that the great men were thinking of seeking terms; the will to fight was failing fast. Then a miracle occurred.

A peasant foot-soldier, Peter Bartholomew, came to the leaders with a story that St. Andrew had come to him in a dream and revealed where one of Christendom's holiest talismans was to be found. The Holy Lance, the spear that had been used by a Roman soldier at the Crucifixion to pierce the side of Christ would be found if men dug where he directed in the floor of the old cathedral in Antioch. The next day excavation was duly made and a spear was certainly found. Even at the time there were cynics who marveled at the opportune nature of the "miracle," but they were overruled. A few days later, with "the Holy Lance" leading them into battle, the crusaders won a resounding victory over the Turkish forces on the plains about the town. These retired, the siege was lifted, and the garrison in Antioch's castle surrendered. The crusaders would continue on their way to Jerusalem, which was to be captured after one of the most notorious sieges in history.

The sack and slaughter at Jerusalem lives in the history of shame for the peoples of western Christendom. Chapter 12 shows how such horrors were all too common and that in the Middle Ages, as today, total war produced scenes of brutality and suffering against civilians as well as the military. Worse even than the atrocities is perhaps the fact that under certain conditions they were actually sanctioned by the emerging conventions as to what we may call the laws of war. In his classic work, *The Laws of War in the Late Middle Ages*, Maurice Keen showed how in the case of the siege these became specialized, even technical in their nature. Chapter 11 explores the matter more fully, but here, at the outset, one should stress that even from the early 1100s, there were formalities governing siege warfare.

### Room for improvement: Rochester, 1215

There were good reasons. The art and technology of defending fortified sites was under constant improvement throughout the medieval period. When King John of England laid siege to the old Norman castle at Rochester in October 1215, held against him by William d'Albini, Lord of Belvoir and one of the ablest commanders in the dissident baronial party that had humiliated the king by forcing the cession of Magna Carta at Runnymede in the summer of that year, the great square corner towers and forbidding curtain walls must have seemed a challenge that could thwart his entire campaign against the rebel forces.

Until just weeks before, the castle had been under the authority of Stephen Langton, Archbishop of Canterbury and theoretically the first minister of the king. But Langton himself had been implicated with the rebels at Runnymede and his lieutenant handed over the fortress to Robert Fitzwalter, self-styled commander of the "Army of God." Rochester secured, Fitzwalter retired back to London, leaving d'Albini with a garrison of 140 well-armed and determined knights and men-at-arms to defy the king.

But John, when roused to anger, was not to be withstood. He put all the ironsmiths of Canterbury to work night and day, forging equipment and armaments. For seven weeks the castle resisted in a siege more hard fought on both sides than any in living memory. Stone-throwers and battering-rams made no headway. The king decided to send in a team of specialist miners and sappers. Driving their mine under the corner of the south-east towers, they brought down large sections of the two adjacent walls and so opened the place to irresistible assault. Though John died with his civil war still to win, his son's advisers secured the royalist cause. Rochester remained a royal castle, but the ruined tower was rebuilt with a circular section much less vulnerable to attack by mining.

Such improvements in castle design, together with innovations in defensive equipment and the fact that the massive thickness of fortifications always presented forbidding challenges to the attacker, meant that immense time, effort and expense were required to capture a well-defended, well-provisioned fortress or fortified town. It was much better if the place could be induced to surrender; and here intimidation rather than suasion was generally brought to bear. Hence the laws governing siege warfare were noted for their "unusual and savage severity."

### The formalities of plunder

In the case of a town that also had a castle within the walls, two groups of defenders came into the equation—the garrison, with their loyalties to king or feudal lord and a commander swayed by military considerations; and the citizens with loyalties divided between king and lord, but also to their families' well-being and their own personal wealth and business interests. In the latter case, a siege went through three phases: first, the occupation of the suburbs, that is, the settlements outside the walls; secondly, the capture of the town proper; thirdly, the capture of the castle or citadel.

The conventions and laws of siege warfare recognized two ways by which a fortified place, whether town or castle, could be taken: by assault, through battery or escalade; or by treaty, that is, using the French terms, *agrément* or *appointement*. We shall see that different legal problems were presented by each type of capture, and the consequences for soldiery or citizenry differed also. Sometimes it happened that the two types of capture were cited in the same siege, or in the legal settlements that could follow the campaign. Following the capture of the French town of Carentan, it was claimed that the suburbs had fallen to assault but that town itself had surrendered by treaty. If the point was accepted, then goods looted in the suburbs were legitimate booty, while anything seized in the town should in theory be returned to the owners.

Since soldiers considered plunder part of their pay package this was something more than a technicality. Pope Pius II (d. 1464) in his fulminations against his arch enemy, that "prince of all wickedness," Sigismondo Malatesta, Lord of Rimini and mercenary commander, charged not only that "he violated his daughters and his sons-in-law (*sic*)" but also that "a slave to avarice . . . he was ready not only to plunder but to steal." Theft was a clear breach of the law, but plunder was something a citizen might have to put up with. Even so, the losses incurred as a result of siege, and the impact of looting on a citizen's prosperity and personal standing, at a time when "worthship," the respect considered owing to a merchant or guildsman, depended as much on physical wealth as on rank in the town hierarchy, was serious. The space devoted to scenes of pillage as such in contemporary manuscript illustrations makes the point graphically. They were scenes of a kind that had surely been repeated many thousand times since the beginning of history.

## CHAPTER ONE

# Fortified Towns and Cities

*"Happy is that city which in time of peace thinks of war."*
Robert Burton (d.1640), citing an inscription in the Arsenal, Venice

From Jericho to Troy, medieval Europe knew a tradition of siege warfare as part of its antiquity. In fact, the siege, a static conflict to capture a strong point, was a type of combat made possible only by the rise of city culture. According to the words of the spiritual, "When Joshua fit the Battle of Jericho . . . the walls came a tumbling down." The biblical text records that the walls collapsed at the sound of the war trumpets of the Hebrew army. This must have been about the easiest victory in the history of siege warfare—and also one of the first.

Naturally, the hand of God played its part in the fall of Jericho. Divine intervention has often been invoked by the religious or the resigned to account for the course of events in war. As he handed over the Alhambra to its Christian victors in January 1492, Abu Abdullah ("Boabdil"), last king of Granada, is said to have recognized the hand of Allah in his disaster and to have acknowledged the sins of the Muslims as the cause of the deity's anger. When, in June 774, Charles the Great, king of the Franks (in French Charlemagne, in German Karl der Grosse) took the city of Pavia, capital of the Lombard kingdom of north Italy, and so laid the foundation for his later claim to empire, it cost his army the rigors of an eight-month siege. In the next century, pious clerics attributed the conquest to a miraculous five-day campaign in which not a drop of blood was shed and during which the Frankish army "built a basilica in which they might render service to almighty God outside the walls if they might not do so within." Indeed, within twelve hours they erected a church complete with ceilings to its roofs and religious painting for its walls of such dimensions that all who saw it vowed it could not have been built in less than twelve months. Confronted with this marvel "that party among the citizens which had favored surrender prevailed." But outside the world of legend or the pages of holy books, siege warfare was a grinding business as old as city culture itself.

The exact dates of Joshua, indeed his very existence, are uncertain, but after excavations in the 1950s led by the British archaeologist Kathleen Kenyon, it seems that Jericho is one of the world's most ancient cities, and is to be associated with the beginnings of the agricultural revolution dated to about the seventh millennium BC. That revolution, which meant the creation and amassing of food surpluses, provided the conditions for the birth of city culture with the storage facilities to secure those surpluses; the administrative personnel to administer those surpluses; and the need for a warrior class to defend them—in short the groundwork for city-based culture or "civilization" (from the Latin word *civis*, "a citizen"). Thus siege warfare, the assault on and the defense of those surpluses, can indeed be seen as the earliest form of organized warfare—as distinct from the raiding-party rivalries of hunter-gatherer tribes.

### Troy VIIa: c. 1250 BC

Homeric legend holds that the war against Troy, which scholarly opinion has placed some time about the year 1250 BC (i.e., the era of Troy VIIa), was the next most famous siege after Jericho. According to Homer, this siege lasted ten years. Archaeology has shown that over millennia the site associated with Troy, in north-western Turkish Anatolia, a few miles inland from the Dardanelles strait, was occupied by a number of cities and subject to more than one siege. The place was a stronghold on a trade route running along the northern coast of Anatolia from Asia to the Dardanelles and crossing into Europe. It was prosperous and powerful and presumably levied tolls on the shipping through the straits, such as Greek merchants plying to ports in the Black Sea.

The siege was prompted when Prince Paris of Troy abducted Helen, wife of King Menelaus of Sparta. He appealed to the other Greek rulers; they joined forces to avenge him and force Troy to return Helen, reputed the most beautiful woman in the world. It is a good story, and anthropologists expert in early cultures suggest that women were often "trophy-traded."

Whether or not it lasted ten years, the siege would, in the nature of things, have lasted a long time. At the start of the conflict, at least, the Greeks had no siege-engines, while the Trojans' battlements were virtually impregnable. The Greeks made a camp on the shore, and it was sometimes besieged by the Trojans. For a long time Achilles, one of the chief leaders in the Greek army, refused to fight because he claimed he had been insulted in the division of the spoil in a successful raid. Many times it seemed that the Greeks would never take the city. In fact, according to Homer, they did so only by deception.

The new cities—rich and above all comparatively well-fed, filled with houses, palaces and temples, crammed with luxury garments and precious objects, and packed with people ripe for enslavement—made mouth-watering targets. But if they were well worth attacking, they were also well provided with defenses. Lightly clad tribesmen and even armored soldiery learnt that success against such objectives called for new ways of fighting, the development of specialized equipment and weaponry, and tactical thinking that developed over time. Unlike the average field battle, a siege did not observe the Aristotelian dramatic unity of time in which the action of a play should ideally be confined to the hours between sunrise and sunset. It was a conflict of weeks, months or even years' duration. Psychological warfare, even simple deception, could be decisive tools to undermine the morale of the garrison or to unbalance the calculations of the commander.

All the world knows that Troy fell to a trick. The Greeks were notorious in the ancient world for their trickery. In his great poem about Prince Aeneas of Troy, the *Aeneid*, the Roman poet Virgil had one of his characters say, "*timeo Danaos et dona ferentis*," "I fear the Greeks [the "Danaians"] even when they come bearing gifts." In the tenth year of the siege, advised by the wily Odysseus (Ulysses), King Agamemnon ordered the building of a massive wooden horse to be left on the plain outside the walls of Troy as if as an offering to the gods. Then the Greek army drew back as if abandoning the siege. The Trojans pulled the wooden monster into the city in triumph. But inside its belly was a detachment of Greek soldiers. That night the soldiers slipped out and opened the city gates to their army which had come back under cover of darkness. Troy was taken utterly by surprise and destroyed, its buildings put to the torch and its citizens put to the sword. The fortunate ones were sent to the slave markets and some may even have made good their escape. One such, Prince Aeneas, voyaged to Italy, where he founded Lavinium, forerunner to Rome. The siege of Troy was clearly an event of world historical importance—at least in Roman legend.

Fire and sword were to be expected by a city that failed in its defense. In exceptional circumstances death might not follow. A Russian visitor to Constantinople, "the second Rome," during the civil turmoil that accompanied the dying decades of the Byzantine Empire witnessed the night-time breach of the city in 1390 by partisans of the line of Emperor Andronikos IV and his son John VII. The streets and squares were in uproar as foot-soldiers and horsemen dashed to and fro, lanterns aloft, among terrified citizenry crowding out on to the streets "in their nightclothes." Brandishing weapons and with arrows notched on bow strings, the soldiery shouted "Long live Andronikos!" and the people—men women and even the children—shouted in response, "Long live Andronikos!" since any who held back even for an instant were threatened with death. In fact, the Russian witness, Ignatius of Smolensk, saw "none slain anywhere, such was the fear inspired by the weapons."

Academic opinion has long accepted that Homer's epic *The Iliad* is a poetic retelling of actual historic episodes. Even so, the story of the Trojan horse seems rather far-fetched: did the Trojans really accept the Greek story that it was a gift to the goddess Athena that would make their city impregnable if they took it in? But perhaps the legend represents a poetic memory of an actual structure: not a model horse but a mobile siege-tower, of the kind known in Assyrian warfare. The Roman army used siege-towers, massive wooden structures on wheels, with ladders inside for the attacking force to climb to bring it to a platform level with the wall of the fortress or city.

Homer had only legends to work with, and the ancient Greeks had some strange legends. When they first encountered tribes that fought on horseback they were so astonished that they are said to have thought they had found a monster, half-man, half-horse—hence the legend of the centaurs. May be the Greek machine at Troy was just a primitive siege-tower dubbed "the horse" by Greek soldiers.

### Heroism of the populace

Just as Troy, site of the most famous siege of ancient history, was on the southern coast of the Sea of Marmara in modern Turkey, so the most famous siege of medieval history was that of Constantinople in 1453 at the other end of that sea. Inaugurated in 330 by Emperor Constantine the Great on the site of the ancient Greek port of Byzantion, it occupied a rough triangle of territory between the Sea of Marmara to the south and the great natural harbor of the sea inlet known as the Golden Horn to the north. It was protected by some fourteen miles of fortifications. Walls ran for five and half miles along the coast, in places rising direct from the shore line and protected by rapid, treacherous currents that made any attack hazardous in the extreme. Another three and a half lines of wall rose behind the docks and warehouses of the waterfront of the Golden Horn. The entrance to the great harbor was guarded at the time of the siege by a massive boom to block the entrance of the Turkish fleet.

The defenses of the city to the landward side were the most formidable in the Western world. Built during the reign of Emperor Theodosius II in the 410s, under the direction of the imperial minister Anthemius, they had been maintained throughout their long history and had never been breached. They comprised a four-mile triple defensive system of a moat 60 feet wide, an outer wall with regularly spaced towers of about 45 feet in height and an inner wall 14 feet thick, 40 feet high and with towers some 60 feet high. On April 2, 1453, the Turkish army of Sultan Mehmet II encamped about midway along the walls at the St. Romanos gate and began to deploy its artillery pieces.

And just as the siege of Troy entered the world of legend so the events of 1453 (see Chapter 6) would acquire almost mythical stature. Well into the sixteenth century, chroniclers of the siege mention the participation of men whose presence is in fact difficult to substantiate and embellish their accounts with feats of heroism that may or may not have taken place. "To have been present at the fall, to have fought bravely at the fall, to be related to someone who had fought bravely at the fall," writes Mark Bartusis in his book *The Late Byzantine Army* (2003), "were marks of distinction that could be supplied by an obliging chronicler."

Local patriotism was often important in the morale of the defenders and so a factor in the military outcome. When, early in 1247, Parma had abandoned its allegiance to Emperor Frederick II and aligned itself, like other cities of the Po valley, with Milan in opposition, it knew that it faced a large and professional imperial army, recruited from the best mercenary troops money could buy. But the Parmese had been determined to make good their independence.

In fact, the city's defection from the imperial cause had been engineered by Cardinal Gregory of Montelongo, the papal commander responsible for its defense, under cover of festivities being prepared for a great society wedding by the imperial party. The cardinal had connived with anti-imperial exiles who, taking advantage of the distraction of public opinion, returned in force and seized the family towers of their opponents. Having won control of the city they next reinforced the defenses, erecting palisades and digging a network of trenches. Their rivals in the city establishment were outmaneuvered, but public opinion was in favor of the new regime. As a result, the cardinal found himself at the head of a body of "citizen soldiers deeply concerned for the safety of their city and for their own freedom." We have already seen how they played a triumphant role in the last days of the campaign. No doubt a learned churchman, the cardinal, in the shrewd estimate of the contemporary chronicler from Parma, Fra Salimbene, was also "learned in war" ("*doctus ad bellum*") and skilled in the arts of dissimulation.

In June, aware that the imperial army was preparing for a protracted siege, Montelongo appealed urgently to the papal emissary for reinforcements—with no result. Facing slow starvation, the patriotic commitment of the citizenry began to wilt. But the refurbished defenses proved more than a match for the imperial forces, and early in November allies from Mantua and Ferrara managed to force the blockade with desperately needed supplies.

Still the siege dragged on. With the approach of autumn, work began on Emperor Frederick's "siege city" of Victoria. The reinforcements looked for by the citizens had failed to appear; rumor said that the pope's agent in Lombardy was in fact in a secret agreement with Frederick. Perhaps he was and perhaps it was for this reason that the emperor felt free to go hunting. But the local patriotism of the Parmese won the day. Two centuries later, similar heroism by the populace of Constantinople could not hold out against the assault of the Muslim conqueror, and that siege ended in defeat and the consolidation of the enemy religion in the Christian metropolis.

# CHAPTER TWO

# Strong Points in a Landscape

*"Our castle's strength will laugh a siege to scorn . . ."*

Shakespeare, *Macbeth*

No structure better embodies the title of this chapter than the legendary crusader castle Krak des Chevaliers. Atop its fortified hill dominating the Homs gap through the mountains between the main Syrian desert and the coast, it still commands the awed respect of the visitor; with the progressive stages of the building program that created it in the twelfth century, it surely appeared as the culmination of the castle designers' art in the Middle Eastern theater of war. Standing at Qal'at al-Hisn in Syria near the northern border of Lebanon, in the site of the Castle of the Knights, on a spur of black basalt rock between two converging wadis, it was often known to Arab writers as the Castle of the Kurds because at the time of the arrival of the crusaders it was held by a Kurdish garrison. By the 1130s it was in the hands of the counts of Tripoli, but in 1144 Count Raymond II ceded the fortress and its rich hinterland to the military order of the Knights of St. John of Jerusalem, the Knights Hospitaller. They made various modifications in the 1140s, then in 1202 an earthquake necessitated an extensive rebuild; today the inner enceinte is essentially the result.

*Sketch plan of Krak des Chevaliers (on the border of modern Lebanon).* Gordon Monaghan

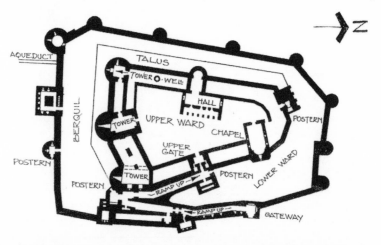

Arguably the greatest military structure to survive from the Middle Ages, Krak is awesome in its strength and complexity of design. The inner curtain wall follows the contour of the spur on which the building stands. The main entrance was by way of a gate approached by a zig-zag path up a steep escarpment. Any attempt at a direct assault meant scrambling up the steep and rugged slope, while to follow the winding path in column meant crossing and recrossing the concentrated fire from the walls of the fortress. An enemy who successfully pierced the gate in the outer curtain wall found himself in a covered passage known as the great ramp, heading up a path flanked by loopholes for archers, pierced by roof holes for the deposit of missiles and liquid fire and broken halfway along its length by a hairpin bend bent back on itself which then led to the upper main gate. Attacking from the south meant crossing a moat before scaling a massive wall defended by a sloping masonry glacis. Should that outer enceinte be breached, the attackers confronted a second water obstacle, the *berquil* or reservoir, over which lowered three massive towers defended by a second glacis whose dimensions were only revealed after the outer wall had been pierced. The place could house a garrison of 2,000 men in adequate accommodation with storage for provisions and water to match.

The soaring vaults of the great hall on the west side of the courtyard with its carved corbels, whose leaf shapes seem to recall the foliage of European woodland rather than the actual, arid setting of the place, provided a dignified setting when the consistory of the Order held its assembly here. In peacetime the chapel was the center of castle life. A large and elaborate building in the Romanesque style, its east end chevet projects a few feet through the curtain wall to form a defensive tower. During its 130 years as a crusader bastion it withstood twelve sieges and repelled an attack by Saladin. The final and victorious siege achieved by the Egyptian army of the Mongol-born sultan Baibars (the name means "panther") began on the morning of March 3, 1271, with the occupation of the township that had grown up below the castle walls. Heavy rains delayed the assault on the fortifications by some three weeks. The first outwork was easily taken and the sultan ordered heavy mining of the great south-west tower of the outer enceinte. But its collapse only revealed the full dimensions of the fearsome inner defenses. These, however, were not put to the test since the sultan resorted to trickery, described in Chapter 9.

### The defense of property

According to the French anarchist philosopher Pierre Joseph Proudhon, writing in 1840, "property is theft." Perhaps he had in mind the vast properties of the French landowning classes, which originated under the old monarchy but survived the French Revolution or were to be matched by grants awarded under Napoleon's empire or the Bourbons' legitimist kingdom.

At some primitive time in Europe's emerging history, with the break-up of Roman patterns of lordship and great villa estates, landownership was a matter of armed dispute. There was, in effect, an age of robber barons: he who could establish himself by main force in a territory and hold it from a fortified residence against all comers, could expect with the passage of time, and by the concession of some one yet more strong than he, a king it might be or an emperor, to be recognized to own the property as of "right." As a noble duke observed with aristocratic pleasantry in a television program *So Who Owns Britain* while fishing a trout stream on his ancestral lands, "An Englishman's castle is his home."

Up to about AD 800, many "castles" were simply converted Roman buildings whose solidly built masonry, even if in semi-ruinous state, was still sturdy enough to mount an effective resistance to ill-disciplined Viking or Saracen raiders. Paradoxically, when Viking raiders attacked York in 867, they overran the neglected Roman fortress and built up its walls as best they could for a fortified base against English counterattack. In Rome itself, the huge circular tomb of the emperor Hadrian was converted into a fortress and, connected to the papal palace of the Vatican by a hidden passage, became in times of danger the stronghold of the popes, who renamed it Castel Sant'Angelo.

Some of Europe's earliest castles were built for protection against invading marauders like Vikings or Saracens. The strong man in his stronghold might offer refuge to his vulnerable neighbors during bad times and expect their loyalty and tribute during good times. From the early ninth century, hundreds of wooden, and later stone, towers sprang up all over Europe. In 862, the Carolingian ruler, Charles the Bald, issued a decree for the building of castles throughout his territories, roughly equivalent to northern and western France, with the barbarian incursions in mind. Of course, the local strong men could as well use them as private strongholds, even against the king. Two years later he had to issue another decree, ordering the destruction of all castles built without his permission. As may be imagined, the decree had little effect.

A century later, with the decay of royal authority, local barons in what we now call France were putting up forts more or less at will. Counts, supposedly royal appointees, established family dynasties ruling their territories with little reference to any king. Castles were the essential factor in the equation. From his power base on the Loire, Count Fulk the Black of Anjou built at least thirteen castles before his death in 1040. For the people of the region it was a very unlucky number indeed. These castles, supposedly built as defense against invaders from Normandy, provided garrison points for the count's soldiery and tax collectors. His rule was so feared that people said the family was descended from the devil's daughter, Melusine. Fulk's great stone tower at Langeais still stands on the banks of the Loire.

Cathedral builders have many admirers; military architects and castle builders as such—kings, marshals, chatelaines, masons—who raised the structures or operated them in combat, hardly any. Yet they, for good or ill, made the larger mark on the medieval landscape even if, today, much of their work has disappeared.

There were, of course, other reasons for castle building. One of the prettiest of all castles is Castel del Monte, called by the German historian Gunther Wolf "a fusion of poetry and mathematics in stone." Located on a gentle hill (the mountain of the name) in southern Italy, it was built in the 1220s by Emperor Frederick II who, the Italians said, "put up castles and towers to stamp the glory of his name so deeply on the memories of men that it should never be forgotten."

Its walls were hung with oriental carpets; its floors inlaid with marble; and it had en suite bathrooms supplied from water cisterns in the roof. The castles of the crusaders could display similar luxuries though their purpose was more warlike—to hold down the populations of Muslims and native Orthodox Christians and defend the conquered territories in the "Holy Land" against Muslim counterattack.

Their fortresses and those of their enemies were becoming quite elaborate in comparison with early stone castles that consisted of single towers accessed by a door at first-floor level reached by a wooden stair scaffolding to be knocked away in last resort. Once outer defenses had been pierced, the garrison, holed up in its last place of retreat, was likely to capitulate within a matter of days, especially if the builder had not had the foresight to locate a well on the premises or within a protective circuit of wall. Other types inevitably followed. As stone-throwing weapons advanced in effectiveness (notably the twelfth-century trebuchet) square towers tended to be replaced with circular ones—corners being more vulnerable to projectiles and to miners digging away beneath the walls who could bring down two lengths of wall if they successfully subverted a corner angle. Another favored technique against stone-built towers was to use skilled sappers prising out the lower courses of masonry. One Byzantine general combined the two in a tower, built "very scientifically" which, according to the historian Princess Anna Comnena (d. 1148), experienced military engineers called a "tortoise."

It was a large circular wooden structure (circular, presumably to deflect missiles), covered in hides and plaited wickerwork, which was moved up to the stretch of wall under attack. It evidently had at least one story since the team manning it was divided into two parties, the first to batter the wall and fight the defenders, the second, expert masons no doubt, working at the foot of the wall with iron instruments to loosen the lower courses of masonry. In fact, they combined a traditional mining technique with their work as sappers: as they pulled out the loosened stone they replaced them with logs serving as pit props to shore up the masonry temporarily. Thus, they worked their way through to the inner side of the wall; as the first chinks of light indicated that they were on the verge of breakthrough, they set fire to the logs—and rapidly cleared out from the area to avoid the collapsing stonework.

The answer to mining was countermining, and brutal underground hand-to-hand combats flared up when a party of sappers broke into the mine of their opponents. These too had their rules, for there were proper procedures to be followed in all aspects of a siege from its formal declaration to the formal surrender of the place.

### Containment by castles

In the late thirteenth century, King Edward I of England built a sequence of castles from Caernarfon to Conwy to Harlech to secure his conquests in the north of the principality of Wales. In so far as the inhabitants of the country were the direct descendants of the British population of Rome's province of Britannia and the last unconquered region of the empire north of the Alps, it has been said that Edward's victories there represented the final fall of the Roman Empire in the West.

The financial outlay on these "Edwardian" castles was huge (in the 1970s it was calculated that each fortress cost in modern terms the equivalent of a Concorde supersonic airliner) not least because the most up-to-date principles and techniques of fortification were used. The strength of these places was to be demonstrated years later when in 1404 the Welsh rebel Owain Glyndwr laid siege to Harlech. For weeks the place was held by just five Englishmen and sixteen Welshmen—when the castellan made overtures to surrender, the garrison locked him up. In fact, the great castle fell not to assault by its Welsh attackers but because, in the end, the skeleton force defending it decided to accept terms and were bought out. Some sixty years later, it was once more in rebel hands, holding for the House of Lancaster when, in 1461, Edward of York became king as Edward IV. These "Men of Harlech" held out for seven years, harrying the neighboring countryside until in August 1468, after a protracted siege, William Herbert, earl of Pembroke, finally recovered the place for Edward. An indication of the effort involved and the obvious strength of the fortress is found in the Public Record Office, where the accounts show some £5,000 paid to the earl for his expenses.

From March 1278, when he arrived in England, the building program was masterminded and supervised by one man, the Savoyard James St. George (his personal career is outlined in Chapter 3) helped by a select band of fellow Savoyards, and under the hands-on direction of the king. In many cases work had begun in July 1277 under the king's then chief engineer, Master Bertram, and presumably to basic designs closely checked by the king. Edward seems to have intended a once for all, pre-emptive solution to the possibility of Welsh insurrection. Perhaps impressed by the gleaming, freshly plastered walls of the recently completed castle of St. Georges d'Esperance in Savoy, where he had first seen the work of its designer, Master James, some years before, Edward grasped the effect of the cold, hard-edged presence of a state-of-the-art modern fortification in the folds of a natural landscape. In Wales, where the people and their leaders hardly disposed of the resources or military know-how for the technically complex operation of a full-scale siege, the aim was all-out intimidation. At Rhuddlan for example, sited in the valley of the River Clwyd, where the ground plan had been determined and building begun well before the arrival of James, two great twin-towered gates guarded the entrance to a double line of defenses. This was technical overkill. Edward gestured his confidence in the security of his measures by having a little pleasure garden (*hortus inclusus*), complete with fishpond fed from the river, created for Queen Eleanor should she be in residence. Of course, in the unlikely event of a siege, the pond would provide additional drinking water for the garrison. However, for a century after the completion of the Welsh castles project not one of the fortresses was taken.

### Under construction

Before work could begin a site had to be cleared out to an extended circumference well beyond the projected site of the castle itself so as to remove anything that could provide protective cover for attackers. At Caernarfon, houses of the existing Welsh village were pulled down; at Rhuddlan, trees of the royal forest were felled. Once the site was cleared, the line of the moat could be marked out and excavation could begin. In the meantime other workmen were erecting a wooden palisade around the site to keep out guerrilla action from the surrounding population. (It seems that the director of operations was liable to be targeted personally; it is certain that, in December 1280, Master James was granted "letters of protection" for the next seven years.) Next the foundations of the main outer walls were dug and the walls themselves built up to about half their intended height.

With the troops posted around this perimeter defense, buildings, generally of wood, were run up to provide living quarters for them and for officials. The residence of the commander, or constable, was a more luxurious affair. At Caernarfon it comprised a handsome suite of rooms in one of the stone towers. When King Edward visited the place he stayed in special timber-built apartments fitted with glass windows supplied by Simon the Glazier of Chester.

Given that building went forward in hostile territory and that work stopped for the winter months (troops were garrisoned to protect the workings), speed was of the essence. Lifting gear comprised a treadwheel-powered winch or windlass or block and pulley; stone as well as timber was usually cut and shaped by hand with specialized saws, adzes, chisels and side-axes. Considering the amount of work entailed, the fact that the superb Conwy castle and walled town was completed in forty months is remarkable. The outer walls were some 27 feet high and had a circuit of, say, 4,200 feet.

From April to November a castle site was swarming with workmen. For the year 1285 the records show 970 men on site at Caernarfon, with another 1,530 between Conwy and Harlech. For 1286, three years into the construction, work at Harlech occupied 170 skilled masons, 90 quarry men, 28 carpenters, 24 ironsmiths, with, in addition, 520 laborers—a total of 832 in the workings. Foremen, payroll and administrative staff amounted to 26 all told, and in addition to all this were three armed horsemen. Soldiers protected the work force—three were there to check desertions and recover absconders. The workmen were paid reasonable wages but were recruited by order of the royal sheriffs from all over England and few relished forced labor at a war front.

### Echo of empire

Begun in 1283, Caernarfon, the most majestic of Edward's Welsh castles, was completed only after the death of St. George. The workings were overrun in the Welsh rising of 1294, and the job of repairing the damage and continuing with the project was deputed to Walter of Hereford, but few doubt that the overall design was conceived by the king's chief architect and "master of works." In April 1284, special temporary residential apartments were run up for the pregnant Queen Eleanor's lying-in, and on the 25th, St. Mark's Day, she gave birth to her fourth child, a son to be known as Edward of Caernarfon (later King Edward II) and designated Prince of Wales by his father. It is to this king that we should attribute the polygonal design of the towers and their decorative banding, which is no doubt an allusion to the walls and towers of the imperial city of Constantinople and trumpets Edward's "imperial" dream for his sway in Britain.

The castles of the Marcher barons and English military activity prompted the later Welsh rulers to emulate them. Llywelyn ap Gruffyd, prince of Gwynedd who in 1258 received homage of the other Welsh princes and was the only Welshman to be recognized by the English as Prince of Wales, took advantage of the baronial wars in England against King Henry III and his heir Prince "the Lord Edward" to consolidate his realm and expand his power in central Wales. One can imagine that Dolforwyn Castle, which he built in Powys as a key to his strategy, was not only an impressive military gesture—the powerful Marcher lord Robert Mortimer protested vehemently against the building—but aimed to match the style and comforts of the English baronial class. No doubt it was also intended as the administrative center of Llywelyn's lordship. Writing in *Current Archaeology* in 1990, Lawrence Butler, who considered that it represented the highest achievement by any Welsh prince in imitation of the Norman castle style, described the site as being well chosen as to its strategic position. However, he noted that despite the massive rectangular keep, the largest built by any Welsh prince, and an impressive round tower at the north end of the enceinte, the structure had no corner towers and the main gate was a simple access through the curtain wall, without the protection of a fortified gatehouse. These weaknesses were revealed when the place fell after only a ten-day siege to King Edward in April 1277.

Edward handed Dolforwyn Castle over to the Mortimer family. Evidently there had been a severe bombardment, for sections of the wall had to be completely rebuilt, the material used being stone from quarries on Mortimer lands in Herefordshire. The castle's builder had remodeled the terrain where necessary with large ditches and stretches of wall determined by the requirements of the design; in this sense it broke with the style of earlier Welsh fortifications, which had generally clung to the contours of the hills.

### Function and type

Where a castle was built depended in part on what it was built for. If it were to be a strong man's base about the only consideration of importance was whether the site was difficult of access. It did not have to overlook an important road or dominate a possibly rebellious town. The early counts of Savoy built their castle of Chillon, focus of Byron's famous poem "The Prisoner of Chillon," near the shore of Lake Geneva. Once there, the count and his men were safe from the angry locals. On the other hand, when William the Conqueror decided to build the Tower of London he wanted more than safety for his soldiery; he also needed a secure base for their operations, a place from which they could control what was even then one of the major cities of northern Europe and a place from which he could, at will, harry the subject population. The result was the White Tower, more or less as we see it today. It was completed about 1087. Over the centuries, beginning with the Bell Tower built by Richard I in the 1190s, additions by other monarchs created the "Tower" we know today, a textbook example of a "concentric" castle with a central keep surrounded by rings of walls.

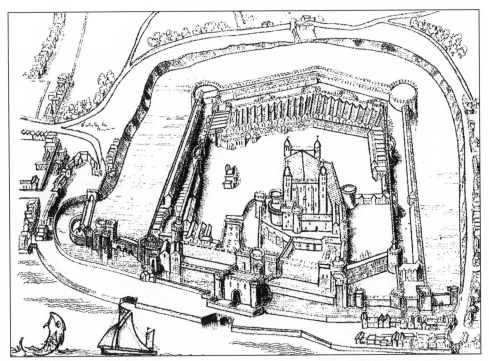

*The Tower of London from a survey of 1597, showing how the original White Tower has become a concentric fortress over the centuries and how, at that time, the place was defended on the waterside by the moat running behind the wharf. It also encircled the Lion's Tower (to the left) and the royal menagerie in the enclosure at its base.* Gordon Monagha

Apart from the simple tower and the concentric fortress, there were various other types of castle such as the "shell" keep, effectively simply a single circular curtain wall shielding garrison quarters and other such service buildings, with perhaps a stone tower at the center. Even prefabricated castles were known at a very early stage. When the Norman invasion fleet beached near Pevensey in October 1066, one of the first items to come ashore was just such a piece of equipment—essentially an assembly kit of ready-made wooden sections, quickly put together by the ships' carpenters. Within a few years of the victory at Hastings, the English countryside was peppered by hundreds of such wooden strongholds, mostly placed on an artificial mound, the "motte," surrounded by a ditch or moat from which the earth had been dug, and beyond that a palisade enclosing a sort of courtyard, known as the bailey. Such fortified housesteads, virtually unknown in Anglo-Saxon England and of little use against serious military assault, were quite sufficient to keep out angry farmers and peasantry and to post an unmistakable signal to a conquered people to heed the alien oppressor and robber of their liberty.

The lesson was inculcated from the very first days of the Conquest by the brutal devastation of the countryside and bloodthirsty terrorization of the people authorized as an act of policy by the Conqueror. It was the way he had fought his own duchy into submission during years of civil war, so humanity was hardly to be expected in his dealings with a foreign population. People knew that a king or great lord was licensed to wreak havoc on subjects who had angered or defied him, but this systematic horror over large tracts of countryside was something new in England, as were the hostile castles raised merely to cow the spirits of native inhabitants. The lofty tower central to the defense of a castle, generally known as the "keep," was, in Norman French, the *donjon*. It could be an awe-inspiring structure: that of Castle Montreuil-Bellay in the Loire valley seemed to "rise to the stars," and was meant to be intimidating. The English word "dungeon" surely tells the story; when the rural Anglo-Saxon population looked across the fields at the donjon of their new Norman master the first thought was of the stinking, subterranean, rat-infested torture cells at its base.

Later, kings of England would built royal castles to hold the line against unruly magnates. The great keep of Orford Castle on the coast of Suffolk survives as an example. It was raised by King Henry II in troubled times, when baronial malcontents led by Hugh Bigod, earl of Norfolk, were stirring up trouble against the new regime after the laissez-faire years of the ineffectual King Stephen— who had in fact raised Bigod to the earldom. Building began in the accounting year 1165, and the tower seems to have been finished two years later. It was to be protected by a curtain wall and outworks, and the whole structure was completed by 1173 at a total cost, as recorded in the royal exchequer rolls, of £1,413 9s 2d—this at a time when the basic annual revenues of the English crown were probably less than £10,000. The year 1173 saw a serious uprising against the king both in his English and continental dominions, led by his sons. By this time Bigod was in his late seventies and yet was recruiting Flemish mercenaries into Suffolk to prosecute his quarrel with the king. During the civil war of 1216– 17 between King John and the rebel barons in favor of Magna Carta, Orford was one of the royal castles in East Anglia surrendered for a period to the army of Prince Louis of France, which supported the rebels. It is highly unlikely that it would have been taken by siege had the commander decided to hold for the king's party.

### Routines of defense

A major castle would house as many people as the population of a decent-sized market town. The bulk of the number would be the garrison—in some cases up to as many as 2,000 men. In addition, there would be clerks to run the church services but also to keep the records and accounts, blacksmiths and armorers, kitchen staff, stable hands and the domestic staff to maintain the household of the castellan in a really prestigious posting.

The castellan had numerous responsibilities even when the place was at peace. Essential, of course, was discipline and diligent attention to lookout and guard duties. The man in charge had to make regular tours of inspection, ensure the well was kept fresh and clear of casual garbage tipped in by lazy kitchen staff. In time of war, the water supply was key to the endurance of the garrison. In time of peace, the castle's requirements would be supplied from nearby streams

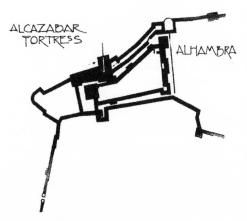

ALCAZABAR TORTRESS

ALHAMBRA

*This sketch plan of the Alhambra shows the hairpin bends of the approach from the Gate of Arms that had to be negotiated, under fire of course, by any attacker.* Gordon Monaghan

and sent in by water carts. Naturally, the fabric of the fortifications had to be maintained in a state of good repair; as important was the condition of the provisions. Quartermaster and chief cook had to ensure that stores were used in rotation—if the barrels to the front were always used and systematically replaced when new supplies arrived, a few months of siege would reveal supplies in the back of the storage area that were inedible, even dangerous, having stood for months, even in extreme cases for years. Storage of firewood or horses' fodder had also to be watched. Bales of straw and hay, or loose timber, stacked for easy access adjacent to the stables would be ready fuel in the case of attack by fire arrows. Such details and many others made the castellan's job or that of his deputy a demanding one. Since his deputy might well be his wife, there was scope for women to excel in the commissariat department, and, since the job had many features in common with that of a chatelaine in great household, many did so. In emergencies, not a few women also proved highly capable at soldiering.

The routines of defense really started with the work of the builder and designer. Ingenuity to match that shown by the designer of Krak is to be found in the *alcazaba* fortress of Granada's Alhambra. There, the Puerta de las Armas, projecting at right angles to the wall with its entrance to the side of the tower, forces the attacker who would enter to fight his way up the approach with his weapon arm and unshielded flank exposed to fire from the fortress wall on his right. Should the entrance gate be forced, the attackers must then negotiate two right-angled turns within the tower itself before debouching into a narrow alley formed by the two outer walls of the defenses. Eventually, having run the gauntlet of a long murder alley leading to yet another gate (at the foot of the Homage Tower), he emerges into the line of the defenses of the Alhambra proper.

For centuries, when the force of the state was concerned more with its own security than with the maintenance of "law and order" as a public service, a household's security was a matter for the householder. The baron had his castle, but many a more modest landowner built for safety first and comfort after. In England, the fortified manor house known as Stokesay Castle, on the Shropshire borders with Wales, is an example of the type. It is also an example of the kind of social mobility that was far more common in England in the Middle Ages than is generally realized. After all, the first earl of Suffolk, William de la Pole, was a wool merchant from Hull before his elevation to the peerage by Richard II in the 1380s.

The original house at Stokesay was built by the de Say family in the early 1200s, and the North Tower of the present structure dates from that time. But the bulk of the house that we see today was built for Lawrence of Ludlow (d. 1296), also a wool merchant who bought out the de Says. His "fortifications" that surround the mansion with its great hall and chambers really seem to be for show rather than warfare. True, the place is encircled by a deep ditch and the South Tower is clearly meant to represent a keep, but the crenellated curtain wall is too thin to have withstood anything but a token siege—good enough to protect Master Lawrence and his family from marauding vagabonds or perhaps Welsh raiders from across the border, but more a (somewhat presumptuous) gesture of a nouveau riche aping the aristocracy than a military structure.

In Italy, where merchant families of the time had reason to fortify themselves against their neighbors and rivals in commerce and town politics, the towers of the city of San Gimigniano remind us of the turbulent conditions in the medieval birthplace of capitalism. A hundred and fifty years after Lawrence of Ludlow's day, the period known as the Wars of the Roses witnessed similar lawlessness among English merchant families, too. Thanks to the famous Paston letters, we know that the Paston family of Norfolk was regularly under threat from powerful neighbors. But they could give as good as they got. They conducted a running feud with "Partrich and his followers," who seem to have lived in permanent fear of a resumption of hostilities. At one point, Partrich was so convinced that his Paston neighbors were intending to "march on him again" that he fortified his town house more like a military blockhouse. The place was fortified with bars at the doors and wickerwork cages around the windows and firing positions "on every corner of the house to shoot out at both with hand guns and bows." Margaret Paston, who reported all this to her husband on business in London, knew they must have guns because, although none could actually be seen, some of the holes punched through the wood and plaster walls of the house were "scarce knee high from the floor and no man could shoot out at them with a hand bow."

The Paston family, prosperous social climbers from their first named ancestor Clement Paston, "a good plain husbandman," acquiring money and land by diverse means, numbered among their menfolk successful lawyers such as William, steward to the duke of Norfolk, and among their women determined and capable household managers. They needed both since they made enemies easily, even among the greatest of the neighborhood such as the duke of Suffolk, who on one occasion came against the house with 300 men and would have entered, "though he said not," had they not fortified the place with guns and ordinance. Times were tough in Norfolk in the 1440s.

## CHAPTER THREE

# Castles and Fortifications: Designers, Builders and Developments

*". . . a great arithmetician, one Michael Cassio . . . must his lieutenant be . . ."*
Shakespeare, *Othello*

The last chapter outlined the typical stages in the building of a castle in Europe. Here I turn to some of the theoreticians, engineers and designers whose work lay behind the practice of medieval warfare—and the evolution of fortification design. We are dealing with a period in which there was much less demarcation between areas of expertise and professional skills than we regard as normal today. According to Anna Comnena, when her father, the Byzantine emperor Alexius I, intervened to help the army of the First Crusade in their siege of Nicaea (Iznik, Turkey), he ordered the building of a number of siege-engines, many following specifications he had himself drawn up rather than "the usual designs of the mechanics" (military engineers). She tells us that people were amazed by this display of imperial technical proficiency: she does not tell us in what way his machines differed from the standard models.

For much of the summer of 1216, Dover Castle was under siege from the forces of Prince Louis of France, called in by the barons opposed to King John in the civil war that followed the king's renunciation of Magna Carta the previous year. The garrison of 140 knights was commanded by Hubert de Burgh, Justiciar of England and Chamberlain (chief officer) of King John's household. He dubbed Dover Castle "the key to England." Built some forty years before by King Henry II soon after he came to throne, standing on its cliff site overlooking the modern town, it is one of the most remarkable fortresses in Europe. Henry, who fortified or refortified some ninety sites in England, spent well over £6,000 on Dover, a sizeable part of a year's royal income. Maurice, Henry's mason in charge (the architect), was clearly a master of military architecture. At the center of the 79-acre site stands the great keep with its square corner turrets and gatehouses finished in the 1180s, with the keep yard or "bailey" protected by its own curtain wall and formidable gatehouse. An angle on the long stretch of the eastern defenses was defended by the Avranches Tower, a structure purpose-built for archers. The circuit of walls forming the outer enceinte was completed under John. The immense fortifications seem impregnable; but at the time of the siege, the French artillery, operating from high ground to the north of the castle, severely damaged the walls, while French sappers mined the northern barbican so that it partly collapsed. The French made an assault over the rubble, but the garrison knights succeeded in holding them. At this point Louis decided to fall back on London, then in the hands of his allies the English rebels. He returned to the siege in May 1217, though in September that year he was bought off and left for France.

By this time Constable de Burgh, after reviewing the defenses, came to the conclusion that the place would be that much more effective as a fighting unit if it were capable of what today we would call a "pro-active" role—if in other words it could carry the attack to the enemy. Still more innovatively, he introduced a network of tunnels that facilitated movement under cover within the garrison but also, with their warren of guardrooms and towers, had sally ports created to enable surprise sorties against a besieging force. He would surely have bridled to be called a mason, master or otherwise, or a mechanic—but his modifications show that he had the skills associated with those callings.

As in so much of medieval life and culture, Roman writers were of great importance, none more so than the fourth-century Roman patrician Vegetius (in full, Flavius Vegetius Renatus), whose military handbook, the *Epitoma rei militaris* ("A Summary of Military Matters"), though primarily a treatise for reforms in the later imperial army, had much to say on tactics and siegecraft. It was, for centuries, the most influential work in its field. (Judging from the number of manuscript copies to have survived, it was clearly a bestseller.) In the run-up to the siege of Antioch in October 1097, Duke Robert of Normandy, following the advice of Bishop Adhemar of Le Puy (the pope's representative on the crusade), adopted a stratagem called the *testudo* or tortoise. In Roman terminology this meant an infantry conformation in which the attackers hold their shields above their heads, overlapping the edges as best they may, to provide protection from missiles as they charge an enemy position. Presuming the Normans used their conventional kite-shaped shield the maneuver would necessarily have been less effective than when adopted with the legionaries' oblong, straight-sided shields. Even so, the novel procedure would have given useful protection. The bishop, being a man of letters, had, we can be sure, read his Vegetius. Remembering that their Byzantine contemporary Anna Comnena used *testudo* to refer to a type of siege-tower, it is possible that it was this that Robert adopted. Finally, while on the subject of tortoises, we find in the illustrations derived from the *De re militari* of the Italian monk and scholar Roberto Valturio, published at Verona in 1472 and much indebted to Vegetius, an engaging picture of a battering-ram projecting from a domed penthouse which has the head of a tortoise! Either way the bishop surely derived his recommendation from his book-learning. Typical of the practical as well as theoretical nature of Vegetius are his comments on siege-towers, warning that a tower repaired with replacement joined timbers is especially vulnerable to capture.

In castle building, the design of the structure and the management of the construction site were jobs for experts, jobs that could bring rich rewards and considerable social prestige. One manuscript illustration for the building of the Tower of Babel shows a robed figure holding a pair of builder's dividers and wearing gloves. He is clearly the master mason/architect, and just as clearly he is in a sphere remote from the laborers or mere stonemasons. An illuminated illustration from a French thirteenth-century Old Testament depicts God himself wielding a pair of architect's dividers.

### James St. George: a career of talent

Master masons had great responsibilities and wielded real power on site. It was up to them to ensure that the plan was realized to the satisfaction of the patron, noble or king; and to this end they were in charge of law and order among the workmen. Walter of Hereford, as director of works at Caernarfon, was authorized to preside over a court where regulations were enforced and fines imposed for misconduct. Such activity was presumably profitable since the fines were paid to him—a valuable perk for a man who already received a large salary. Above Walter came James of St. George, who was considered a friend by King Edward. He became Keeper of the works at Conwy Castle, and in 1290 was appointed Constable of Harlech, the kind of position that usually went to a nobleman. Contemporaries recognized the status of men like James, commoners by birth who had risen to prominence by mastery of the skills and technology associated with the artisan class.

By 1293, St. George's annual fees from various sources amounted to 100 marks, that is, in today's decimal currency £66.66, or $91.90 (the great hall and royal apartments at Conwy cost just £100, or $140, to build). Since 1284, St. George had been entitled to a pension of three shillings a day, in a full year £54.75—royal governments were notoriously unreliable paymasters, but in the case of Master St. George it seems reasonable to assume that he got his money more or less on time.

We first encounter him working, with his father, Master John, who was a *cementarius* (or skilled artisan builder) on the castle of Yverdon for the count of Savoy, an influential cousin of the King of England, Henry III, and Earl of Richmond. By the mid-1260s James had risen from artisan status to that of "chief master mason." He was now directly responsible to the count's military engineer (ingeniator) on such projects as the castles of Chillon and St. Georges d'Esperanche. It was here, returning from his crusade in 1273 that Edward, as a guest of the new count, Philip of Savoy, first encountered the architect's work. At that time the count was having three other castles built or renovated within a day's ride of "d'Esperanches"; so the king could have been shown over the works by Master James and his superior John de Masoz the *ingeniator*. When in March 1278 he first appears in English records, as successor to Chief Engineer Bertram, it seems that St. George had made it to the top of his profession.

In Savoy the works' accounts spoke of tasks being assigned to the teams by *dominum* ("lord") de Masoz the *ingeniator* and *magistrum* ("master") Jacobum

(James); in Wales it is Master James *ingeniator* alone who "ordains the works of the castles," as "master of the king's works in Wales." Later records also call James "machinator," which suggests the skills of military engineer—certainly, in January 1283 he was at the siege of the castle of Dolwyddelan, a crucial objective in King Edward's campaign in Snowdonia.

From 1298 to 1305 the great military architect and engineer was with the king on his campaigns in Scotland working on Linlithgow Castle and, it is thought, directing technical operations at the siege of Stirling in 1304 (see Chapter 7). In 1306 he was found back on site at Beaumaris, but died some time within the next three years. For more than forty years, he had been a leader in his field as master mason and military engineer: for thirty of those years had been the valued collaborator of the king of England, as master of the king's works in Wales. Commander of Europe's most successful armed forces, Edward valued the company as well as the expertise of his military men. It is hardly surprising if people considered James of St. George a man of influence.

With St. George's pension went the office of "king's serjeant," and his widow Ambrosia was assured an annual pension of some £27. One assumes that she and her husband were paid in coin of the realm—the workmen on site were not necessarily so lucky. We know that they sometimes had to accept payment in tokens. By the 1290s royal finances were sorely stretched. In 1294, the last Welsh rising was defeated and the following year St. George's last great commission, the textbook concentric stronghold at Beaumaris on the island of Anglesey, was started. In 1295, more than 2,600 men, many of them Welsh and 400 masons were at work for a weekly wage bill of £250. (In the first eighteen months total expenditure amounted to more than £10,000.) But soon troubles in Gascony and Scotland called for attention. The annual expenditure at Beaumaris dropped to about £300. In the later twentieth century, archaeologists unearthed a cache of leather token coinage on the island.

### The man on the spot: Gabriele de Tadini de Martinengo

We do not know that St. George ever "road-tested" one of his designs, so to speak, by being present during a siege, but there are certainly cases of military engineers who either by choice or under compulsion did find themselves participating in hostilities. The Italian city of Brescia, as we shall see, owed its survival of siege by Emperor Frederick II to the Spanish engineer Calamandrinus, bribed away from the imperial service. Some 300 years later, the man estimated to be the best military engineer of his age, Gabriele Tadini de Martinengo, was head-hunted by the military Order of the Knights of St. John to remodel the defenses of Rhodes for the great siege of the island by the Turks in 1522 and was present throughout the siege. He proved a hero of that epic engagement, second only to the Grand Commander of the Order, who directed the defense.

Retained in the service of the Venetian authorities on the island of Crete (who made what historian Desmond Seward termed, "frenzied attempts" to prevent the engineering genius of the age from defecting), Martinengo was induced to join the defenders of Rhodes by Grand Master Villiers de l'Isle Adam. He was lured not so much by an irresistible financial package but, as a devout believer,

An idyllic battle scene, with the swan in the moat and the unwarlike windows of the château, from the Chroniques d'Angleterre by the chivalric writer Jehan de Wavrin, soldier, courtier and bibliophile. He commended Henry V of England for maintaining "the discipline of chivalry as did the Romans in former times." In the foreground are three "pots" mounted on somewhat unstable gun carriages. Taylor Library

by the idea of contributing to the defense of this eastern Mediterranean bulwark of Christendom against the advance of Turkish power. When he reached his new posting he was so impressed by the religious dedication of the knights that, as an unmarried man and so entitled to be considered, he asked to be admitted to the Order. De l'Isle Adam immediately inducted him. Martinengo's advice in the placement of such defensive works as V-shaped double trenched "ravelines" projecting from the bases of the bastions was invaluable; his siting of the artillery batteries (Rhodes had far more guns than in 1480) to maximum effect; or the insistence that especially vulnerable elements in the defense be further protected with the contemporary equivalent of sandbag walls, were perhaps to be expected, but his authority as high-powered professional saw the work carried through with maximum efficiency and speed and his willingness to adopt ingenious solutions no doubt fired enthusiasm and admiration. Typical was a primitive vibration detector comprising a tensioned drumhead modified to trigger a bell signal by any mining activity.

This remarkable man had the character of a true hero, physically tough and rich in the quality that validates all others—courage. In the early weeks, his head was pierced by a bullet that entered through the eye socket and, miraculously, exited without having caused mortal damage; within the week he was back at his duties, an inspiration to a now flagging defense.

### Security never guaranteed: Harfleur, 1415

Of course, even when the design of its fortifications followed approved theory, a place might succumb. The defenses of the strategically significant town of Harfleur at the mouth of the Seine, called by the French chronicler Monstrelet the principal key to France, were certainly formidable and apparently followed state-of-the art principles. The surrounding wall, though pierced at three points, was strongly defended; each of the gates had drawbridge, portcullis and, we are told, "angle towers according to the theories of Master Giles." The "Giles" in question was the theologian, political philosopher and polymath Aegidia Colonna, "Giles of Rome" (d. 1316), whose treatise on government, *De regimine principum* ("On the Rule of Princes"), a standard work on its subject, was translated for Henry V when he was still Prince of Wales. A deep ditch gave further protection to the town wall at Harfleur, while the port could be closed to ships by a boom or chain even at high tide.

On August 14, 1415, Henry V landed with his army at the mouth of the Seine at the beginning of what would come to be known as the Agincourt campaign. He was unopposed and five days later had the town invested by land. The English ships packing the Seine estuary might not be able to force an entry to the harbor; but they did bar any relief from the seaward. Meantime, Henry's soldiers dug themselves in with protective trenches and his miners (mostly experts from the Forest of Dean) began tunneling toward the wall. Rather surprisingly perhaps, given the quality of the defensive design, the king reckoned he could take the place in three weeks. He was counting on the supine indifference of the French high command. Neither Charles the Dauphin at Rouen nor the French constable with his force at Honfleur on the south bank of the Seine estuary made any move to raise the English siege, while that doyen of chivalry, the Marshal Boucicaut (d. 1421), appointed commander-in-chief by the mentally unstable King Charles VI, held his position at Caudebec-en-Caux upriver, content to allow the English their bridgehead on French territory, confident that he could destroy them once they began their march inland. (In the event he was among the prisoners at Agincourt and died in captivity.)

For his part, the English king found that his calculations were thrown out because many of his troops succumbed to dysentery and camp fever brought on by the marshy terrain and its fetid water. This slowed up proceedings and depleted his effective forces. Nevertheless, Henry pressed the attack and after a night-long barrage by his siege, artillery had opened a breach in the wall; on the morning of September 19 he was able to order the first assault, immortalized in the words of Shakespeare. As the English recovered themselves preparatory to the decisive attack, the duke of Clarence commanding on the east of the town received a deputation from the garrison offering to capitulate on the 22nd if no help reached them by that time. Accordingly, on September 23 King Henry of England and, as he claimed, of France, made a solemn entry barefoot into "his" town of Harfleur, where he offered thanks to God in the parish church of St. Martin. The fall of the town had been a clear case of demoralization on the part of the defenders. But they could claim various justifications for their behavior. In the first place, to defy one's rightful liege lord meant, by the laws of war, unrestrained sack and pillage in the event of defeat; in the second place, there were influential people in France prepared to consider the legitimacy of the English claim to the crown and, finally, the court party had done nothing to reinforce Harfleur.

### Developments in castle design

In places the landscape of Iron Age Europe showed numerous massive hill forts, comprised of earthworks thrown up to emphasize and enhance defensive features of the natural contours of a hilltop. In Britain, the most famous instance is Mai Dun in Dorset. As the Roman armies conquered the Celtic peoples of northern Europe so they built walled garrison towns and garrison forts, at first of timber and then of stone. With the decay of imperial authority, so these places were taken over by invading Germanic tribes, principally Franks and Goths, or fell into disrepair. In the eighth century these peoples, in their turn, came under attack from outside raiders—Vikings and "Saracens" among them—and began to build fortresses as safe havens for agricultural populations outside and remote from the Roman urban centers. These structures, free standing in the countryside and often built of timber, are the first castles as we understand the term—often starting life as refuges against invading marauders.

During the medieval centuries, the castle became a major element in warfare. As we have noted, the success or failure of a campaign was generally measured in terms of the number of strongholds or walled towns that had been taken and subjected to the new lord. But for centuries, the castle was also the focus of the cultural life of the European nobility. The *fabliaux* and *chansons de geste* of the *jongleurs* were declaimed in the great hall, and here the songs of the troubadours were first performed. Even the conventions of the chivalric courtly love and new fashions in the dance were born within the walls of the castle. Its kitchens competed with those of the great abbeys in refining the delicacies of the table; and the arts of the tapestry maker were devoted to the adornment of the castle walls. In short, the grim exterior of the castle sheltered the luxury life that would be the preserve of the residential palace as the pattern of war changed and walled cities increasingly became the target of siege warfare.

### Castle to palace: the Alhambra, 1492

In October 1492 Columbus made landfall in the Caribbean; the following year he would return to Spain with the news. His voyage was to open a "New World" of conquest for the monarchs of Spain, new territories and immense wealth; the birth of an empire and mass conversions to the Christian religion were to follow. But in January 1492 all this lay in the future; the triumph, to which all Christian Spain rang for the rest of that year and long after, was the capture of the last stronghold of Moorish Spain, the Alhambra or Red Fort of the Muslim rulers of Granada.

A natural fortress, the site had been fortified for centuries but the work as we see it today was begun by Muhammad I, the first ruler of the Arab Nasrid dynasty, who reigned from 1238 to 1275. The conquest of the great Muslim metropolis of Cordoba by Ferdinand III of Castile in 1236 meant that Muhammad needed both diplomacy and vigilance to maintain his position against further Christian advances. He made submission to the Castilian king, agreed an annual tribute and even supplied troops to Castile in its conquest of the neighboring Muslim principality of Seville. But he also redesigned and rebuilt several fortresses within his own territories, among them the *alcazabas* of Malaga and Granada. In the latter case, he extended the walls of the fortress to embrace what was to become the most majestic, the most beautiful and the most cultured palace complex in Western Europe. Emblematic of the combination of military and cultural considerations is the Puerta de la Justitia (Gate of Justice), built in the reign of Yusuf I (1333–54). Its entrance, embellished at the top of its horseshoe arch with the open hand, symbol of the five virtues of the Muslim faith, is protected by an outer flanking tower and, within itself, forces any would-be attacker through the hazards of a double bend access. According to tradition, the courtyard within the gate was the site of the open-air court of justice of the Muslim rulers.

The fall of the Alhambra came as the culmination of an investment of Granada that had begun in the summer of 1490. An early gain by the Christian armies of Aragon and Castile had occupied the coastal strip from Adra to Salobreña with its hilltop alcazar. In fact, Granada was effectively isolated from any hope of support from Muslim North Africa even had the rulers there been willing to intervene in its support. Its ruler, Abu Abdullah "Boabdil," seemed unable to consolidate his position there and this was not compensated for by the fact that the month before he and his commander, Musa ibn `Abd al-Malik, had recaptured three important castles in the plains before the city. When, on June 18, 1491, Queen Isabella of Castile accompanied her husband King Ferdinand of Aragon (who was directing the campaign) to the important Spanish position at La Zubia to view the prospect of Granada across the valley, it was very much like collectors inspecting the goods they were shortly to acquire. By October their forces had completed the building of a fortified base camp and the net was closing in. On November 22, secret negotiations of surrender had been agreed by representatives from the opposing sides. Apparently news leaked out among the population; at all events, in the night of January 2, Spanish soldiers were admitted secretly to the Alhambra as a body guard for the king at the formal surrender the following day.

After eight hard-fought months the siege was over. The bishop of Avila entered in solemn procession and encountered the fallen king, who saluted him with the words, "Enter and occupy the fortress which Allah has bestowed upon you as punishment to us for the sins of the Moors." Meanwhile, to the horror of the Muslims, the silver cross of Christ was being raised above the Alhambra. Boabdil, with an escort of fifty horsemen, rode on to meet the Spanish monarchs Ferdinand and Isabella who greeted him honorably and delivered back his son who had been their hostage during the siege.

Granada was assured of honorable terms in defeat and the privilege to retain the Muslim religion. Within a short time the concession was rescinded. But the reverse for Muslim power in the western Mediterranean was soon to be counterbalanced by success in the east.

### The thunder of the guns and the siege of Rhodes, 1480 and 1522

Following the Ottoman triumph at the siege of Constantinople in 1453 (see Chapter 6) the eventual dominance of Islamic power seemed at last assured in the eastern Mediterranean; and yet Muslim shipping was still prey to the pirate galleys of the Knights of St. John of the Hospital, based in Rhodes city harbor on the island of Rhodes. For more than a century the Hospitallers had held the place, the defense of the walls parcelled out among the various langues (languages) from which the knights came—England, Italy, France, Provence, Aragon, Germany—and had harried the trade routes of Islam. The nuisance had to be abated.

The decisive role played by Sultan Mehmet II's Turkish artillery at Constantinople was a sign of the times, and when, in 1480, his generals laid siege to Rhodes, they had again brought their guns to bear with great effect. A French illustration drawn just ten years after the siege shows a stretch of the high curtain wall of the city, evidently recently damaged by artillery fire, made good as a temporary measure with what looks like an artist's impression of rubble-filled gabions. Whatever they were, they seem to have done the job, since the Turks called off the siege, having been unable to capitalize on the breach made by their guns and suffering heavy casualties in repeated assaults.

For their part, the Knights made important modifications to the defenses of the city. At various points the walls were remodeled to take gun emplacements; above all, the walls were reduced in height so as to offer a target of lower profile. In the next century the low-profile fortress would be found in many parts of Europe, classically at the coastal fortress, built by King Henry VIII, of Deal in Kent where a cluster of low circular towers surrounding a low contour central "keep" crouch in an immensely wide but shallow pit so as to present almost no elevation to the cannons of enemy ships. Other measures to counter enemy artillery at Rhodes included the digging of a second dry moat to allow a first line of defense and bastions carefully positioned along the walls to give maximum fields of fire against attacking infantry.

News of the heroic and successful defense of Rhodes rang throughout Europe, as did the name of the man who had organized it, Pierre d'Aubusson, nobleman by birth, churchman by profession. A crusader to the manner born, austere, deeply religious and a strict disciplinarian, he also observed the Christian convention that an oath sworn to an infidel had no force: so when Cem, the pretender to the Ottoman throne, fled to him for protection, he in fact accepted a bribe from the prince's brother, Sultan Bayezid II, to hold him in prison. It is said that Bayezid presented the Grand Master with a reliquary containing the severed arm of John the Baptist.

Fifty-seven at the time of the siege, Aubusson, its undoubted hero (he took five wounds in one day of fighting), had been master of the Order for four years. When it was over, he was well qualified to oversee the reconstruction of the fortifications, for this charismatic leader was knowledgeable in mathematics and a trained engineer. Design innovations like those found at Rhodes are found in other Hospitaller fortresses associated with his twenty-seven-year rule as Master, and it seems likely that they were first tried out at Rhodes.

Bayezid's son and successor, Selim I, called "the Grim" (who forced his father's abdication and probably had him poisoned for good measure, murdered his own brothers and all but one of his own sons to ensure an untroubled succession), in a whirlwind campaign in 1516–17 conquered the Arab rulers of Syria and Egypt and so won mastery of Cairo, Alexandria and Beirut, the three greatest ports in the Levant. It was known that he was determined to eliminate the "nest of Christian pirates," whose depredations on the empire's shipping was more deleterious than ever, but he died in September 1520 before he could put his plans into execution. They would be taken up by his successor.

In July 1522, his son, Suleiman I the Magnificent (ruled 1520–66), the richest potentate in the history of the Ottoman Empire, having dispatched a fleet of some 300 ships for the island, led a force estimated at 100,000 to Marmaris on the southern coast of Anatolia opposite the northern point of the island on which Rhodes city stands. In addition to the fighting men, the army was accompanied by tens of thousands of Balkan peasants. Among other methods in the Turkish panoply of siege warfare was the construction of huge flat-topped earthen ramps thrown up as gun platforms with sloped approaches. This called for massive resources of disposable labor since manpower losses were inevitably high. Hostilities got under way in the month of August.

Even their improved fortifications could barely withstand such a concentration of force as the Knights of St. John, under their Grand Master Villiers de l'Isle Adam, now faced. The garrison comprised just 300 knights of the Order and 6,000 additional fighting men. The defense was apportioned between the eight *langues* of the Order, France, Provence, Auvergne, Germany, Italy, Aragon, England and Castile. There was no hope of relief from Catholic Europe, where France and Germany were at one another's throats, and at one point it seemed it might very well come to a near suicidal last stand.

Forty years on since the last great siege of Rhodes, the technology of war had progressed. The Turks had new weapons—a mortar that fired almost vertically and could drop its bombs with deadly effect within the fortifications, and the use of gunpowder in mining operations; and new tactics—above all their artillery practice was more scientifically calculated to maximize its effect. Operating from the serf-built earthen ramparts, they were able to fire down on to their targets, now fully visible and open to systematic demolition.

On September 4, two of the terrible new mines blew the English bastion sky high, brought down some 36 feet of wall, and, most fortuitously for the attackers, more or less filled the moat or fosse at that point with debris. The Turks fought their way along the whole front line planting their horse-tail standards. The English, responsible for holding this stretch of the walls, under the towering figure of their standard bearer Brother Henry Mansell, blocked the advance long enough for de l'Isle Adam to rally a relieving force that drove the Muslim soldiers stumbling back from their moment of vantage, leaving the newly opened breach to be occupied by the defenders and the Turkish standards to be hurled to the ground in contempt.

But while the Turks had lost many men and three senior captains, the defenders, who could absorb such loss far less easily, had lost many men in their turn and had seen Mansell brought down with a fatal injury. Another English charge across the treacherous and cutting stones of the rubble repulsed a new surge from the Muslim ranks, and when they were now backed up by brethren from the German *langue*, forced Mustafa Pasha, the sultan's brother-in-law and general commanding, to throw himself into the front line. Once more the Christians carried the fight to them. For by this time the Knights had maneuvered light-weight field artillery into position. There were two types, firing three-pound and six-pound rounds, as much an advance on the guns of forty years earlier as anything in the Turkish arsenal. No one questioned the courage of Mustafa, but with these cannons dealing death at close range and men falling in blood-torn heaps about him, his aids dragged their resisting high commander back to some degree of safety. In an age when serious religion was all about fundamentalism, the opposing forces at Rhodes were men of extreme courage, extreme conviction and, as the West would see the case today, extreme fanaticism. The next day, September 24, Mustafa Pasha having ordered a renewed general assault, the sultan himself, surveying the conflict from a rise in the ground behind the lines, tears of frustration in his eyes, watched as four of the *langues'* bastions were mercilessly pounded by his artillery to no apparent effect. Worse still, these infidel warriors of the devil threw back the soldiers of the Faith again, in yet another charge of screaming and fanatical heroism. He had to recall his men, yet again.

For the Christian defenders, it was obvious that despite their glorious achievement only one end to the fighting was possible. By now, not only was the breach virtually un-defendable but the enemy had broken through in two other places; Turkish sappers had managed to push their trenches into the town to a distance of about 100 feet; the reserves of fighting men had been used so that laborers were being called on to fill up their ranks. The Knights had the choice to end that fighting rather than die, to the last man of the garrison, for the glory of their religion. And many were in favor of martyrdom. Others realized that if they chose a glorious death for themselves, their defeat would spell pillage, rape and death, the price of defiance, for the townspeople.

A pitiful deputation of citizens, led by the Orthodox bishop, came to the Commander of the Order begging him to yield. After much deliberation among themselves, the knights decided that to seek terms and sue for peace would be more agreeable to God since it would spare the lives of the ordinary people. A truce was called. It held for little more than a week before the emaciated remnant of knights and soldiery found themselves called to sally against the infidel yet once more. But now the people of Rhodes, their appeal to the honor of their fanatical neighbors having been aborted, began deserting to the "enemy" in large numbers. The sultan was offering generous terms. In return for Rhodes, which in fact he had already won, and its dependencies, the surviving Knights were to be able to quit the island with all their goods; the islanders were promised continuing freedom of worship; their churches would not be desecrated. De l'Isle Adam capitulated on December 23, 1522, accepting a safe conduct for himself and his men and also for any of the islanders who wished to leave. The sultan confirmed his pledge to recognize Christianity on the island.

The great siege of Rhodes was over. With the first day of January 1523, their armor burnished and their helmets glinting in the sun and, to the sound of their drums and the snap and flutter of their banners in the winter breeze, the last members of the Order marched out in good order. Their days of crusading warfare in the eastern Mediterranean were part of history past. In fact, their role in the western Mediterranean would belong to history's future.

It was later said that, thanks to a spy in the sultan's harem, the Knights had to some extent been prepared for the attack—though truth to tell they surely knew that had he lived Selim would have got round to attending to them in due course, and no less was to be expected of his son. As it was, the fame of the siege and its champion, Grand Master Villiers de l'Isle Adam, transcended that of forty-two years earlier, even though, this time, the warriors of Islam won. Nowhere would it resonate more thrillingly than in England, thanks no doubt to the roll of the English *langue* and its standard bearer, Fra" (Brother) Henry Mansell.

In his book, *The Ottoman Impact on Europe,* Paul Coles wrote, "the capture of Rhodes in 1522 . . . and the withdrawal of the Knights of St. John to a new citadel on Malta marked the passing of crusading initiative in the Mediterranean from Christendom to Islam." The judgment of the Holy Roman Emperor, Charles V, was, "Nothing in this world was ever so well lost as Rhodes."

In 1656, a remarkable London playbill advertised *The Siege of Rhodes,* a "Representation by the Art of Prospective Scenes and the Story sung in Recitative Musick" to be performed at Rutland House, Aldersgate Street. The pioneer work of English opera it was doubly remarkable for the facts that it was to appear "under the express license of Oliver Cromwell, Lord Protector" and that a female character was to be performed by a Mrs. Colman—the first time a woman's name is found in an English theatrical cast list.

# CHAPTER FOUR

# Machines of War

*"For what hope remains when the defenders confident in the height of their walls see them over-topped by the tower machine (machina bellatores) of the enemy."*

Vegetius

The Merriam-Webster American dictionary defines artillery in its first meaning as "weapons (as bows, slings and catapults) for discharging missiles"; in its second meaning as "large bore crew-served, mounted firearms." Because gunpowder transformed the design of artillery weapons, I have devoted a special chapter to its introduction and the military arm developed from it; here I am concerned with the kind of artillery used in Western warfare at least since the time of the Romans up to the fifteenth century. We start with a discussion of the counterweight trebuchet, a weapon unknown to Roman technology and developed, probably by European engineers, in the late twelfth to early thirteenth centuries.

The Chinese military deployed a missile weapon in which a pivoted lever arm, with a missile pouch or sling at the long end, was secured by a trigger mechanism until the machine was to be activated. The force was provided by men hauling on ropes attached to ropes at the short end. (Such traction weapons seem to have been used in the siege of Toulouse in 1218, during the wars of the Albigensian Crusade.) The range of the weapon was roughly related to the number of hauliers on the ropes, which may have been as large as 200. When the trebuchier released the trigger mechanism, the lever arm was suddenly flailed upwards, hurling the stone on its trajectory (and presumably leaving the troops to heel over backwards: one well-known manuscript illustration shows an engineer clinging on for dear life to a trebuchet rope). Perhaps it was the trigger mechanism that gave the European version of the weapon its French name, since *trebucher* is the French for "to trip." Manuscript illustrations show such traction weapons in use in European theaters of war. It is a fact that such stone-throwers were unknown in Europe before the First Crusade but are often depicted in manuscript illustrations of crusading warfare and were common in European sieges from about 1200 onwards. The first use of a counterweight trebuchet in Chinese warfare was at the siege of Xiangyang in 1275, when it is described as a "Muslim" weapon—clear evidence of West–East diffusion and suggestive as confirmation of its origins as a European invention. It is said that the Egyptian Mameluke force that finally recovered the port of Acre on the coast of Palestine (modern Akka, Israel) for Islam in 1291 employed no fewer than ninety-two counterweight trebuchets to force the surrender of the place after a long and heroic defense.

Stone-throwers had been used by both sides in the twelfth century campaigns of Christian against Muslim in the Middle East. It seems that the counterweight type was in use from the 1160s, the brain child of either a Muslim or Christian inventor. An illustration in a treatise on war presented to Saladin depicts a contrivance with a counterweight basket and what looks like a trigger mechanism, but there is no sign of the all-important sling and, all in all, the draftsman does not seem to have seen an actual, working model of the device. At the siege of Acre during the Third Crusade, the Turks of the garrison deployed a weapon they called "Bad Kinsman" against the crusaders' *petraria*, "Bad Neighbor." Built for King Philip II of France by his military engineers, it plied day and night against the principal wall of the city. The team manning the Turkish machine were clearly expert marksmen since although their target was a single enemy war machine, as opposed to a stretch of wall, they made several direct hits that "broke it in pieces." Nevertheless, the French eventually won

*Based on a near-contemporary illustration of a traction trebuchet deployed by the defenders at the siege of Toulouse during the Albigensian wars of the early thirteenth century. It will be seen that the team of hauliers powering the weapon included women.* Gordon Monaghan

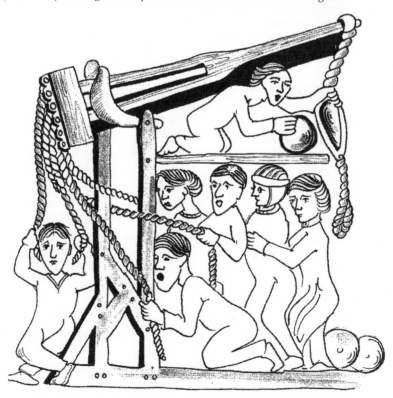

this round in the artillery duel: each time "Bad Neighbor" was knocked out, Philip's engineer corps brought it back into action, so that it managed to bring down a stretch of the wall.

Such "artillery duels" were only possible because of the accuracy of aim that could be achieved thanks to the all-important sling-shot action of the trebuchet. An excellent example comes from the siege of Tournai in Flanders, in 1340, at the opening of the Hundred Years' War. An "artillery engine" manned by a team of Flemings, allies of England's Edward III, were targeting the St. Fontaine gate in the north-west wall of the town. The French defenders countered with an "engine" just inside the gate, which quickly knocked out the enemy piece. The Flemings dragged their "engine" out of line of fire, repaired it and returned it to the attack—only to see it smashed once more. It is perhaps possible that the imprecise term "engine" conceals the presence of a gunpowder weapon, such weapons having being known in the West for at least twenty years. The fact that the Flemings were able to make running repairs strongly suggests that the "engine" in question was a trebuchet rather than a cannon, but it does not necessarily rule out the latter possibility. An early cannon was little more than iron tube (the barrel) mounted on some kind of carriage. Possibly the French missile had merely unseated the barrel from its mounting. But the historian Froissart, who reports the contest, uses the word cannon elsewhere, which suggests that in this case he has in mind the more conventional style of "engine."

At the siege of Acre there was much rivalry within the Christian camp between the various commanders. The duke of Burgundy's trebuchiers worked to outdo the Templars' team, and the Knights Hospitaller waged an unceasing bombardment on their own account it seems. The count of Flanders had financed two machines, one of them the largest yet seen in the campaign. When King Richard of England arrived at the scene of operations, he supervised the building of two *petrariae* of "choice workmanship and selected materials of top quality" and remarkably effective range. A third apparatus designed by Richard himself, the finest military architect of the age, was a compact piece fitted with steps for the operator to mount when checking the settings. This the army dubbed the "*Berefred*." In addition he had two "mangonels" constructed, one of which acted with such violence and velocity that it was capable of dropping a missile in the center of the city. It fired huge stones which Richard had acquired at Messina during his stopover in Sicily en route to the Holy Land. One of these killed twelve men at a single shot—the missile was brought to Saladin for his inspection. From a very early period it seems, specialist ammunition was demanded whether for trebuchet or, later, gunpowder artillery. Edward I had nearly 800 stones prepared for his stone-thrower artillery at the siege of Stirling in the 1290s.

For the vast majority of the army, warriors and camp followers alike, the "crusade" (the word was only coined much later) was in the first place an armed pilgrimage rather than a campaign of armed conquest, and for them, one imagines, the rivalry between the teams of artillery men, the counts and the kings and the crews of the "Monks of God," must have seemed impious. Perhaps

*An artist's impression of a massive counterweight trebuchet with pulley "gearing" to facilitate the pull down of the lever arm carrying the all-important sling and pouch, in which the missiles were loaded.*
Gordon Monaghan

it was for this reason that the "other ranks" clubbed together to finance the building of what we might call a communal petraria. Soon known as "God's stone-thrower," it had its own crew, chief among them "a priest of great probity." His job was to preach the word of God and exhort passers-by to contribute to the costs of the machine. He was also charged with recruiting volunteers to search for suitable stones as ammunition and bring them to the firing platform. It is tempting to suppose that these, to our minds, clumsy pieces of apparatus hurled any old rock that came to hand and that their crew captains were indifferent to any quality apart from the weight of the missile and its adaptability to the weapon's sling. However, a comment in the Itinerary of Richard I from which much of this account is drawn, indicates that things were more complicated. Talking of the stone inspected by Saladin the account says: "Nothing could withstand stones and flinty pieces of rock, such as this one, of the smoothest kind; they shattered any object that they struck."

This suggests that ammunition was being shaped and produced for trebuchet firing from the very start of the weapon's career in western warfare. The pilgrim soldiers who volunteered for ammunition duty on what one might call the "God's stone-thrower detail" may have worked to quite specific instructions in their search—custom-made ammunition stones hurled from the opposing batteries would, one supposes, have been ideal. The passage in the Itinerary with its report of stones having been brought all the way from Messina is a practical instance of King Richard's renowned professionalism as a military man: it also indicates how highly prized specialist ammunition was.

Archaeologists working at the site of Dolforwyn Castle in Powys in the 1980s unearthed round balls of dolerite, a fine-grained igneous basaltic rock. It seems safe to assume that these, brought from Montgomery Castle, some eight miles distant as the crow flies, were ordered up as projectiles for the English siege-engines that reduced the place to surrender in April 1277. One imagines they were carried part of the way by barge along the River Severn. This would have added perhaps three miles to the journey, but at a time when inland waterway was almost always quicker and cheaper it would probably have been well worth it. This kind of decision would have been all in a day's work for the quartermaster in charge of supply for a medieval army.

While smaller models may have been of use in sweeping a fortress wall of defenders in preparation for an assault, a large trebuchet was not of course primarily an anti-personnel weapon, though we have seen that a chance direct hit would be lethal and even a near miss could be dangerous. At the siege of Stirling in 1304, Edward I was thrown from his

*Medieval war illustrations were often the work of monastic illuminators with little military experience. It is hard to believe that the flimsy contraption bottom right could ever have existed as shown, let alone been deployed. However, the principle of the counterweight and, more important, of the sling action is clearly understood here.* Taylor Library

horse when it was brought down by a missile stone that landed just by. So far as we know, the first great trebuchet that might have been seen in England was the one brought over for Louis of France (later king as Louis VIII) when he came to help the baronial rebels against King John in the war of Magna Carta in the 1210s. "Might have been seen," because the massive contraption capsized the transport vessel carrying it when the French invasion fleet was driven back by English ships off Sandwich on August 27, 1217. We do not know whether it was salvaged for inspection by the English—probably it went to the bottom with the transport. Reportedly it had a counterweight box that could hold over 12 metric tons of hardcore and rubble and could hurl a 300-pound missile some 200 yards (185 meters). We are told, tantalizingly enough, that it too was dubbed *malvoisin* ("Bad Neighbor") by the French invading force. Was this the name routinely applied by French builders to a certain type of trebuchet? It would be nice to think that here we have a glimpse of a range of artillery manufacture; nice, but pretty far-fetched perhaps.

At this time we also find an English reference to "Turkish mangonels," though it is not clear what the term meant. Historians of warfare have traditionally taken "mangonel" to refer to a stone-throwing artillery piece powered by torsion; though in this reference the word could perhaps be merely an alternative term for a trebuchet. The adjective also poses problems. Does it mean a weapon learnt from the Turks or a weapon developed by Christian knights in the Holy Land in their wars with the Turks?

Modern trebuchet reconstructions suggest that engines like "Malvoisin" were indeed quite accurate—once the range was established such a weapon could play heavy missiles on the same target area over many hours until the masonry crumbled or suddenly collapsed. But they were massive contraptions—timber beams up to 18 feet long were required—and took many hours to set up. It was also difficult to shift the direction of fire. By increasing or reducing the weight in the counterweight box it was possible to alter the range with some degree of precision, but once the chosen target masonry had been demolished it was an arduous business to traverse onto a new target area. A manuscript

*The artist may not have been clear as to how the sling contraption actually worked but he gives a vivid idea of one of the nastier ploys used to demoralize the opposition. It is not unusual to find reports of the heads of prisoners seized in a failed sortie from the garrison being fired back into the town or fortress.* Taylor Library

illustration from Spain seems to show a trebuchet with a wheeled frame. It is not clear what this was for, but it may have been to improve the performance of the counterweight. On a fixed frame engine the weight would necessarily fall in an arc and waste part of the gravitational energy in forcing against the rigid frame. But if that structure was free to move (ideally on a rail track) then the weight would fall vertically thus exerting the full force of the drop on the lever arm and the missile sling. Modern trials on reconstructions have, incidentally, demonstrated that the whiplash of the sling contributed essentially to the centrifugal power of the lever arm.

### The crossbow: a hand-held machine

If we take a "machine" to be something that involves a mechanism, then the crossbow was an early war machine found on European battlefields. Known in some form or another from the earliest times in ancient China, it comprised a short bow mounted "crosswise" on a wooden stock. This meant the string could be hauled back two-handed by the bowman and, looped over a hook, could be braced to a much higher tension than in the simple bow and the tension maintained until the projectile (either arrow or bolt) could be loaded in a trough hollowed out in the stock. The weapon was then raised to the shoulder and "fired" by activating a trigger mechanism that released the string. The loading procedure made for a much slower rate of fire than in the case of the simple bow; but the projectile was delivered with much greater force. Even more important, the two-handed system of bracing the bow meant that the soldier did not require the long training needed by the longbow man to develop the muscular strength and poise to handle the simpler but more responsive weapon. Perfection in longbow practice was all about training to improve the man's strength and rate of fire. In the case of the European crossbow, improvement was much more about mechanical R & D to increase the weapon's firepower. A hook suspended from the bowman's belt, together with a stirrup attached to the foot of the stock, meant that he could brace the string to still higher tension than by the simple use of two hands since he could now pull back with the whole weight of his body. Later, a lever fitted into lugs on the stock was used to increase the pull weight on the bowstring. Finally, in the early 1400s, a cranked windlass or *manivel* that could be removed before firing was fitted to enable a still greater pull. This type, sometimes called the *arbalet*, was more lethal than the early handguns beginning to appear at about the same time. A further development was a type of rack-and-pinion mechanism called the *cranequin*.

From an early period the crossbow fired a specialized projectile, a short wooden bolt with a flat base to absorb the impact of the high tension string and often with a broad metal head. A crossbow bolt could punch a hole in all but the toughest plate armor, and on the exposed body caused a splayed and jagged wound (somewhat like a dumdum bullet one supposes). As early as 1139, Pope Innocent II issued a bull to ban its use in warfare between Christian states—a prohibition somewhat less effective than modern Geneva conventions governing chemical and biological warfare in the world arena.

In place of feathers the bolt was guided in flight by clumsy leather fins which made it less accurate than the longbow; it also had a shorter range, which coupled with its slow rate of fire, put it at a disadvantage as a weapon in the field, except in the hands of specialists, most renowned of whom were the Genoese companies of mercenaries. The crossbow came into its own in siege warfare. Here, the garrison bowman was secure behind the fortress battlements during his loading procedure while the attackers could take cover behind special heavy shields, known as pavises, carried on the back on the march (or transported in a wagon) and pitched in the ground when the soldier was in action. A heavy ground, frame-mounted crossbow, known to the Romans as *ballista*, seems to have been used as a siege artillery weapon. The Turkish artillery at the siege of Constantinople in 1453 certainly deployed large frame-mounted crossbows in addition to numerous types of gun. At the other end of the scale, as will be seen in Chapter 10, it seems that the crossbow might be preferred to the longbow in what one might call domestic use, that is, when defending one's house against unruly neighbors if the ceilings were too low for the deployment of longbows.

### The battering-ram: simple but effective
Although hardly a "machine," the battering-ram could prove highly effective in forcing an entrance against a poorly guarded or inadequately reinforced

timber gate. In its simplest form a log or beam of wood anything from 22 to 33 feet long, wielded by a body of men, it was swung against the obstruction until it yielded. In fact, the ram was very rarely as simple as that. If it was to be used against masonry it would be shod with an iron point (sometimes, if contemporary illustrations are to be believed, shaped like a ram's head) and was more often than not slung by leather or rope collars from a ridge beam supported on a sturdy wooden frame. This of course relieved the team of the ram's weight but also enabled them to work up a rhythmic swing and so built a momentum of travel. The objective was not so much to batter a hole through the wall—given the thickness of most defensive walls that would be impossible— but rather to dislodge or crumble the lower courses of the masonry so that sappers with picks could dislodge and remove the stones; this done, the wall was expected to collapse, though the entire job

*A crossbowman cranking up his bow string with rack and pinion, comes from a painting of the early 1500s. The head of the short missile or "bolt" held between his teeth, guided by two leather fins, is splayed so as to cause a ragged open wound. A papal edict against the weapon in Christian warfare had been issued in the 1130s.* Gordon Monaghan

might take several days. The men working the ram were naturally vulnerable to overhead attack; so the combined apparatus of ram and ridge beam was most often provided with a penthouse covering, the sides perhaps draped with water-soaked leather as protection against fire weapons. Usually it was mounted on wheels.

The late Roman army knew an elaborate version of this kind of ram. In fact, at the sixth-century siege of Rome it was used against the city by the Goths, who had presumably learnt the design from their imperial enemy. It comprised a four-sided hut of wooden beams covered in animal hides and mounted on wheels; the beam acting as the ram was pointed either like an arrow or like a flattened pyramid. A team of up to fifty men operated the machine, pushing it from within. "Machine" seems the right word here because a contemporary description records that when they had maneuvered it close up to the wall they drew back the beam "by turning some sort of machinery."

The ram as described may have originated with the Romans but the principle was well known at least from the seventh century BC. A relief carving of a battle scene from Nineveh depicts a wheeled tower with archers firing from the battlemented top stage while below them a massive pestle-like beam projects upward from the tower at an angle of 45 degrees. If it is a simple ram, the angle is problematic since it would be more effective if swung horizontally; moreover, the end is not pointed but in fact flairs somewhat. In any case it is not attacking the lower part of the wall but dislodging stones from near the top. It is presumably pivoted within the tower and is perhaps being manipulated with a hammer-like action by the team within— certainly a lot of masonry is being dislodged.

*Based on a ninth-century* BC *Assyrian relief carving, this illustration shows what may be the earliest depiction of a siege tower. A massive armored vehicle is fitted with a pivoted arm, operated from within to tear at the presumably mud brick walls. This is not a ram as understood by medieval commanders, but they would have recognized the mobile tower concept.* Gordon Monaghan

The ultimate triumph of the rammers could be considerably delayed, if the walls of the fortress were not too high, by suspending heavy mattresses from the battlements so to absorb the impact of the ram head. But there were other measures, sometimes ingenious, sometimes desperate. In 1111–12 at the siege of the coastal Muslim city of Tyre, in modern Lebanon, the crusader king Baldwin of Jerusalem, used a number of large siege-towers with battering-rams slung in their bottom stage. The defenders on the walls could not really do much harm to the ram team as they were covered by the heavily protected tower structure. The Arab commander's daring solution was to have his men break up a stretch of masonry along the top of their own wall. The stretch in question was exceptionally high and defended by two projecting towers. The detached stonework was now toppled down, destabilizing the tower, and, as it cascaded down and outwards from the base of the wall, it formed a slope or glacis or counter-batter which protected the footings of the wall, so that the tower-ram could not resume its operation until the rubble had been cleared. In addition, of course, the fallen rubble had blocked or even filled in the damage already made, and clearing it would cost the Christian attackers many lives. They decided to shift the point of attack and begin the laborious process over again at a new point along the wall. Even so, the Muslim defenders were, not surprisingly, delighted with their check on the Christian attack. Citizens flocked to the top of the walls to look down on their triumph.

### Innovators on site, named and unnamed

Among the spectators was a sea captain who had brought a ship with supplies down the coast from Tripoli. By the time he arrived to view the recent triumphs, the Christian tower-ram had already been moved and was systematically pulverizing the lower masonry of a new section of wall. This time the garrison commander would not sanction any further dilapidation of his defenses. The seaman described a maneuver based on the idea of the grappling-hooks used in sea fights. At his suggestion the defenders let down massive hooks from the parapet: once they engaged a ram shaft it was possible to drag the thing off target. Since the Christian troops had to go right to the foot of the wall to neutralize the grappling-hooks and so became sitting targets for the hail of missiles from the battlements, the attack in this sector was stalled.

The clumsy counter-tactic had an unexpected benefit from the defenders' point of view. The rams, fitted with iron shoes about 20 pounds in weight, were so long that they projected out from the back of the siege-towers. Once the defenders had grappled the front of the ram they continued to haul it up, the rope of the grapple was wound about the drum of a windlass mechanism so that a large pull weight could be achieved and maintained. With the rear end of the ram timber stuck in the mud the front end strained against the cross piece of the tower's lower stage. The tower structure was necessarily unbalanced and, if the ram did not snap under the strain—and some did—was liable to be overturned, the men climbing the ladders on it sides being thrown to earth.

But the crusader army continued its attack. The sea captain, clearly an engineer of inventive genius, now came up with an entirely novel weapon that, if it worked, would deliver a virtually unbroken deluge of fire onto the enemy siege-tower from behind the safety of the battlements. In the absence of a Byzantine-type siphon it was the nearest thing to a flame-thrower possible at the time. As before, the captain's contraption was an adaptation of maritime equipment he was familiar with. Under his direction, carpenters constructed what amounted to a massive crane or derrick. Two large wooden beams were set up in the form of a "T," the cross piece, about 60 feet long, pivoting on the upright member and fitted with an iron extension carried a system of rings and pulleys that could be controlled from behind the battlements. These supported a running line along which a chain of buckets, charged with flaming incendiary materials, could be run out over the siege-tower and emptied on the structure and its unfortunate occupants. The result was an intermittent river of fire that forced the would-be attackers back down into the lower stages or to jump desperately for their lives. Within a matter of minutes the massive wooden tower was abandoned, the twelfth-century equivalent of a "towering inferno." King Baldwin had fought a determined siege but the sight of his massive machines of war reduced to charred ruins with such ease seems to have decided him to abandoned the operation. Tyre remained Muslim for another forty years.

From the introduction of Greek fire at the siege of Constantinople in the 670s by a named inventor (see the following chapter) it seems clear that individual inventive genius and innovative expertise on the spot must have made decisive contributions on many occasions. We know about the ingenious hero of Tyre only thanks to the survival of the text describing his prowess; his name is not recorded, but the account offers a rare glimpse of an individual making a vital contribution to the outcome of a siege.

The case is quite different for the siege of Brescia in the summer of 1238. Here the citizens, in arms against the oppressive rule of Emperor Frederick II, probably owed their survival to an expert whom they pressed into their service and whose name is recorded in the account of the siege. Allied with Milan, leader of the Lombard city communes, the Brescians knew full well that they could expect no quarter in the event of an imperial victory. As the siege progressed they made a number of sorties, and it was a rare occasion if they recovered the safety of the city walls without having inflicted serious losses on the besieging German troops and bringing in valuable captives. The greatest prize was won in a particularly daring raid that managed to return with a renowned Spanish military engineer called Calamandrinus who was actually on the staff of the emperor's chief adviser, Ezzelino of Romano. Apparently he was a cool-headed professional who owed allegiance only to his own career: he now willingly sold his services to his new employers, on the offer of a fine house complete with attractive housewife. He made a thorough study of the city's defenses and made designs for important improvements based on his knowledge of the capabilities of the imperial artillery.

Before the arrival of Calamandrinus, Brescia's antiquated defenses were proving quite inadequate to withstand the battery of state-of-the-art siege weapons brought to bear under Ezzelino's command. Many, it seems, had been built to designs by the Spaniard who was now directing the defense of the place they had been devised to destroy. It is rare indeed for one side to acquire such hands-on expertise relating to the enemy's resources.

Then, on a moonless night early in October, probably with advance notice of celebrations in the enemy camp, the Brescians achieved another coup; they forced their way through the tents of the confused imperial soldiery, "heavy with wine and sleep," almost to the quarters of the emperor himself. When the raiding party withdrew, they left scores of enemy dead in their wake and a demoralized opposing force. This was the decisive moment in the siege. That the defenders had survived long enough to deliver this coup was due to the improvements they had been able to make to their defense works under the expert guidance of the Spaniard, the innovator on site they had bought over.

# CHAPTER FIVE

# Fire Hazard

*According to Sun-tzu, there are five targets for attack by fire, and the first is men. The others are, in the order given, supplies, matériel, store houses and lines of communication.*

A fter the collapse of the imperial Roman army, barbarian Europe's use of fire projectiles was probably limited to fire arrows. The Romans had deployed various forms of incendiary weapon both on land and at sea, and Vegetius has a certain amount to say about them. He describes petroleum oil-based mixtures and recommends an army hold reserves of bitumen, sulphur and pitch as well. He also makes specific recommendations as to the best methods to adopt for the burning of wooden structures. However, the chief fire weapon of the Middle Ages was unknown to Vegetius: this was the notorious "Greek fire" of the Byzantine naval arsenal. As it was developed at Constantinople, founded as the new first city of the East Roman Empire, though the home of Greek culture, Vegetius would surely have pointed to it proudly as a Roman innovation. It may be the first example of a "secret" weapon in history—it is probably also the most successful ever.

## Greek fire: a legendary technology

From its first appearance in warfare at the blockade siege of Constantinople by the Muslim fleet in the 670s, its reputation was fearsome. The principal quality of this Greek fire was its combustion on contact with water. Four hundred years later the Byzantines were still using it, this time to disperse Christian shipping en route for the Holy Land. Vessels from Pisa raiding Greek islands for supplies and carrying crusaders found themselves under attack from the Byzantine flotilla of light galleys, each with a siphon flame-thrower mounted in the prows. The nozzles were in the form of a lion's head or other predator, so that it seemed as if these land monsters were vomiting fire on to the sea.

The invention is attributed to an architect/engineer called Kallinikos of Baalbek, a Syrian refugee, presumably Christian, in the great city at the time of the blockade. Combustible materials of various types had long been used in warfare when Kallinikos revealed the secret of his new "wet fire" to the emperor. Given that water played so important a part in the combustion, it has been suggested that quicklime was the new secret ingredient, in addition to sulphur and a naphtha ingredient. The mixture was projected from copper

*The famous incendiary weapon known as "Greek fire" was usually deployed at sea. The secret recipe included petroleum and resinous extracts so the burning liquid would float on the surface. Based on a ninth-century Byzantine manuscript, the illustration shows how the nozzle of the flame thrower might be cast in some monstrous shape, sometimes like a lion belching flame.*
Gordon Monaghan

tubes and ignited on contact with the moist side of the enemy ships, or with the sea. (The Byzantine navy was soon equipped with siphonophores, specialist "siphon-bearing" vessels.)

If reports are to be believed the weapon developed truly remarkable properties over the centuries. In 1081, Byzantine power in the Balkans and the Adriatic coast was under threat from Robert Guiscard, duke of Apulia, the chief of the Norman brigands then in southern Italy. Venice saw his expansion as a threat to its trading interests and was happy to support Constantinople in the area. Indeed, Venetian galleys seem to have had access to Greek fire technology, whether actual weapons or siphonophore crews assigned to their commanders.

In the summer of 1081, Guiscard was preparing to lay siege to the Adriatic port of Dyrrachium (Durazzo or Durrës) when a Venetian squadron swept down to do battle. It was a night engagement and the scene must have been dramatic. John Julius Norwich notes a report in the contemporary *History of Sicily* by the Norman Benedictine monk Geoffrey of Malaterra, relating the deployment of the weapon during the action. The Venetian vessels, he says, discharged "the fire that is called 'Greek'" through pipes operating from beneath the surface of the sea and so "burnt one of our ships under the very waves." There is a well-known illustration in an eighth-century Byzantine manuscript of a siphonophore operating at sea, its flames living on the sea's surface having perhaps ignited there, but there appears to be no other source to confirm that the fire-jet could actually surge beneath and through water and so combust the target. Was the equipment actually operated by Byzantine technicians?

After a long and hard-fought battle, the Venetian ships were able to force their way through into the harbor at Durazzo as dawn was coming up. They had found a safe haven; but the ambitious Guiscard was not to be deterred by a single sea fight, no matter how dramatic. He was still in command of a sizeable army and prepared to invest the port city. Defeated outside the walls of Durazzo in October, in an attempt to raise the siege, a Byzantine army led by the emperor himself had to retire. Even so the place held out for the best part of four more months and then was won only through the treachery of a Venetian resident. It turned out that he had betrayed the interests both of homeland and his adopted country in return for a promise that he might marry into the duke of Apulia's family.

The precise secret formula of Greek fire has never been fully deciphered. Its potency was never in doubt. According to Chaucer's highly sexed Wife of Bath some men could find her kind of loving "like Greek fire, The more it burns, the fiercer its desire / To burn up everything that can be burned." In an article published in 1979, Jim Bradbury suggested that one mixture included crude petroleum, and that the Byzantines may have been able to refine the crude, since Arab sources referred to them as "cooking" it. (But descriptions of the fire-pots hurled by trebuchets speak of the oil in them bubbling as it boiled.) Inevitably, fire inspired terror whenever deployed, and it seems that any particularly vicious fire weapon whether flame-thrower or not was dubbed "Greek" fire. A typical incident was recorded by the Sieur de Joinville campaigning on the Nile in 1249 in the crusading army of King Louis IX of France. One night when he was in charge of the guard on the crusaders camp, the "Saracens" brought forward a stone-thrower, something they had not used before, and put a barrel of "Greek fire" into its sling. De Joinville recalls that, seen head-on as it hurtled toward them, it seemed it must be a large barrel of verjuice, with a fiery tail the length of a long lance. It came on with the roar of a thunderbolt and the whole effect was of a dragon, while the mass of flames emitted so much light that the entire camp was lit up as clear as day. Such fire weapons were still being deployed three centuries later by Turkish forces at the siege of Malta, and they were notorious for the speed with which the flames devoured everything in their path. The Russian siege of Constantinople by a Black Sea fleet led by Prince Igor in 1043 was thrown into confusion by the dreadful weapon. Attacking the seaward walls, the Russian ships found themselves assailed by "liquid fire . . . like sky lightning . . . that was shot out from long tubes emplaced in the battlements" that burned men and ships "so that we could not overcome them." The Venetian ships that led the 1204 siege of Constantinople were protected with water-soaked awnings of animal hides; there is no mention of any vessel being put out of action by flame-thrower.

The classic Greek fire weapon then was the siphon flame-thrower of the Byzantine navy. Oddly enough, although, thanks to a portage of ships from the Sea of Marmara ordered by the sultan, Turkish warships were active in the Golden Horn, according to Mark Bartusis, an authority on the late Byzantine army, there is no reliable evidence that Greek fire as such (known to the Byzantines as "liquid fire") was used by the defenders at the siege of Constantinople in 1453. It may be a question of terminology. Tursun Bey, an Ottoman official present during the action, claimed to have seen fire weapons using what he called Greek fire.

No one else it seems was able to duplicate the naval application of true Greek fire that ignited on contact with water. Nor it seems was the action of

*An illustration from the German handbook on incendiary weapons Feuerwerkbuch of the 1420s shows, in addition to the incendiary arrows, a large cannon in its gun carriage. Back up transporters would carry a gun cradle or frame on which to mount the weapon for action; a winch with which to lift the barrel onto the cradle; ammunition; and gun powder.*
Taylor Library

the siphonophore devices ever exactly replicated. However, pump-action appliances were used by other military forces, and almost as effective was the "trump," an infantry weapon comprising a metal or metal-bound wooden tube with a rear-mounted bellows pump and filled with an inflammable mixture of resins, sulphur salts and linseed oil. The muzzle was smeared with a viscous "fuse" and once this was lit, the liquid forced out by the pump became a spear of fire, with a range of several yards, "snorting and belching furious flames." Some writers used the word trump for another highly effective combustible weapon—the fire wheel. As its name indicates, this comprised a wheel or hollow hoop coated with pitch or tar and simply bowled toward the enemy; in the hope, presumably, that it would not tip onto its side before it reached him.

It is possible that Greek fire was introduced into Western European warfare during the first half of the twelfth century, though the evidence is confused; certainly the ruling of Pope Innocent II, at the Second Lateran Council of 1139, prohibiting the use of the crossbow in warfare between Christians also banned the use of incendiary weapons. This pope had a special interest in military matters since early in his pontificate he had been opposed by a rival for the papal throne and had recruited the Holy Roman Emperor to fight his cause. Whether the banned "incendiary weapons" also included Greek fire as such is not clear, but the chronicler Jean de Marmoutier names the weapon in his description of the protracted siege that Count Geoffrey of Anjou deployed in 1151 against the castle of one of his rebellious barons, recounted later in this chapter. Given that chroniclers can rarely have been familiar with the technology involved, it seems probable that many of the references to Greek fire are simply records that fire was used in the engagement concerned.

## Fire bombs and underground infernos

But for all the drama of these anti-personnel liquid combustion weapons, fire delivered its classic and most telling results either as incendiary bombs hurled by siege artillery ammunition or in the subterranean operation of the miners' and sappers' corps. The principle here was simple enough. The aim was to dig a tunnel to the fortress wall and widen it into a gallery under the foundations supporting them. When all was ready, fire was set to the tinder so as to burn away the timber uprights at the time calculated to bring down the maximum possible amount of masonry. It is obvious that success demanded technical expertise, sound judgement and professional experience as well as a cool head and some courage.

The mine-head should ideally be situated out of sight of the enemy; the length of the drive tunnel had to be calculated with accuracy; the gallery had to be spacious enough to facilitate sufficient combustion. Since the chemistry of combustion was not understood and neither was the very need for air, experience of what conditions favored the work was the only guide. And of course, the excavation work had to be carried out as quietly as possible. The sinking of listening shafts was a more or less routine precaution for the defense.

Sometimes the mine-head was sunk in full view, so to speak, of the defenders under the protection of a framed penthouse or mantelet. Often it was well behind the siege army's lines and in any case the miners could change direction underground if it seemed likely the garrison had identified the start. The defenders would combine their observations on the ground with their own assessments of their defensive weakness to calculate where the enemy might be aiming for. At the siege of Caen in 1417, the defenders experimented with bowls of water atop the walls on the theory that the vibrations of work below ground would set up sympathetic ripples in the water surface. Simple but quite sophisticated, this sensing device, if it was to work, obviously depended on the officer in charge ensuring silence within several yards of the placement.

Finally, the director of the operation should ideally be able to collapse the wall to coincide with a prepared assault. A breach made too far ahead of schedule would allow the enemy defenders to make good the damage, or at least throw up obstructions to slow the attackers. A well-conducted mine offered the possibility of serious gain. If at all possible such an operation had to be foiled.

The standard response was the countermine. Having satisfied themselves that the attacker was driving a mine and having also decided, by judgement, spies' reports, careful listening and luck, where it was heading, the defender sank a mine in his turn—aiming to confront and break in on the enemy tunnel before it reached the wall foundations or at least before their opponents had time to extend the gallery. Similar tactics were used in the twentieth century in the trench warfare on the Western Front in the First World War. For all miners, medieval or modern, it was nerve-racking work. Long minutes of listening for the vibration of the enemy picks, ears strained for the slightest sign; followed by stealthy scraping away at the face of the tunnel and then, as it became apparent that the enemy was near at hand, fierce hacking down of the last arm's length of intervening earth. Then the opposing teams met and plunged into a fearful struggle of picks and daggers in the muddy claustrophobic tunnels.

Surely such encounters must have furnished the most brutal, the most bestial episodes of medieval warfare. If the officer in charge of the mining team could alert his commanding officer in good time of an impending breakthrough into the enemy tunnel, the opposing miners would find themselves confronting properly armed soldiers rather than another mining party. At the 1107 siege of Durazzo the Greek defenders successfully countermined the enemy tunnel and, bursting through on their unprepared opponents, drove them back with "Greek fire" trumps. The effect of these fire weapons, whatever their mechanisms, were surely as horrifying for the targets as anything depicted by film special effects for battle scenes from the Second World War.

Sometimes the garrison got really good intelligence as to the location of the mineshaft behind the siege lines. For most of the summer of 1377 the fleets of Castile and France swept the English Channel, pillaging from the Isle of Wight to Hastings and even sailing up the Thames to Gravesend, which they put to the torch. Edward III , hero of the Hundred Years' War, died in June; England was in despair. In 1378 his son John of Gaunt, duke of Lancaster, led a fleet to the Normandy coast to deal retribution, but the French had retired up the Seine. Rather than head home with nothing to report, the duke laid siege to St. Malo—strongest port on the north coast of France still in French hands. While his artillery battered the walls and his men-at-arms delivered assaults, the main attack was to be a follow-up to a mining operation that, by early August, was nearing completion.

It seems that the Maloines were well informed. Under cover of the confusion of a night attack, a raiding party succeeded in completely wrecking the mine so that the workings had to be abandoned and, since it was decided pointless to start a new mine, so was the siege. On the night in question Richard Fitzalan, earl of Arundel, was in charge. But, as commander of the expedition, Lancaster was held responsible. It was a bad business for the aristocrats—the more so since John Philipot, merchant of London, had recently fitted out a fleet at his own expense that had captured the notorious Scottish pirate, John the Mercer.

### True Greek fire on the River Loire? 1151

With its massive keep, double-walled enceinte and wide rock-cut dry moat, Montreuil-Bellay, near Saumur on the River Loire was, boasted its proud lord, Baron Gerald Berlai, impregnable. Of course, it wasn't. But it had held out for the best part of three years before Count Geoffrey of Anjou deployed his incendiary weapons. Since blockade was not working (the defenders clearly had a protected water supply, among other advantages) Geoffrey at length decided on assault, and the use of fire—perhaps the long delay in deploying this weapon can be taken to mean that the count actually had come by a dramatic new technology, genuine "Greek" fire. We know from the chronicle record that he had been reading his copy of Vegetius (he was known as learned Count Geoffrey). He employed a civilian labor force to help his troops fill in the moat and so was able to bring up specially constructed siege-towers. With bowmen keeping defenders off the walls, his engineers were able to hurl Greek fire that burst in balls of flame so that the whole fortress was quickly ablaze. Even so, and even though his artillery was able to breach the walls in one or two places, the garrison still held out, managing to patch up the damage with heavy timbers during the night. These were reduced by the use of fire-bombs comprising iron canisters ("jars," the chronicler calls them) on a length of chain, filled with nut oils, linseed and hemp seed oils. They were then firmly sealed and heated in a furnace until the metal was glowing red hot and the oils within boiling. When the chain had been chilled in water it was attached to the arm of an artillery piece, the vapors of the bubbling contents were ignited and the contraption hurled, flaming, against the timber repairs in the wall. Since the canister burst on impact, the flaming contents exploded across the timbers and spread to other parts of the defenses, "vomiting an extraordinary surplus so that men barely had time to escape the conflagration."

Since Jean de Moutier, a contemporary chronicler of the siege, makes no mention of any type of siphonophore flame-thrower and there is no mention in his "recipe" for the inflammable mixture of naphtha, considered by some an essential ingredient of Greek fire, it seems likely that for him, as for many of his Western contemporaries, the essential characteristic of Greek fire was that of a combustible missile. However, the fact that we find a Robert de Greco and other Greek names among Geoffrey's courtiers tempts speculation. Geoffrey's final assault ended the siege and the rebel baron Gerald Berlai spent time as a prisoner of Count Geoffrey's.

Unfortunately for the count, he seems to have been such a devotee of Vegetius that he also followed the old Roman's advocacy of swimming as healthy exercise. To his contemporaries swimming for pleasure was a mark of eccentricity, and they would not have been surprised when it was reported, in the very year of his triumph at Montreuil, that the lord of Anjou died of a feverous chill after going for a bathe.

### Were flame-throwers chivalrous?

Somehow, one does not look upon fire as a weapon proper to the age of chivalry, but that is perhaps to misunderstand that rather eccentric and self-delusional epoch. There was a code, which at times could amount to an ethical system of the secular world, to match that of the churchmen. But its devotees, pre-eminently the knightly class, were warriors first and foremost and professionals in the art of war. As such they considered any weapon or armament as part of their expertise—even the subterranean warfare of the mine had its conventions, as we have seen, and in time gunpowder artillery, too, came to be integrated into the traditions of chivalric propriety. It was the same with incendiary artillery. Classic was the encounter between Edward of Woodstock, Prince of Wales, and the French commanders Lord Boucicaut and the knight known as the Hermit of Chaumont shortly before the prince's triumph at the Battle of Poitiers in 1356.

An English force had driven the Frenchmen to bay in the castle at Romorantin. When he heard of it the prince decided "to ride that way to take a closer look at them." By the time he arrived at Romorantin the town was filled with

English debating the best way to take the castle. In fact the French position looked hopeless: Edward, "mounted on a black charger," asked his friend Sir John Chandos at his side, to ride up to the castle palisades and offer the French honorable terms of surrender. Of course they rejected the idea. So Edward, thinking none the worse of them, ordered a full-scale assault the next day. Archers lined the banks of the moat, putting down such a withering fire that the defenders hardly dared show themselves; sappers negotiated the moat with picks and mattocks to hew away at the masonry footings of the wall. Boucicaut and Chaumont and the Lord of Craon headed a sturdy defense, themselves hurling down stones and flints and pots of quicklime. As night fell, both sides retired to tend their wounded.

The next day, still without a result, Edward, now indignant that he had been resisted for so long by a "hopeless case," vowed to take the place unconditionally, that is without mercy. Losses continued to mount until the prince agreed to bring up the cannon and to have Greek fire hurled into the courtyard in the hope that it would spread. It did indeed spread, and the thatched roof of the great tower where the three knights were leading the defense went up in a rush. With an inferno roaring above their heads, courage deserted them and they begged for terms. Perhaps recognizing that he had forced them by less than chivalric means, Prince Edward withdrew his earlier vow and granted quarter. The prince's men plundered castle and town of everything they could carry. The castle was left a burning ruin and de Boucicaut and the other gentlemen of the defense rode with the prince's entourage as his prisoners.

It is a revealing account of just one small engagement among hundreds such during the Anglo-French War. As is his wont, Froissart, the gentleman chronicler, has little interest in the horrors suffered by the ordinary soldiers and the ruined lives of the citizenry. But he does contextualize the values and conventions by which the gentry thought it proper to wage war. It seems that terror by fire razed also dishonor and could rescind the "laws of war" so that slaughter was no longer the legitimate consequence of enforced unconditional surrender.

# CHAPTER SIX

# Artillery

*"Oh villainous saltpeter . . . digged . . . from the bowels of the harmless earth,*
*which many a good tall fellow hath destroyed so cowardly . . ."*
Shakespeare, *Henry IV*, Pt. I

This chapter is concerned with artillery in its now conventional sense of projectile weapons powered by gunpowder or some other explosive mixture.

The first mention of cannon is in a Florentine source, the *Registro delle Provisione* of 1326, and the first illustration of what appears to be a gunpowder weapon showing an arrow being shot from a bottle-like "barrel," in the manuscript of Walter de Millemete (also of the 1320s), owned by the already warlike teenage King Edward III of England. From that time on, from being a kind of giant scare weapon, it slowly developed into siege equipment. Gunpowder itself has much earlier origins—as in fact do gunpowder weapons.

According to Joseph Needham, numerous firearms of various types were used by Chinese forces at the siege of Khaifêng-fu in 1232. Gunpowder certainly originated in China, and it is now generally accepted that it reached Europe by diffusion westward. However, Needham also showed that it was a mistaken idea that in China it was known only in firework displays and that its application in warfare was a Western adaptation.

Gunpowder is made of three things: saltpeter—potassium or calcium nitrate—sulphur, and powdered charcoal. Of the three, saltpeter is the essential as it provides the oxygen vital for combustion. Historically there have been two basic types: the earlier, based on calcium nitrate, and the post-medieval type based on potassium nitrate. Six parts of saltpeter and one part each of sulphur and charcoal will make the best proportions for a mixture that will explode rather than just fizzle.

It is now reckoned that the earliest written formula for gunpowder dates from the AD 1040s, in Song Dynasty China; that it was a by-product of Chinese alchemy's centuries-long concern with nitrate compounds; and that the Chinese devised numerous gunpowder weapons for military purposes, such as "fire-lances" (i.e., flame-throwers), percussion and incendiary bombs, rockets and possibly even cannon. It came to the West, possibly via Arab sources, as an innovative military technology. Europe found its own recipes for quality gunpowder by trial and error. However, because its geology and meteorology meant that the Continent had very few naturally occurring nitrate deposits, it also had to develop methods of cultivating and purifying nitrate salts. At first it depended on Asian imports for these ingredients.

Although the English Franciscan and polymath Roger Bacon, writing in the mid-1200s, gave directions for the making of gunpowder and speculated as to its possible applications in warfare, Professor Bert Hall, on whose work much of this chapter is based, states that Europe's earliest workable recipes come in the *Liber ignium ad comburendos hostes*, attributed to Marcus Graecus, about 1275–1300. Claims made for a certain German-Swiss cleric from Constance, named Berthold der Schwarze, to have produced a gunpowder recipe in the 1310s and to have been the first to cast a bronze cannon, are not now generally accepted.

For the next hundred years, saltpeter, known then as "Chinese snow," was imported through Venice, where it arrived along the spice route. It was expensive and always in short supply. In 1346 Edward III's agents purchased in London 912 pounds of saltpeter and 886 pounds of sulphur "for the king's gunnis." It is tempting to assume that the record refers to materials of war purchased for the Crécy campaign. But from this bare record it is hard to make any useful conclusions. The proportions indicated would not have yielded a satisfactory mix. Normally one would want about four to six times as much saltpeter as sulphur. Did Edward's ordnance experts supplement the mix from stores of

*The guns, without trunnions (i.e., lugs to support them in a gun carriage) and so mounted in wooden frames, consist of barrel and detachable powder chamber with touch hole. With the ball rammed into the barrel, the cylindrical chamber is tamped down with powder and wedged hard against the breech for firing. The pavilions would not, in reality, be within range of enemy fire – not that there is any!* Taylor Library

saltpeter in hand, or did they simply store the surplus sulphur? Were people still experimenting with proportions? Expert opinion as to whether Edward deployed cannons at the battle is still divided, but if he did so they can have had little impact on the outcome; indeed, the two English chroniclers with Edward's army make no mention of guns.

It is therefore surprising to find that five other apparently independent contemporary sources do in fact refer to cannons, and two of these authors were dead by 1348, that is, within two years of the battle. One of these says that the English had "guns that cast iron balls by means of fire." An Italian, he speaks of the Genoese cohort of crossbowmen in the French army being shattered by this fearsome weapon. It has been argued that his being an Italian discredits his testimony on the grounds that it was a fiction to save the honor of the Genoese who, apparently, fled the field. But three rather later French sources, among them a version of Froissart of about 1376, also refer to cannons in the English line. We know that Edward III's quartermaster bought quantities of saltpeter and sulphur, and we know that the king ordered "gunnis" to be constructed for him to take to France. We also know that he had already encountered artillery. The fact that two English clerks present at the battle made no mention of guns is not telling; neither of them gave any details of the encounter, not even the decisive role of the English archers. Four years later English chroniclers also do not record the presence of the new weapon, but one presumes that they based their accounts on their predecessors.

Even so, it is certainly curious that nothing is said of the matter by six near-contemporary English writers. Perhaps they were unwilling to lessen the glory of the victory by admitting to the use of the terrifying effect of the relatively new firearm; or perhaps they had heard nothing of it because, *au contraire*, the little primitive fire tubes made insignificant impact on the outcome. In any case, we are talking about small bore guns. Until it was destroyed by bombing in May 1940 a house and café on the rue de l'Hôtel de Ville in Abbeville was said to have on display an iron cannonball some 1.25 pounds (560 grams) in weight and 3 inches (79 mm) caliber, reported by the local paper *L'Abbevillois* as being unearthed on the ancient battlefield in September 1850.

### Early kanons: Tournai, 1340

Six years before, Crécy gunpowder artillery had undoubtedly been deployed by the French defenders at Edward's siege of Tournai. Froissart's account of the action refers to *l'artillerie, engiens, espignalls et kanons*. In that list the first three words may or may not apply to guns—for example artillerie, which first enters the English language in this century, seems to derive from the French artillier, "to equip with weapons"—but there can be no dispute about the word *kanons*.

The siege of Tournai could be called the engagement that inaugurated the Hundred Years' War between England and France. It was preceded by a letter of challenge to single armed combat from the 34-year-old Edward III of England to the 47-year-old Philip VI of France, addressed contemptuously as Philip of Valois. The son of Count Charles of Valois, brother of King Philip IV, he was not in the direct line of descent whereas Edward, grandson of that king through his daughter Isabella, was. In fact, Queen Isabella herself urged her son's right while she was still regent for the under-age king. The French, of course, would assert that this descent through the female line, perfectly valid in English law, disqualified Edward's claim under French law. Edward may himself have advanced it in the first instance to win military support of Flemish towns in his projected campaign in France. Nominally subject to the king of France, the Flemings would have welcomed a formula offered to legitimate their rebellion. At all events, in the month of July 1340 Edward was preparing to lay siege to the strategically important town of Tournai on the River Scheldt at the head of an army drawn from Flanders, Brabant and Hainault, as well as England.

The place was well stocked with food against a long defense. The walls and gates had been reinforced where necessary and some of the gates blocked up entirely (a precaution not commonly adopted in besieged towns, though Hubert de Burgh had had the North Gate at Dover walled up in the improvements he had made after the French siege of 1216–17). Booms blocked the river both upstream and downstream and siege-engines, guns and perhaps others, were emplaced at the principal gates. Edward's forces were stationed by "nationality," the English against St. Martin's gate on the south-west, the Flemings against St. Fontaine's (north-west), the Brabanters against the Marvis gate (north-east), and the Hainaulters against the Valenciennes gate (south-east). It appears that each contingent was equipped with its own artillery "engines."

Among them were ribaudequins, anti-personnel guns described by Froissart as comprising three or four barrels bound together. The separate explosive charges for each of the separate barrels were presumably fired with one multiple linstock (or equivalent) wielded by the gunner, thus allowing a single man to discharge three or four shots at one firing. Commenting on the use of the artillery, the military historian Alfred Burne explains that "in order to hit the defenders upon the battlements, plunging, or at least horizontal fire was required." Special towers were constructed so that the weapons could be raised to the required height. We do not know how effective they were, but we do know that when the siege was over the towers were dismantled and the citizens of Tournai were happy to buy the shaped timbers from which they had been constructed—army surplus sold to the former enemy to raise funds!

### Early recorded injuries from gunshot

At the French siege of the English fortification at St. Sauveur-le-Vicomte in 1375, a lucky cannon shot blasted through the window of the bedchamber of the English commander, Sir John Chatterton, smashed some furniture and then crashed through the floor. Chatterton, who was in bed at the time, may have been unnerved—he certainly opened peace negotiations. He had no guns, and while only four French guns actually fired during the siege, a further thirty-two were on their way to St. Sauveur. Four guns had achieved little, but the threat posed by eight times that number was another matter. What Sir John probably did not know was that the entire siege train was supplied with just thirty-one pounds of gunpowder, less than one pound a piece.

Sir John may also have reflected that he had had a close shave. In fact, the first recorded fatality from an artillery round seems to have been at the English siege of Orleans when Thomas Montacute, 4th Earl of Salisbury, died on November 3, 1428, of a fearful wound incurred six days before while inspecting the city from a window in the bridge tower of Les Tourelles. It is said that "half his face was blown away." The agonies of his death can hardly be imagined; his demise was fatal for the English cause. At the "siege of Paris," some twenty years later, a trumpeter with the household of the count of Charolais was killed while bringing the meat course to the count's dining-room by a cannon shot that flew past the young count as he sat awaiting his dinner and ricocheted down the stairs—mincing the entré, presumably, even as it also eviscerated the serving man.

Yet it was possible to survive even quite serious wounds from artillery fire. An archer at the siege of Liège (1470s) received a ball from a culverin that traveled through the fleshy part of one thigh and lodged in the other. Death from gangrene could have been expected, as powder and fragments of clothing that had carried through into the wound festered. Evidently the unnamed soldier was lucky in his surgeon and his injury was carefully dressed.

At St. Sauveur, we have seen that the French problem was gunpowder availability, not money. Chatterton made a good bargain, negotiating a surrender bonus amounting to 55,000 gold francs, and on July 3 the English garrison marched out of St. Sauveur, collected its pay-off, and went on its way unmolested. "In other words," comments Professor Hall, "the French could afford the cost of bribing the English to surrender, but no amount of money could buy enough powder to force the issue."

### Saltpeter and other technicalities

The restricted saltpeter supply in the fourteenth century also limited the size of firearms. The Tower of London accounts of the mid-1380s mention eighty-seven new guns: the largest nearly 737 pounds in weight, but most of them around 350 pounds. The average cost (at about 4 pence per pound) was not excessive—about £5 8s, that is, wages for a day's campaigning by 230 archers. Contemporary foundry techniques could have produced much larger weapons, had the supply of quality powder made that desirable. Then, a technological breakthrough in the manufacture of "cultivated" saltpeter, first indicated in the Frankfurt-am-Main area in the late 1370s, meant that from the 1390s the output of saltpeter, from specialized "plantations," dramatically increased. As a result, the pattern of siege-gun development radically changed.

These plantations were, essentially, stone-lined pits where rotting organic waste was composted with urine under controlled conditions to yield crude saltpeter deposits that were then, presumably, scraped from the lining walls. There are no detailed descriptions of the workings but the chemistry is well enough understood. Nitrates are produced by bacterial action as part of the process that converts once-living tissues into their chemical components. Readily soluble, they serve as a main ingredient in commercial fertilizers (they are common ingredients in contemporary terrorist bomb-making). Two genera of bacteria, nitrosomonas and nitrobacter, are also very fond of calcium carbonate;

so when nitrates are leached out of composted manure or other organic matter, calcium nitrate is a predominant by-product.

The boost to European domestic saltpeter production slashed gunpowder prices and expanded availability dramatically. Between about 1385 and 1425 in France, the price of gunpowder fell by 50 percent and by the 1480s, French gunpowder cost less than 20 percent of what it had a century earlier. Prices for Frankfurt saltpeter fell even more rapidly, from 41 florins per hundredweight in 1381–3 to less than 10 florins by 1440. All the data for England show a similar trend.

Fourteenth-century purchases of saltpeter are measured in hundreds of pounds weight; fifteenth-century accounts speak of tens of thousands of pounds bought, sold, or in storage. Preparations for a siege of Calais anticipated in 1406 involved the purchase of some 20,000 pounds of gunpowder. Fifteen years later Parisian dealers had 10,000 pounds of *poudre à canon* on hand, and material to make 10,000 pounds; in reserve, surplus to immediate needs, lay nearly 8,000 pounds of that former rarity, saltpeter. The production of this essential ingredient developed like a peasant "cottage industry" based on limitless supplies of animal manure and urine.

A telling instance of how gunpowder became cheaper and guns larger and more numerous comes from a Florentine chronicler, who calculated that during the fifty-five-day siege of Constantinople in the spring of 1453 the artillery train of Sultan Mehmet II, the conqueror consumed 1,000 pounds of powder per day. In any army it was the business of the quartermaster's department to ensure sufficient supplies were in store and properly stored. On the side of the besiegers this was, in the last analysis, a matter of transport—if he valued his head, Mehmet's transport officer presumably made certain that the guns were fully supplied for the duration, however long that might be. On the side of the besieged it was more a question of foresight and calculation.

The longer a siege lasted through the devoted efforts of the defense, the longer it should have been provisioned for. At the 1522 siege of Rhodes just when it might have seemed, miraculously, that the Knights of St. John had seen off the tactics of attrition of the Turkish attackers and, it was rumored, Sultan Suleiman the Magnificent was planning to raise the siege, a deserter brought news that so many of the garrison had been killed that they could no longer hold out. Certainly the artillery was critically low on gunpowder. A rough and ready powder mill was effectively botched up in the hope of manufacturing further supplies on the spot, but then it was found that they had run out of saltpeter. One feels that no one was to blame—the heroic, protracted defense was the cause of the shortage. However, when a few days later the Turks' powder was rendered useless by torrential rain, the officer in charge of storage would surely have been questioned, even though the damage was probably caused when the powder was actually being loaded into the guns.

In fact, storage was a constant problem. Calcium nitrate is a lively oxidizing agent so that gunpowder made with calcium or "lime" saltpeter will combust brilliantly. But it will also spoil very quickly in storage (a matter of weeks, months at the most) as it avidly absorbs atmospheric moisture. (After 1500, when it became the practice to mix a solution of partly refined saltpeter with potash, the resulting potassium nitrate saltpeter gunpowder would have a shelf-life measured in years.)

There were numerous recipes for restoring moisture-damaged powder, by techniques that can now be seen as attempts to minimize the calcium content. As early as 1280 the Arabic *Treatise on Horsemanship and Stratagems of War* by the Syrian writer Hasan al-Rammah Najm al-Din al-Ahdab, who clearly had an extensive knowledge of Chinese practices as to gunpowder and firearms, contains a recipe for using a wood ash additive in making *barud* (saltpeter). Unfortunately, the versions of the recipe in the available texts are very difficult to interpret—though they perhaps describe a process for making potassium saltpeter. There is early European evidence for the use of ashes in saltpeter-making, often confused and technically improbable. A 1420s recipe from Germany recommends using "dyer's potash," while in the 1474 municipal accounts for Winchester we find payments for vats and firewood and also "asshez for . . . to fine . . . saltepetre," which suggest experiments in refining crude saltpeter into potassium saltpeter.

Because gunpowder is a "mechanical mixture" of three solids, the gunpowder-maker, so as to ensure rapid and even combustion, must consolidate or, as the trade calls it, "incorporate," the particles of the ingredients as closely and as evenly as possible into a homogeneous mixture. It was the discovery of a method of successful integration as much as the discovery of ingredients and recipes that made possible what we can call the "gunpowder revolution," which in turn transformed the technological basis of siege warfare.

Early powder-makers achieved incorporation by mixing the dry ingredients in a mortar under the repeated blows of a pestle. The shearing action of the pestle head on the side walls of the mortar helped consolidate the ingredients. The continuous stamping-and-grinding process over many hours would eventually, in the highest qualities of handgun powder, yield a product of the consistency of cosmetic talcum powder.

To facilitate incorporation, the ingredients under the pestle came to be wetted during the later stages of grinding with just enough liquid to make the contents of the mortar into a pasty mass. Such wetting caused the small particles of saltpeter to dissolve partially and coat the inner micropore surfaces of the pulverized insoluble charcoal, carrying particles of the poorly soluble sulphur along with it. (Woods of high porosity were used for the charcoal in the best quality powder.) This led to the production of "corned" or granulated gunpowder, a transforming technique because of the way gunpowder burns. In effect, each grain burns from the outside to its core, hence the size of the gunpowder grain has a powerful influence on the burning characteristics of each charge. For maximum burn speed and thus maximum gas pressure and maximum ballistic effect, just the right size of "corn" was essential and the ingredients had to be properly mixed.

### Improved gunpowder and some consequences
When Henry V of England's invasion fleet sailed for France from Portsmouth in mid-August 1415, contemporaries commented on the large numbers of siege

artillery pieces and other firearms it carried. The French chroniclers emphasized the "unheard of size" (*inaudite grossitudinis*) of Henry's weapons, as well as their noise and smoke, during the siege of Harfleur (1415). (One of these great guns is recorded with a barrel 12 feet long and 2 feet in diameter. It threw a stone shot of about 400 pounds in weight). After Agincourt, in the campaigns of 1417–22, Normandy was returned to its allegiance if only for a time, as city after city fell. Henry's new guns may not have been the decisive factor, but they undoubtedly played their part.

Each firing of a 400-pounder meant a charge of up to 120 pounds. Twenty-five years earlier, the financial outlay involved would have been ruinously expensive. Henry's artillery train matched state-of-the-art military theory and practice after a century of R & D and was decisive. France learnt the lesson. Charles, the French dauphin derided by Henry, would, when he became king as Charles VII, boast the finest artillery train in Europe. This expensive arm of the French military continued to enjoy royal favor under his parsimonious son Louis XI: in 1470 it was estimated that expenditure on the *gens d'armes* and the artillery came to 907,000 livres—getting on for three times the total sums paid out in pensions to the princes of the blood.

Because corned powder was so powerful even in small quantities, effective portable or shoulder arms became possible. Within thirty years of corned powder's appearance the *Hackenbüchse* or arquebus, ancestor of the musket, had been invented. (It was often mounted on a stake or post and secured by a hook [German *Hacke*] to absorb the recoil). But if the new powder made it possible to generate supersonic missile velocities in small caliber weapons, siege-guns were slower to benefit. Barrels and breaches were often too weak to contain the high pressures it generated. Exploding guns were a constant threat to gunners. The able and tough-minded King James II of Scotland died thus aged only 29 when directing his siege artillery at the siege of Roxburgh Castle in 1460. It was a severe loss to his kingdom; it was also a cruel irony. The great hooped gun that exploded and killed him was called "the Lion"—which is of course the heraldic emblem of Scotland.

Adaptation to the new gunpowder led to radically new designs for heavy guns. Barrels had to be cast from tougher materials, usually bronze, and grew longer. The more robust weapons were able to fire shot made of high density cast iron rather than stone. Corning evolved from earlier powder-making practices. As we have seen, the basic requirement for any powder was that the three constituents, saltpeter, sulphur and charcoal be compounded, or "incorporated." A recipe for "plain" or simple gunpowder (i.e., one without fashionable additives like sal ammoniac [ammonium nitrate] to achieve what we may call "super-charged" gunpowder) in a text in the Austrian National Library suggests that this technology was being pioneered as early as 1411, though as a means of prolonging storage life by reducing absorbency. The anonymous writer recommends that "some camphor" be dissolved in good wine and all the ingredients be crushed together—the mixture to be left to dry out in the sun.

It is a classic instance of technological advance in one direction resulting from a procedure aimed to achieve a different objective. For the writer of the recipe, the camphor is the essential new ingredient; it slows down the deterioration of the mixture. The fact that it will also make the gunpowder stronger and more fiery (German, *brunstig*) is mentioned as a fortunate by-product. For him, the wine is there merely as a solvent for the camphor. In fact the camphor affects the powder neither one way nor the other; the key new ingredient was the liquid, and water would have done just as well as wine.

This text is critical in understanding the development of corned powder from earlier wet-mixing processes. If you are to granulate a loose, dry, powdery mix, wet incorporation must come first. A suitably mixed slurry can then be ground in a carefully designed powder mill (an early effective design was produced in the 1420s by the French artillery commander Jean Bureau). But the 1411 manuscript says nothing about shaping the pasty mix into grains: its concern is with preservation rather than improving ballistic characteristics. Why should that be so? Because, argues Bert Hall, the 1411 recipe appears just at the time that inferior home-made saltpeter was flooding the European market. The hygroscopic qualities of this cheap calcium nitrate reduced the shelf-life of gunpowder significantly by making it even more prone to spoilage from the damp. So the "research program" was aimed at rebalancing the problems of gunpowder's unfortunate tendency to go off through absorbed moisture. In terms of the theories of the elements then accepted, camphor was a dry resinous substance, calculated to counteract water. It is also mildly flammable—no doubt a point in its favor.

The vital step of moisture-incorporation was thus originally intended as a means of enhancing the shelf-life of gunpowder. So was the next step toward corning. In the 1420s German *Feuerwerkbuch* ("Firework Book") there is a recipe for "lump-powder" (*Knollenpulver*), in which the standard ingredients are mixed with vinegar (not wine and no mention of camphor). These "lumps" are next dried, either in sunshine or in heated sheds, depending on the season. Because such globular shapes minimize the surface exposed to atmospheric moisture relative to the volume that they contain, they would absorb less moisture, and so would last longer in storage. A very similar method was apparently used in the making of fireworks in rural Spanish Galicia well into the twentieth century. The wet gunpowder was worked into bolas about 4 inches in diameter and set out to dry in the sun. Writing in the 1470s, Francesco di Giorgio Martini describes a "secret" method to preserve powder on long expeditions: Shape the wet powder into loaves, like bread, and let it dry. Before use, these loaves of sun-dried gunpowder must be crushed into a granular consistency. Professor Hall's fascinating account now moves on to the sixteenth century.

### Giant guns and the naming of guns

The first half of the fifteenth century was the first golden age of giant guns—a number survive. "Mons Meg," now in Edinburgh, fired a stone shot weighing about 550 pounds; "Dulle Griet" or the "Great Bombard of Ghent," one of over 750; and the "Pumhart von Steyr" ("the bombard of Styria"), in Vienna, a mammoth of 1,530 pounds. Given that the explosive force of gunpowder was still relatively weak, such weapons nevertheless made sense, for that powder

*Mid-fifteenth century cannon achieved giant dimensions. "Bombards" like "Mons Meg" (caliber 20 inches; barrel length 13½ feet; weight 5 tons) or "Dulle Griet" were often by Flemish founders. Typically, they were built up from iron bars welded together round a wooden core (subsequently drilled or burnt out) and reinforced with iron rings welded round them. For firing they were lodged in a cradle or frame.* Gordon Monaghan

was now easily available in quantity and cheap. The energy needed to break down walls with stone shot demanded a large missile, and large missiles were now feasible. These monster guns were certainly difficult to transport and slow to fire, but they got results.

Christening guns with women's names, which continued into the twentieth century with "Big Bertha" (the monster artillery piece made by the Krupp Company in the First World War and named after Frau Bertha von Bohlen, head of the Krupp family), may actually pre-date firearms if the etymology in the *Oxford English Dictionary* is accepted. Noting a record from Windsor Castle in the 1330s of the presence there of *"una magna ballista que vocatur Domina Gunilda"* ("a large ballista which is called the Lady Gunilda"), the dictionary surmised that the word "gun" may itself derive from the Scandinavian woman's name Gun. (It also noted that in Old Norse both *gunn-r* and *hild-r* mean "war.") There is nothing to show that this ballista was a firearm—as late as 1398, when Pierre Roy was appointed *artilleur* to the duke of Burgundy the service he headed "included cannon, ammunitions and siege-engines of all kinds." However, a London record of 1339 seems unequivocal. "Item," it runs *"in camera Gildaule sunt sex instrumenti de latone, vocitata gonnes Item, peletae de plumbo pro eadem instrumentis . . . Item xxxii librae de pulvere pro dictis instrumentis."* "Six instruments of brass called guns together with balls of lead . . . and 32 pounds of powder for the said instruments," shows that the lady's name, wherever it started, has translated to the firearm service. (We find a "gret brasen gunne" in action against the Flemish town of Guisnes during the Burgundian campaign against Calais in 1436.) It is interesting to find that the Guildhall housed artillery: did it also have its own corps of gunners, as the artillery men of the Bruges militia seventy years later did, who had their own distinctive blue headgear?

Gunners generally worked behind a screen of heavy timber shuttering with gunports of the exact diameter of the barrel cut in them, if contemporary illustrations are to be trusted. Often it seems bombards were mounted in pairs, sometimes on a gun-carriage consisting of a simple flat bed with a protective timber housing mounted on a frame.

### A great gun against "the Great City": Constantinople, 1453

Probably the finest siege-gun of the period was the one built by Urban, a Hungarian engineer for the Turkish sultan Mehmet II, conqueror of Constantinople. Cannon had been used in the earlier siege of the city in 1422 (the Byzantine sources use the Western term bombardi to describe them). And the Hungarian army had used them in the crusade of 1443–4. In the summer of 1452 Urban arrived at the court of its last Christian emperor, Constantine XI Paleologus, offering his services as a master gunmaker.

Apart from territories in southern Greece, the empire now extended barely beyond the walls of the great city preparing to face siege by the Turkish army and already blockaded by the Turkish fleet. Constantine could not provide the raw materials required, not even sufficient timber for the foundry fires, nor could he raise funds to pay for the work nor match the professional fee Urban was demanding. As a Hungarian, Urban was no doubt also a Catholic and, since the pope had consistently refused to sponsor assistance to the schismatic Orthodox emperor until he should submit to Rome, could, as a result, square his conscience for his next step. Within weeks Urban was at Adrianople (modern Edirne) explaining his plans to the 20-year-old military genius Sultan Mehmet II, who at once commissioned him at a fee four times greater than he had asked and with all the materials and technical assistance he required. Within three months a massive gun was emplaced on the walls of the sultan's new fortress of Rumeli Hisar overlooking the Bosphorus—it sank the first Venetian galley that tried to run the blockade.

The sultan now commissioned a cannon twice as large. With a bronze barrel of some 26.5 feet in length, and capable of throwing stones of some 1,440 pounds, it was cast at Adrianople and ready for trials in January. The citizens were warned of the huge noise to be expected (in fact the report was heard over a distance of ten miles) and after hurtling down a range of more than a mile, the missile buried itself to a depth of 6 feet in the earth. Mehmet ordered the construction of other, though smaller, guns, while 200 navvies began work to level the way for the transport of the monster to Constantinople, a distance of more than 150 miles. Thirty pair of oxen were needed to drag the gun-carriage and 200 men marched beside it to steady the load. On April 5 Mehmet and his entourage arrived before the walls of the Great City with the last detachments of the army. His artillery, headed by Urban's lumbering masterpiece, offered doom-laden omens of their fate to the citizenry. By order of the sultan, the great gun was sited opposite the San Romanos gate; it was here that the Turks would make their final breakthrough.

Accepting the statistic that in a siege situation the defense has the advantage, and given that contemporary Greek accounts inevitably colored the Turkish numbers, up to 120,000 in one estimate, the Byzantine defenders were nevertheless heavily outnumbered. The empire approached its destiny with a functioning bureaucracy reporting to a man who was, in the emperor's words, "skilled in arithmetic and able to guard secrets." And George Phrantzes, the official in question, records a total of 4,773 Greeks and some 200 foreigners at disposal for the defense. The second figure was no doubt a "guestimate," but the first represented the total of local neighborhood censuses carried out by district officials, at the emperor's command, "as to the exact numbers of laity and clergy" available for conscription and the reserves of weapons and missiles.

Yet Phrantzes does perhaps offer, in all good faith, an underestimate. His figure may be an accurate total of the reports submitted to him, but the reports themselves may have been faulty—other contemporary reports on the Greek side give estimates of as many as 6,000 citizen and military effectives and up to 3,000 foreigners. Perhaps the "200" were the foreigners under direct imperial command in the localities and did not take account of the Genoese and other expatriate communities who came under their own governors. But the Turks cannot have been fewer than 60,000 and the defenders more than 9,000—so the defenders were outnumbered by at least six to one, probably, in fact, by much more.

The city did have artillery, it is true, but nothing to redress such an imbalance of forces. The weaponry in question included old-fashioned frame-mounted ballista crossbows, but also some small cannon and apparently guns supplied by the Genoese with their colony in Pera, but nothing on either side was a match for Urban's monster. In any case they were restricted by limitations of powder and shot. They did have one or two large guns, but these, it seems, they hardly used; according to one observer their largest cannon burst on its first firing. Another piece, mounted on the walls and capable of throwing shot up to 75 pounds in weight did some practice against the sultan's great gun, but its own vibrations shook the ancient walls so severely that its use was discontinued.

Discharging the huge gun was a laborious business for the Turkish artillery men: the barrel had to be loaded with gunpowder tamped down with wadding rammed home and then the massive gun-stone forced in. The power of the explosion was liable to throw the barrel from its seating, so that it had to be remounted and of course thoroughly cleaned of smoldering debris before reloading could commence. Apparently, it rarely hurled more than seven missiles a day. Even so, the immense damage it caused may well have been the decisive factor in the fall of the city.

This came on the fifty-third day of the siege at a time when, despite their overwhelming superiority in numbers, the Turkish forces were beginning to lose their assurance of victory. The air on both sides was laden with prophecies and counter-prophecies about the fall of the city, some reaching back to the seventh century. The garrison and the citizen defenders had held out with desperate endurance, despite the best efforts of the sultan's team of miners recruited from the silver mines in Serbia, heroic assaults by the Turkish infantry and, of course, the bombardment.

Over the weeks, though the massive fortifications had been punctured in numerous places, the defenders had made good the damage, plugging the walls with mud and masonry infill which proved more resilient than stone rubble alone. However, despite heavy matting hung before the walls to lessen the impact of the missiles, much of the wall facing the Hungarian monster was leveled and the moat filled with the rubble. Thanks to the inspiring leadership of the soldier-like emperor Constantine XI, morale remained surprisingly high, although most defenders must have known the case was hopeless. Day after day chains of women and children passed rocks and stone fragments hand-to-hand up to the walls to be hurled down on the attackers. Other non-combatants crowded the churches to pray to the Blessed Virgin, who was considered the divine protector of the place, to save her city, and on the last day of the siege, May 29, the vast cathedral of Hagia Sophia, "the Holy Wisdom," was packed with supplicants.

Priests led daily processions through the streets, the sound of church bells adding to the cacophony of sound that filled the air from dawn to dusk. Beyond the walls the roll of Turkish kettledrums kept up a constant roar; trumpets brayed on both sides and the Greeks would surely have deployed performers on the raucous sounding hydraulis organs, traditionally used in the hippodrome races and never an instrument of church music in the Orthodox Church service, blasting the air with pipes that could sound like steam whistles.

Second only to the emperor himself, the great inspiration of the defenders appears to have been the Genoese Giustiniani, commanding a force of 700 (which he had recruited and paid out of his own pocket) in the place of danger on the outer wall, opposite the great siege-gun. On what proved to be the last day, he was wounded and, despite the emperor's entreaties, had himself carried through the gates to receive treatment for his wounds. Venetian chroniclers would claim his nerve had finally broken and he had deserted his post. His absence from the wall certainly dispirited his men and correspondingly heartened the attackers.

The end came with shocking suddenness. The Turks made no attempt at surprise, indeed the dread inspired by well-heralded preparations of attack was part of the softening-up process. It seems the removal of Giustiniani from the opposing wall was signal for a renewed assault that was able to force the inner gate into the city. The defenders trapped between the two outer walls were cut down and the attackers burst in. There followed three days of looting and massacre, as allowed to most armies, Western or Eastern, when a city had failed to surrender voluntarily. From Sir Steven Runciman we learn that "blood flowed in rivulets down the steep streets . . . toward the waters of the Golden Horn." The emperor was reportedly last seen battling sword in hand against the wave of incoming Turkish janissary troops. He had the day before calmly told his faithful secretary, George Sphrantzes, that as Christian emperor he was charged with the defense of the great city to the end—certainly his body was never recovered. Sphrantzes lived to a venerable age to record the last days of the Christian metropolis and Urban, the Hungarian whose great siege-gun had opened the way to the Turkish victory, was rewarded with a splendid mansion in the conquered city.

With Constantinople secured, the historic "empire of Rum" (i.e., "Rome") effectively ceased to exist, though there were pockets of resistance in Thessaly and parts of the Peloponnese. In the spring of 1458 the conqueror embarked on a systematic campaign to reduce all resistance, his powerful artillery a principal weapon. At Corinth he bombarded the acropolis with stone ammunition chipped by masons to the required diameter for the caliber of his great guns. One of these was capable of hurling a ball weighing 900 pounds over a range of about a mile and a half with a force that demolished the bakery and arsenal building of the citadel. The Greek garrison, led by Matthew Asan, refused to capitulate, though their provisions were all but exhausted; the besiegers, by contrast, were reinforced at this stage by a foraging party that had rounded up thousands of head of cattle. Asan seems to have been prepared for last-ditch heroics but the majority of the garrison was not with him. On August 6, Corinth, the key to the Morea, gave up its citadel to the Turks: for them it was the "star" castle of this part of their extended empire.

### Guns advance the reconquest of Spain from Islam . . .

At the other end of the Mediterranean it was Christian guns that were turning the tide of religion. In the spring of 1485 King Ferdinand of Aragon left his city of Cordova at the head of a force of some 30,000 men dedicated to the ending of the Reconquista of Spain from Islamic domination, a fitful campaign of reconquest that occupied Iberian war and politics for seven centuries and more. His objective was the town of Ronda, today famed as the ancestral city of the rituals of the modern bullfight, then the second city of the western province of the Moorish kingdom of Granada.

The king was accompanied by the Masters of Spain's monastic orders of the crusading knights of Santiago and Alcántara, and also by an awesome train of artillery. Their destination is itself almost awe-inspiring, set on its mountainous outcrop among precipitous ravines. Virtually unapproachable and so virtually impregnable, the place was home to a confident citizenry, intrigued but not, it seems, intimidated as they watched monstrous guns being hauled up the mountain slopes overlooking their town. But finally ensconced in their placements, the muzzles of the monster bombards nosed down toward the houses and mosques, mansions and market squares as if sniffing their prey.

It would be interesting to know what ammunition they had. Iron shot had been increasingly favored since the early 1400s, though very large cannon, like Henry V's great siege-gun at Harfleur with its 2-foot bore and 400-pound stone, kept to traditional stone. In the 1430s, we hear of artillery gun-stones (meaning stone shot—Shakespeare's coinage, from Henry V) being transported to the Burgundian siege of Calais and in the 1450s the artillery of Sultan Mehmet was firing stones chipped to the requisite caliber by specialist masons. However, by the time of Ronda, German and Italian artillery men hired by Spain's Catholic Monarchs were using marble shot, fireballs of compacted tow soaked in oil and what were, in effect, shrapnel shells, being spheres of friable stone that shattered into rough shards on impact with all but the most absorbent surfaces, such as mud.

On May 5 the gunners at Ronda opened a hail of fire-balls and gun-stones down upon ramparts and buildings and towers—and upon the now terrified people. Four days were enough to bludgeon the outer walls into rubble. The enemy swarmed into what the week before had been peaceful suburban communities; the gunners wheeled their ordnance up to pulverize the next line of defense. Just ten days after this provincial Armageddon had started, it was all over. On May 15 Ronda's town officials made their unconditional surrender. Battering-rams and stone-throwers had helped complete the job, but it was the baying and roaring of the artillery that reverberated around the doomed kingdom. The following year the palatial residence of Boabdil fell to the guns of Aragon; and six years after that Granada, "jewel of Islam in the West," would face the plunderer.

### . . . and France from the English

Even at this early stage in its history the artillery gun, though primarily of use as a siege weapon, was being deployed against infantry. The English, from being pioneers of the practice, were late to realize the possibilities of artillery in the field and were taught a sharp lesson by, of all people, the French. The cannons reported in the English lines at Crécy, if indeed they were there, probably did little more than frighten the French cavalry horses and may indeed have been used solely with that intention in mind. However, a century later in the dying days of English rule in Gascony, Charles VII of France used artillery to deadly effect against the finest general of his day and the bogey man used by French peasant mothers to frighten naughty children, John Talbot, earl of Shrewsbury.

On June 30, 1451, a French force entered Bordeaux, there being no English army in the area to oppose them. They were not hailed as liberators. As Charles himself later observed in a letter to James II of Scotland, then campaigning against English outposts in his country (and himself to be killed by an exploding cannon), it was common knowledge that "after having been English for 300 years, the people of that region are at heart completely inclined toward the English party." Indeed, early in 1452 the Bordelais sent a deputation to London begging an army be sent to their aid. Talbot landed with a force of 3,000 men in October; Bordeaux expelled the token French garrison and opened its gates, as did many neighboring towns. But the English expeditionary force was always going to be too small for the job in prospect and its field artillery inadequate—a military tradition used to triumph with the longbow had little time for other missile weapons in foot combat, despite early experimentation. The following spring, determined to expel the national enemy once and for all, the French king ordered three armies against the rebellious province.

By the middle of July 1453 the French commander, Jean Bureau, arrived before the fortified town (*bastide*) of Castillon, commanding some 8,000 men and numbers of siege- and field-guns. Charles had the finest artillery train in Europe and his captains were developing new theory and practice in its use both in the field and at siege. Convention might have expected encirclement of the town,

*This sixteenth-century engraving shows, to the right, a "fort newly built to bombard and besiege [the Italian city of] Civitella." At Castillon in 1453 the French artillery commander Jean Bureau built a similar (if perhaps less permanent) emplacement for his guns. Talbot, the English commander ordered a direct attack, acting on faulty intelligence that the French were preparing to decamp.* Taylor Library

possibly with walls of circumvallation. Bureau ordered the construction of a fortified encampment, effectively an artillery park, some 700 by 200 yards, so aligned as to give his guns maximum effectiveness by oblique and enfilading fire.

Before the French could begin the bombardment Talbot, misled by false intelligence and believing that the enemy were abandoning their position, came up. Instead of the disorder of an army preparing to decamp, he found a well-defended site, its guns trained at the ready. Nevertheless, he decided on a frontal attack with foot-soldiers. For a time, the outcome seemed to be in the balance until a concealed force of Bretons debouched from woods to the north of the battlefield. Even then, it was the collapse in English morale caused by the death of their commander that precipitated the English defeat. Talbot was killed when his white palfrey, a talisman for his troops, was struck down by a cannon-ball.

### Guns and chivalry?

It was a sign of the times. For crusty old military types, nostalgic for what they supposed had been the age of chivalrous warfare before the advent of powder and shot on the battlefield, the death of the Burgundian knight Sir Jaques Lalaing on July 2, 1453, at the siege of the Ghentish castle of Poeke was yet more poignant. When on active service in the duke's army he might be found leading light cavalry on scouting duty or, as at Poeke, performing the functions of an officer in the observer corps, marking the fall of shot of the ducal bombards. But by this time Lalaing had been felled by a stray cannon-ball from an enemy gun, aged just 32. When not on campaign, he had been noted among the most distinguished champions of the joust.

Had he known how Lalaing met his death, Don Quixote de la Mancha, "the knight of the mournful visage," would have been melancholy indeed. The Burgundian gentleman was among the most celebrated knights errant of his day, the kind of man whose exploits were, second only to the romances of chivalry, the Don's favorite reading. In fact his life, in all its bizarre detail, recorded by an anonymous admirer under the title *Livre des faits du bon chevalier Messire Jacques de Lalaing*, has been said to read more like a romance than a biography. But Lalaing was also a serious soldier, though he would probably not have recognized any real difference between the tournament and the battlefield.

The hero of many a skirmish against a garrison's sorties, he delighted in reporting back to the duke those "who had aided him by their valor." On one occasion, during the siege of Ghent, these numbered Andrieu de la Plume, court jester to the duke's heir, Charles Count of Charolais. After this encounter Duke Philip, "who well knew the hardships to which they had been exposed, ordered his supper be laid on tables set at the [outer] earthworks . . . and he had 'Sire' Lalaing sit next to him, saying he would observe the good old custom of honoring the doughtiest hero of the day." At the month-long jousting known as the Passage of Arms of the Pilgrim Lady (*Pelèrine*) Lalaing continued in the lists even though his opponent had disabled him in the left arm; at the Passage of the Weeping Lady, which he himself organized, he waited the umpire's ruling before abandoning a joust, even though his lance was split so as to be useless in combat. Such, the knight of La Mancha would have reflected, was the paragon laid low by the brute machinery of modern war.

### Organization of the artillery arm

Of course, the hero of Cervantes's great novel lived in a fantasy world: but even at the birth of Lalaing in the 1420s the profession of the artilleryman was well over a century old. In this same decade, it will be remembered, the first reliable water-powered mill hastened the mass production of effective corned gunpowder. Any European potentate of consequence had an artillery train as part of his military establishment. Chief among them were the dukes of Burgundy who, by dint of marriage policy (for example with heiress of Flanders) and successful war-making, extended their territories to become Europe's middle "kingdom" in all but name. Henry IV of England's "thirty-nine guns and cannons" stored at the Tower of London in the early 1400s would be considered a modest enough number by later military establishments—like that of Burgundy.

We get some idea of the size and careful organization of Burgundy's military establishment at the height of its power from the dossier drawn up by officials at the Hague at the request of Duke Philip the Good in January 1456, in preparation for the crusade he proclaimed as a response to the conquest of Constantinople by the Turkish sultan, Mehmet II, a little less than three years earlier. In anticipation of the siege warfare that would be needed if once Christian cities were to be recovered, Philip purposed to take with him a considerable artillery train. Tall, with a bearing "worthy of a king or an emperor," an outstanding player in the "real" tennis court, always polite to women because, he said, they ruled their menfolk, Philip also had a penchant for what one can only call arts and crafts, having a special room for his gadgetry, including soldering irons. It is surely a telling detail that although the duke was a noted champion at the joust and a stickler for the etiquette of chivalry, his favorite heraldic device was the steel and flint with a scatter of flames and sparks.

"As regards the artillery," ran the Hague dossier, "the duke should at once send to his master of artillery to ascertain the state it is in." After consulting with Sir Daviot de Poix, the master, Duke Philip was recommended to select what he reckoned he would need for the expedition, make an inventory for the records of the master traveling with the expeditionary force, and leave the rest of the artillery behind under the charge of a deputy master with a duplicate inventory. The master was to have command of twenty-five lances whose pay was to be grouped with that of the troops detailed to help and transport the artillery. The document reckons that up to 600 gunners, carpenters, masons, smiths, pioneers, miners and workmen would be needed, complete with their tools, armed so as to be able fight, if need be in the ranks of the pikemen but paid at the same rate as archers.

Daviot de Poix is the fifth we know of in a line of Burgundian artillery chiefs back to Joseph Colart, appointed as cannoneer by Duke Philip the Bold in the 1380s. He was evidently an ironmaster for besides guns he supervised the casting of the metal work such as the bells and chandeliers of the convent of the Charterhouse of Champmol. Pierre Roy, the *artilleur*, we have met. After him comes Jehan Manus, canoneer, perhaps less a gunsmith and more an artilleryman for he was directing the bombardment at the siege of Velloxon in October 1409. He is followed by Jaquemart le Mahieu, *maître charpentier des engins* to Duke John the Fearless; he was a master craftsman who had cast the bombard "Griette" at St. Omer, where it had been tested outside the town gate in the presence of the duke himself in the summer of 1411 before being hauled south to the siege of Bourges, where it almost single handedly reduced the defenses of the town. Then in 1414, Duke John appointed Germain de Givry *maître d'artillerie*, another artilleryman one presumes more than gunfounder, with the brief to look after cannon and siege-engines of all kinds through out the ducal territories. John instituted a new accounting system exclusively for the artillery service and established a specialized arsenal facility at Dijon for all the weaponry when not in active service. His son and successor, Philip the Good, continued to nurture this vital military arm so that, in the 1460s, at a muster near Honnecourt (Nord-Pas-de-Calais) just a part of the Burgundian artillery establishment required 236 wagons loaded with bombards, mortars, serpentines and other types of cannon.

On July 16, 1465, during the French civil wars known as the League of the Public Weal, Charles the Bold, count of Charolais, Philip's heir, drawing support from individual nobles like the lords of the château of Bonaguil in the south to the great dynasty of Burgundy in the north, led the Burgundian forces against King Louis XI of France at the Battle of Montlhéry. He claimed the victory, but so did the king, and Charles's allies, the dukes of Berry and Brittany, began to waver in their commitment. So, the following week, to silence argument as to his supremacy he lined up his artillery at Etampes and had his gunners fire off all the pieces, twice, for the benefit of his uncertain allies. His victory in the battle may have been open to question, but this demonstration of his gunners' fire-power not only impressed the dukes but "overawed the king for months to come."

The citizens of the Franco-Flemish city of Dinant no doubt also took note. Shortly after Montlhéry, hearing that the count's defeat had been total, a group of the citizenry had hung the count in effigy and then issued a proclamation that, far from being the son of Duke Philip he was a bastard of Jehan, bishop of Liège, a serial fornicator, and Duchess Isabel of Burgundy, Charles's virtuous mother. Charles marched to avenge the insult. As a result Dinant, which boasted in its long history successful resistance in no fewer than seventeen sieges, fell within a week to an unrelenting artillery bombardment by Charles's artillery. On August 25, 1466, the count of Charolais made a triumphal entry to the town. In the days that followed, the place was systematically sacked and then put to the flames. The punishment was terrible but was to be expected.

## Cost-effectiveness

The cost of early gunpowder artillery was considerable, but in the view of many modern commentators its effectiveness over the first century of development was very doubtful. According to Professor Hall, for instance, "before about the year 1400 gunpowder artillery in action barely influenced military outcomes." In his biography of Duke Charles the Bold of Burgundy (1973) Richard Vaughan reckoned that even Burgundy's state-of-the-art equipment, impressive though it could be, also had a somewhat checkered balance sheet. He analyzed ten sieges set by the duke in the 1470s and found that, while six major cities fell to the ducal army, the artillery was not actually brought to bear in a single case; on the other hand, of the four occasions where siege artillery was deployed the garrisons held out until relieved. By contrast, in his campaign against the rebel earl of Northumberland in 1405, England's king, Henry IV, was able to force the capitulation of the earl's castle of Warkworth with just seven salvos from one of his great cannon. The town of Berwick was also reduced to seek terms by cannon fire. A comparatively small-bore gun demolished a stretch of the walls and then a larger caliber weapon removed the staircase corner of the Constable Tower, killing a man climbing it.

Effective or not, from the 1360s onwards guns in all their variety—bombards cannon, spingards, spingardels, serpentines—were the military must-have for any ruler with serious pretensions: not that these gentry necessarily met their bills. In late 1453, while at Lille, visiting the arsenal there presumably, the duke of Burgundy received a note from his bailiff in Hainault asking whether he was intending to pay ready cash for a bombard he had ordered there.

*An artist's composite impression of siege weapons. In front of an archery firing stage complete with pivoted protective baffle a light artillery piece can be seen mounted on an ingenious, if perhaps not very effective, elevation mount. Center foreground is an unmounted gun barrel of the type sometimes termed a "pot."* Taylor Library

Mindful of their "worship" (i.e., "worthship" or status), aldermen and burghers of Europe's greater cities also acquired their own ordnance establishment. In England, London and probably York had their own weapons from an early date while the "loophole" gun ports still to be seen in the West Gate of the city walls of Canterbury, dated to about 1400, indicate that here too the city authorities must by then have had guns at their disposal. On the Continent, Strasburg, Liège and Nürnberg were just a few cities to boast their own artillery—with greater or lesser success, it must be said. The great gun of Strasburg, named *"der Strauss"* (no doubt from the old German for "battle" punning on the other meaning of the word "ostrich" for its long "neck" or barrel), was engraved with the city's arms. This monster, we are told, "buzzed" and "danced" when fired with a "crop" well packed with powder; it required a team of eighteen horses to shift it and though capable of only fourteen shots a day was obviously an object of smug self-satisfaction to the Strasbürger. Raes de Lyntre of Liège on the other hand, who commissioned the building of the huge bombard *le Liègeois*, had less cause for pride: it exploded on its second test firing.

Henry IV of England was no more lucky with his two-ton monster "the Messenger," which also blew up, possibly because of ill-adapted gunpowder. On his crusade into Lithuania in 1390, before the advent of the improved gunpowders, the 24-year-old Henry of Bolingbroke as he then was, had perhaps discussed their "art" with the gunners traveling with his entourage. He was certainly "into" gunnery for a decade later, early in his reign, the records speak of "a large cannon newly invented by the king himself," while an entry in the royal accounts notes £210 paid to a gunsmith for supplies of iron and coal to the making of cannon (there is no mention of charcoal).

In a letter to his ally Henry VI of England complaining about payments outstanding, Philip the Good of Burgundy noted that he had expended 40,000 *saluts* (a gold coin worth about forty English silver pennies) on the artillery prepared for the siege of Compiègne.

In addition to the expense of the weapons, costs mounted if the advice of an outside expert master of artillery was called on. In the numerous officers of his son's extensive household, where rank was precisely indicated by the quality of one's robes of office, the controller of the ducal artillery was just one of twenty officials whose perks included a half-length black damask gown adorned with needlework pourpoints of violet-crimson satin. Yet, despite maintaining an officer of such standing on his regular roll of expenditure, during the siege of Neuss Charles thought it worth engaging the renowned cannoneer Hans of Nürnberg for seven weeks. His fee may be judged from the fact that his wife was handsomely compensated to defray the expenses of running the household in his absence. One hopes that Charles did not have to pay a consultation fee as to the gun emplacements at Neuss when his half-brother Anthony, the "Grand Bastard of Burgundy," passing through on his way to London in the course of a diplomatic mission to King Edward IV, was asked to cast his eye over the dispositions.

From its faltering beginnings in the 1340s, the skills of the gunner had evolved into an increasingly complex expertise so that by the end of the period covered by this book the profession of artilleryman was a recognized branch of the military arm and the manufacture of artillery weapons a highly specialized business offering high rewards from patrons able to meet the bill. Urban the Hungarian had even been willing to enlist on the payroll of the champion of Islam to get his price. By the time of the siege of Ronda some master gunners seem to have turned freelance to take advantage of a seller's market in war-happy Europe, hiring themselves out to any potentate who could afford their fees.

# CHAPTER SEVEN

# Attack and Defense

*"Once more into the breach dear friends . . ."*

Shakespeare, *Henry V*

So far, the aim here has been to give some account of the structures and fortified settlements liable to be targeted in siege warfare; the principles of design involved; details of the careers of a few of the known designers; together with some account of the kind of weaponry at the disposal of both attackers and defenders. This chapter outlines the thinking in respect of the deployment of those weapons and the tactics and strategy behind the conduct of operations.

## Basics and essentials
In the summer of 1452, during the Burgundian war against the city of Ghent, the castellan of the Ghentese fortress of Overmere knew full-well he could expect a siege, from the preparations being made by the duke of Burgundy. Messengers were bringing in reports of the scouting party of twenty-five lances led by Sir Jaques de Lalaing; they were reconnoitering in the vicinity for signs of possible hostile action against gangs of pioneers and laborers, equipped with saws and drills, billhooks and other tools, under the command of the duke's master of artillery, Sir Daviot de Poix. Making the highway straight involved filling in ditches, remaking roads and demolishing any barricades that had been thrown up. De Poix also commanded a detachment of foot-soldiers, on the payroll of Burgundy's artillery establishment. Lalaing was clearly on the lookout for any more serious forces ambushed in the woods.

Fifteen years earlier, Burgundy's siege of Calais (1436) had involved the assembling of an artillery train of pieces from all over the Burgundian state, such as the three large bombards together with 275 gun-stones as ammunition, from the province of Holland. The guns coming up from ducal Burgundy (capital Dijon) severely damaged the bridge on the main road at Chatillon-sur-Seine. A major siege could have an impact on the country for miles around laying considerable indirect costs on the local regions.

At its most basic, the defense of a medieval fortress depended on its extreme solidity of construction—walls could range from 15 to 30 feet in thickness. Well provisioned and well commanded, the garrison might hold out for months, even a year and more. Even so, the objective was to neutralize the place while

An illustration of an episode in the Hundred Years' War from the Chronicles of Froissart. Scaling-ladders had to be sturdy to carry the weight of several men in armor; it seems that the defender to the right of the picture is thinking of shoving one of them away from the wall. Taylor Library

operating elsewhere in the enemy's territory: if the attacker had sufficient forces in the field, he might consider this a reasonable trade-off—though of course he would have to keep his own troops supplied with arms and provisions. The attacker who wished to storm the place had the choice of three types of solution: over, under or through—all of them laborious and costly in materials and manpower.

To take a wall by escalade (the word is French derived from the Italian *scalare*, "to mount") required, naturally enough, scaling-ladders either constructed on site, supposing there was sufficient timber available, or supplied as part of the baggage train. Contemporary illustrations depict what appear to be carpenter-made ladders with the rungs let into planed side pieces, and a more rough and ready apparatus of rungs roped onto untrimmed poles on either side. Once ready, they had to be raised against the walls; for ladders of any length this meant using forked poles to steady them in place. Of course similar poles would be probing out from the walls to thrust them down. At the siege of Neuss (1476), Charles Duke of Burgundy ordered the construction of a crane that would lower the ladders into place with less risk to his soldiers' lives. To the general hilarity of the defenders, but unfortunately for the duke's tactics, it got stuck in the mud before it could get near enough to the target wall area.

Soldiers mounting the scaling-ladders were of course horribly vulnerable to missiles—not only rocks but fragile pots of quicklime that shattered on impact, scalding water, or burning pitch. A shield held over the head would protect but would also impede a man's ascent—speed was very much of the essence. Defenders might let a ladder fill up with men and then attempt to lever the head away from the wall, to send the attackers plummeting down to the ground or into the moat. Of course, if too many soldiers were allowed onto the ladder, then bodyweight might combine to nullify the leverage force that could be applied by the defenders. Should one of the attackers make good his ground on the top of the wall it was for him to defend the ladder head as best he could so that colleagues could join him.

In the course of the Spanish reconquest crusading wars, the Christian armies used a specialist form of siege technique depending on teams of specialist *escaladores* ("ladder-men") equipped with lightweight ladders and grappling-hooks, ideally three fluked anchors on ropes and hand weapons of hand-axes or knives. Their task was to scale walls as rapidly and quietly as possible with the aim of rapid sneak attacks.

### Towers and siege-towers

A siege-tower provided a protected platform for the attackers that would deliver them to the top of the wall without the need for escalade. Of course this was the ideal. Here as elsewhere, reality rarely matched or even approached the textbook prescription. At their most elaborate such towers comprised a wooden structure in several tiers, hung with soaked animal hides as protection from fire-arrows and with ladders going up inside the structure to the top platform; there might be a drawbridge, held in the vertical and affording protection to the troops waiting for the assault. As soon as a cohort was assembled the bridge was swung down and the troops forced themselves across as best they could. Ideally, before the charge, bowmen in the tower would sweep the enemy wall to clear it of defenders. Bowmen manning a turret stage above the swing bridge could provide covering fire for the assault party. A large siege-tower had to be constructed out of range of the defenders and mounted on a wheeled base so that it could be rolled against the enemy fortress on the orders of the commander. Such a wheeled tower was a "belfry" (from the French *befroi*), and, if we are to believe the sources, could achieve truly enormous dimensions. Reporting on the siege of the rebel town of Bréteuil in Normandy (loyal to Charles of Navarre) in the 1350s by King John II, Froissart records a giant belfry (the "cat house" as some called it) of three stories in height, capable of accommodating 200 men on each story with room enough to wield their weapons.

Before such a siege-engine could be wheeled into place the castle moat had to be filled in and leveled. At Bréteuil the king had the peasants of the district rounded up and put to work carting great quantities of wood to the site, offloading them into the moat, spreading straw and finally tamping down a rammed-earth carriageway. In the nature of things we must be talking of a stretch of moat no more than 40 feet long, just wide enough to carry the wheeled tower. The work took a full month to complete and, although Froissart says nothing about casualties among the workforce (they were, after all, only serfs belonging to a rebel lord), it would have cost many lives. The defenders had not been idle, hurling fire and cannon shot against the work in progress and raining missiles down on the peasant laborers. If the job followed precedents, the infill would have been augmented by workmen's corpses and severed body parts.

Job done: and, we are told, knights and squires were lining up to man the structure before it was rolled across to the wall, desirous of winning distinction in the fighting that lay ahead. For members of a social class for whom petty warfare was a habit of life, such desire for glory was part of the style. They may

*A visualization of a medieval siege tower in action. The moat has been filled in, perhaps rather tidily, with bundles of withies; animal hides protect the tower from fire while the attackers' trebuchets are evidently hurling incendiary devices at the defenders. Soldiers are streaming across the drawbridge under covering fire from archers on the top stage.*
Taylor Library

also have calculated that fighting out from the protective structure of a siege-tower was measurably less hazardous than assaulting across the treacherous, sharp-edged rubble of an open breach. Such "forlorn hope" work might be detailed off to the common soldiery.

Even so, John's gentlemen soldiers had a fight on their hands. The defenders met them with equally ambitious and also brutal hand-to-hand infighting; "many fine feats of arms were performed," Froissart notes with approval. He would have had his evidence from eyewitnesses, possibly heralds whose job included monitoring battle action and keeping a tally of notable feats of arms, as well as acting as emissaries before hostilities and recording losses afterward.

After a time the defenders retreated back onto the walls. While they fended off the attack their artillery men fired shot and fire canisters onto the belfry so that some attackers were killed and the rest were forced to abandon it to avoid being incinerated when the whole contraption went up in flames. When the men of Bréteuil saw this they burst out in cheers and shouts of "St. George! Loyal to Navarre!" followed by jeers like "Wasn't so easy to get us as you French thought it would be, was it then?" The charred ruin in the moat had failed, and the French command decided on a general assault which meant filling the remainder of the moat—Froissart guessed 1,500 men were committed to the work, with common soldiers working alongside the peasants.

In fact, though his siege-tower attack was aborted, King John forced Bréteuil's capitulation thanks to the remorseless 24/7 play of his siege artillery. With their lord Charles of Navarre in a Paris prison, his scattered fiefs in Normandy under pressure themselves, and their English allies away to the south, the citizens realized they could expect no relieving force to come to their aid and that if the town eventually fell to assault, which seemed inevitable, "they would all" as Froissart succinctly but accurately puts it, "be slaughtered." Accordingly they offered up the town on the guarantee of their lives. This John granted, together with as much of their possessions as they could carry and a safe conduct as far as Cherbourg, the best part of 140 miles distant. For his own part, the king was glad to be finished with an episode that had cost him much and immobilized forces that should have been fighting the English.

### Tactics and heroism

Obviously, once it had been decided to deploy a siege-tower, one needed as accurate a measure as possible of the height of the target wall and this required an expert eye or some aid to calculation. At the siege of Rome in 537–8 the Goth commander, familiar with Roman masonry standard measures from other city walls, counted the number of courses in the wall confronting him and so was able to make a reasonably accurate estimate of the height of towers he needed. A number were duly constructed with wheels at the four corners and traces anchored to the structures so that these could be dragged up to the walls by teams of oxen. An eyewitness recalled the terrifying impression made on the defenders as the monstrous war machines lumbered inexorably on, dragged by the "milk-white Etrurian oxen." People shouted to the army's commander, Count Belisarius, to unleash the ballistae on the walls against the towers, but he merely looked on with a smile on his lips. Nearer and nearer came the contraptions until, judging the moment to a nicety, Belisarius drew a bow on a Goth chief in the front line, armed with breastplate and Roman-style mail and shot him through the throat. The crowded walls cheered, relieved no doubt to see some action (at last) and excellent shooting. And then the commander gave the order for general archery fire—at the oxen. Within moments the animals had slumped dead in their traces. The fearsome towers had been immobilized well short of their objective but within easy range of the Roman ballistae.

In treacherous, muddy terrain, siege-towers might be mounted on runners rather than wheels. Construction could take weeks: when finished, one siege-tower required thirty wagons to bring it to the front, but while the carpenters were at their work troops labored to prepare the road to the walls and, in most cases, fill in the moat at the point where the attack was to be made. This meant relays of men carrying baskets of earth and rubble to be tipped into the moat. Anything that came to hand was used—even decaying corpses.

Two large siege-towers, one 75, the other 60 feet high, were deployed at the siege of Tyre, the important fortified seaport on the coast of Palestine, as, after their capture of Jerusalem, the crusading army expanded their presence in the Holy Land to the dimensions of a kingdom. In November 1111 the army of King Baldwin arrived before the city and dug in, preparing to starve the place out. The Muslim defenders had sent a desperate plea to Tughtigin, the ruler of Damascus about seventy miles inland. But his relieving force, when it did arrive, proved too small to dislodge the Christian army. It could not even stop work on the towers under construction among the huts and tents of the crusader camp. The Muslim relieving force launched attack after attack against the construction site, hoping the garrison would be able make a sortie and set fire to the structures. But the Christians had dug trenches round the position and were able to hold off the attacks. After eleven weeks the towers were ready for action. Each was equipped with a battering-ram slung between the posts of the bottom section.

It was now February. The massive contraptions had to be manhandled up to the walls against a hail of missiles. When they were nearly in place the garrison made a sortie and succeeded in setting fire to the smaller of the two, and flames and sparks from the conflagration spread to the larger one so that it also began to smolder and in places take fire. Though it had to be withdrawn from action while repairs were made, it returned to the attack again and again; the garrison fought with equal determination. The battle of the towers dominated the action at Tyre for days, but eventually the army from Damascus forced Baldwin and his army to retreat and they had to fight their way back up the coast to Acre. The army of the kingdom of Jerusalem did not finally conquer the port of Tyre for another thirteen years.

In crusading warfare, once the breach was made, the honor of leading the assault and so of being considered the captors of the town was often competed for among the attackers—none moreso than in the warfare of the Holy Land. In fact, at Ascalon in 1153, such competition almost lost the crusader kingdom of Jerusalem a prize that had eluded it for half a century.

The great port had been there for the asking as far back as 1100 when its authorities offered to surrender the place. However, the horrifying memories of the dreadful slaughter at the capture of Jerusalem the year before meant that they were prepared to hand over the keys only to Raymond of Toulouse, the one crusading leader to have shown any humanity. Godfrey of Bouillon, sovereign of the new kingdom and jealous of Raymond's reputation, refused to consider the idea. For the next fifty years the greatest port on the southern coast of Palestine remained under the rule of the Fatimid caliphs at Cairo.

King Baldwin III, dubbed "the ideal king" by his Christian subjects and admired even by his Muslim opponent Nur-ad-Din, decided that the strategic prize simply had to be won. Mustering the army of the kingdom with all available siege-engines, he appeared before the walls on January 25, 1153, and summoned it to surrender. All the grandees of the kingdom were with him, including the grand masters of the two military orders, the Temple and the Hospital. In the words of Sir Steven Runciman, "Ascalon was a tremendous fortress, spreading from the sea in a great semicircle, with its fortifications in excellent repair." It was also well-stocked with armaments and provisions. Baldwin made a complete blockade of the city from the landward side, but his siege-engines seemed unable to make any significant impression on the walls and the Egyptians could supply it from the sea. In June, an Egyptian fleet, far outnumbering the twenty galleys of the Christians, sailed unopposed into the harbor, laden down with supplies of all sorts and troop reinforcements.

It was now that the crusading army made full use of its principal siege-engine, a tower that literally towered over the battlements, so that its team could rain missiles and flaming tow and torches down into the streets of the city. It was situated on the stretch of wall assigned to the Templars, but a night sortie from the garrison caught the guard by surprise and successfully fired the huge structure. As the flames were fanned by the rising wind, it rapidly flared up like a giant torch and, buckling under its own weight and blown off balance by the gusting wind, it collapsed against the city wall; in due course, the intense heat of what was now a roaring inferno cracked the masonry. By morning a sizeable breach gaped.

And now the Templars decided to take the road to glory. Forty of their number, magnificently armored and equipped, forced their way in, hoping, presumably, to hack their way to the Muslim command post before the full garrison was raised. Their colleagues outside the wall actually fought off attempts by fellow Christians to join the assault, determined that the Templars alone should have the honor of forcing the city's surrender. The outcome was a fiasco. The forty heroes were soon surrounded and cut down, their corpses hung out on the city walls. A truce was called to allow both sides to bury their dead.

That Ascalon was not lost a second time was due to the grand master of the Hospitallers, great rivals of the Templars, who took their side in urging that the attack should be resumed. The king was persuaded and the barons followed. A month later, on August 19, the garrison capitulated. The soldiers, together with such citizens as wished, were allowed to go as refugees to Egypt. Thousands streamed out of the city, which had been honored on both sides of the religious divide as "the bride of Syria." A treasure-house of luxuries and armaments had fallen to the kingdom. Ascalon was its last major triumph, but it had so very nearly been a disaster, thanks to a rivalry for honor in victory.

### Weaknesses and strengths

In a siege, as in any department of war, the first rule of hostilities was to know the enemy's weaknesses and exploit them. Procopius, the historian of the reign of Emperor Justinian, tells us that when the Ostrogothic king Witigis laid siege to Rome in 537–8 he had the city's aqueducts cut. The complex of public baths ceased to function and of course drinking water was in desperately short supply—but so too was bread, as the city's flour mills were water-powered. Animal power could not be used as a replacement since all the animals, except the horses needed by the military, had been slaughtered to economize on feed. Count Belisarius, heading the defense, found a brilliant solution. He had a row of boats moored side by side across the Tiber at a point where the current flowed strongly, then two mills were placed in each boat and a waterwheel suspended between each pair of boats. Water power was once again driving Rome's flour mills.

Under the pressure of siege conditions Belisarius, who apparently was the inventor, had introduced a new technology. Getting reports of the mills from deserters, the Goths floated logs and Roman corpses down the Tiber to clog the paddles: Belisarius strung heavy chains between the bridge arches upstream. Procopius says nothing about where the aqueduct waters were diverted to—if they were simply allowed to flood the plain, the resultant swamps and stagnant water would have been ideal breeding terrain for flies and might in part explain the sickness that plagued the besieging army.

The siege of the island of Malta in 1568 witnessed the deployment of virtually every technique of siege warfare. It included a notably ingenious exploitation of a weakness the attackers were surely unaware of until the defenders unmasked artillery where none could be expected to exist.

The Turkish commander of the attacking force had had a huge tower, complete with drawbridge, wheeled right up to the walls of the Fort of St. Angelo. Sharpshooters were able to fire down on defenders beyond the walls. The machine, draped with sheets of leather that were kept constantly wet by streams of water from tanks inside the tower, seemed impregnable to fire and indeed any other mode of attack since gunners on the fortress walls were picked off by the sharpshooters. However, the defending commander had masons open a hole in the base of the wall opposite the tower. Since the outer stones of the wall were left in place to the last moment the Turks in the tower did not realize that the defenders had rolled a cannon into place. As soon as all was ready the outer masonry was removed and the cannon smartly run out. It was loaded with chain shot; when the gun was fired the shot whirled out somewhat like the whirling blade of a circular saw. Repeated discharges of this lethal ammunition pulped the wooden beams of the siege-tower which buckled and crashed down, bringing the soldiers inside with it, as well as a cascade of water from its tanks.

## Panic

There can have been few protracted sieges during which, at some time or another, there was not a moment of panic. Anything, of course, might set it off; resolute action might stop it in its tracks. During the "siege" of Paris, King Louis XI of France was roused from his bed to answer a panic report that across the city a Burgundian commando unit was setting fire to the capital. Taking the precaution to order out the militia, he rode to investigate and discovered that the fire alarm had been occasioned by the "bright tail of a comet"—more probably a meteorite shower.

Sometimes rank incompetence was to blame. During Burgundy's campaign against Ghent, the city sent out a detachment to relieve the pressure on their ally, the town of Gaverre. Presumably the field battery was manned by experienced gunners, but in a shocking lapse of elementary security an uncovered barrel of gunpowder stood near enough to the guns for a flying spark to ignite the explosive mixture. As the smoldering mass sprang into flames the gunner yelled a warning to his colleagues. They panicked and the scare spread to the Ghentish infantry. Capable and brave but lacking battle experience, it was soon in rout, driven from the field by the Burgundian troops.

The fortress within the city of Antioch.
(Taylor Library)

A sapper's-eye-view of Rochester Castle, Kent. Soldiers trying to lever out the lower masonry courses would have worked under a hail of missiles. In fact, the corner tower to the right is a 1217 replacement of the square structure brought down by King John's miners in the siege of 1216. The circular cross section was supposedly less vulnerable.
(Taylor Library)

A section of the triple defensive walls of the ancient Christian capital Constantinople (now Istanbul), the so-called Theodosian walls begun in 413 on the orders of Anthemius, regent for the then 12-year-old emperor Theodosius II (401–50). (Taylor Library)

The majestic presence of Krak on its rocky eminence still inspires admiration—in its "active life" so to speak, it surely intimidated any would-be conqueror. Between the great towers can be seen the massive *talus* or batter to protect the base of the walls. Below it lies the concealed *berquil*. (Taylor Library)

Krak des Chevaliers: A view of the *berquil* which, as well as acting as a defensive hazard, served also as a reservoir for the winter rains. (Taylor Library)

Castel del Monte, "the Crown of Apulia," built by Emperor Frederick II, has luxurious living quarters, no doubt indebted to Arab and Byzantine models. Probably used as a hunting lodge, it would have been an effective strong point in case of war. The mullioned windows are in the Gothic style of the emperor's German dominions; the classical style of the gateway looks back to imperial Rome. (Italian Tourist Office)

A view of Caernarfon Castle in Wales, built by Edward I of England, from across the River Seiont. The banding of dark stone, reminiscent of walls at the imperial city of Constantinople, may have been intended to signify Edward's ambitions to create an "empire" in Britain. The stone revetment cladding the motte of the earlier Norman castle projects from the bottom of the wall to the right of the picture. (Courtesy of www.CaernarfonOnline.co.uk)

The massive double towered gateway at Rhuddlan, North Wales, and the strength of the fortifications overall, seem a somewhat exaggerated response to any threat that might be posed by the under-resourced Welsh princes it was intended to repel. (Taylor Library)

In 1216 Dover Castle, today one of the best preserved medieval fortifications in northern Europe, held out against a siege from Prince Louis of France. After the siege, these foreworks were built to afford added protection.
(Taylor Library)

Just in shore across the Menai Straits from the coast of Wales, the last of the sequence of Edwardian castles to be built, Beaumaris (though never completed) could garrison a sufficient force to maintain the English presence in the island of Anglesey. From the air it can be seen to be a classic version of concentric design, even without a keep. (Taylor Library)

Bodiam Castle, Sussex (1380s), restored by Lord Curzon who presented it to the National Trust in 1926. Built by Sir Edward Dalingrigge, perhaps to defend against French pirate raids (the Channel coastline then ranged further inland). A concentric "courtyard castle" and, like Beaumaris, lacking a central keep, it had luxury domestic apartments and a textbook moat: it suggests an old soldier's dream of perfection. As British viceroy of India (1898–1905), in 1895 Curzon initiated the restoration of the Taj Mahal. (Taylor Library)

A dramatic shot of the restored portcullis ("sliding gate") at Bodiam. The sharpened stakes conjure images of skewered attacking soldiery not fast enough on their feet. (Taylor Library)

The castle of Bonaguil standing on a spur of rock ("fine needle," *bonne aiguille*) between the Thèze and Lemance rivers (Lot-et-Garonne) in France, a major tourist venue, dates largely from the 1480s–1520s. Originally (*c.* 1250) a simple tower, it was extended during the Hundred Years' War (1350s–1450s), when Bonaguil held for the English. (Taylor Library)

The comparatively narrow gateway and the massive round towers that flank it make a powerful defensive statement at the main entrance to the castle of Rhodes. Atop the towers, the business-like battlements continue the theme, while projecting stone corbels supporting them provide machicolations (murder holes from which to drop incendiary missiles on an enemy attempting to sap the base of the walls). (Taylor Library)

The towering cliffs on which the southern Spanish town of Ronda stands, seemed to make it impregnable to siege—and yet it fell. Time and again, the history of medieval warfare demonstrated that the term "impregnable" meant little in the face of determined attack. (Author)

The windowless towers of the austere Alcazaba fortress seen from the adjoining grounds of the Alhambra de Granada. (Author)

The castle of the counts of Flanders at Ghent, or "Gravensteen" (literally, "the count's stones"), was for a period during the nineteenth century used as a factory. During the 1880s, however, a faithful reconstruction, down to the hinged wooden shutters to protect the archers on the battlements, also restored the moat. To the left of the massive keep can be seen the counts' residence. (Ghent Tourist Office)

Within the walls of the great citadel Cairo built on the rocky promontory known as the Muqqatam, by Saladin, sultan of Egypt (1168–93). To the right can be seen one of the great towers of Saladin's structure and ahead, beyond the walls, the famous Alabaster Mosque built by Muhammad Ali, ruler (1805–49) and founder of modern Egypt. (Author)

The town walls (*murallas*) of Avila, Spain survive as a classic reminder of the kind of defenses once presented by every major town in continental Europe. (Avila Tourist Office)

In 1265, the keep at Dover Castle was the site of a desperate last stand by Countess Eleanor, widow of the rebel earl of Leiccester, Simon de Montfort, defeated by the Lord Edward (later Edward I) at the Battle of Evesham on August 4. The baronial cause was lost. But in Dover, the countess hired a group of archers and prepared to hold out in the hopeless cause. (Taylor Library)

The "Castel Nuovo," Naples is noted for the triumphal archway built to celebrate the accession of Alfonso of Aragon as king (1442–58) of Naples. The first castle was built (1279–82) for the court of Charles of Anjou, king of Naples and Sicily, though he never lived here. The place was much modified by his successors. (Author)

The hill on which the fortress at Aleppo stands has been fortified for thousands of years. At the time of the crusaders' siege of Damascus (1147–8), Aleppo was the great Islamic power center in Syria. However, the citadel as we see it today owes much to the work of Saladin's son, az Zahir al Ghazi (d. 1216). (Rachel Lewis)

Auguste Rodin's masterpiece *The Burghers of Calais* was commissioned by the city council of Calais in 1884 but not in fact accepted until 1895—the councilors had hoped for defiant heroes, but they got real men, broken and suffering. This cast was installed in Parliament Gardens, Westminster, in 1913 to honor the memory of Philippa of Hainault, queen of England, who persuaded her husband King Edward III to spare the burghers' lives. (Taylor Library)

The sequence of round and square section towers at Dover testifies to the changing fashions in castle design. The almost exaggerated batter at the base of the gate tower would surely have frustrated any attempt at mining this section of the fortification. (Taylor Library)

Built at a time when the sea lapped the outer walls of the "Castel Nuovo," this indented batter would surely have made any attempted approach by ship extremely hazardous. (Author)

The ruins of Château Gaillard, Richard I of England's "Saucy Castle," overlooking the River Seine in Normandy; the river valley can just be seen in the background. It was once covered by a complex of causeways, river barrages and defensive towers, yet Philip II of France took the place in 1204 and the rest of Normandy followed within months. (Author)

With its militia neutralized as a fighting force, Ghent had to submit to its ducal overlord. Luckily for the city, Duke Philip, called the Good, was also clear-headed. When a vengeful member of his council urged the duke to destroy the rebellious city now at his mercy, Philip coldly enquired how he would then replace the huge revenues that flowed to his coffers from this commercial powerhouse.

In one form or another most types of warfare known to us today were practiced in the Middle Ages. The first known instance of biological warfare set in motion the most notorious event in European history. In the summer of 1346 a mysterious and lethal illness was reported among the population of the Genoese commercial colony at Caffa in the Crimea, on the Black Sea coast. Europeans may not have seen it before but there was no doubt about the source of the infection. The colony was under siege by the Tartar tribes of the region; there was an epidemic raging through their camp and, being equipped with siege artillery, the Tartar commander decided to share his good fortune with the besieged population by lobbing plague-ridden corpses over the city walls to break the defenders' resistance with the ultimate terror weapon.

Within weeks the Genoese galleys were rowing, panic-stricken, from the place; the Tartars made no attempt to interfere with their departure—they knew too well the dangers of tangling with the victims of this plague. In October 1347 at Messina in Sicily, the Franciscan friar Michael of Piazza Armerina noted that "twelve Genoese galleys . . . fleeing the vengeance which our Lord was taking on their nefarious deeds entered the harbor." He does not specify what these deeds may have been—perhaps for a Sicilian the mere fact that the perpetrators were Genoese was sufficient. In any case, the fallout from the siege of Caffa reached the rest of Europe with lightning speed.

# Chapter Eight

# Logistics

*"The art of moving and quartering troops, i.e., quarter-master general's work . . ."*

*The Athenaeum*, 1898

It seems that the word "logistics" arrived in English in the fifteenth century as a derivation of the French word *loge*, a small house or lodging. Thus it might seem that the science and art of arranging for the movement and maintenance of military forces in the field was in the first instance a matter of finding accommodation for those on campaign. And to a certain extent it was just that. When a medieval army went to war the military personnel, those doing the actual fighting, were just part of the huge body of men and women involved. In addition there were the servants of the knights or men-at-arms (according to Edward III's military establishment men with at least 450 acres of land to their name) and the household staffs not only of the monarch himself but also of the great nobles who might be accompanying him—their butlers, chefs, wardrobe masters, footmen, trumpeters and many others, including chapel staff. During the English invasion of France in the first quarter of the fifteenth century, for example, the sheer numbers of the English choral establishments astonished the French. The capture of Joan of Arc on May 30, 1430, was celebrated with the singing of a special Te deum by the duke of Bedford's choristers at Compiègne.

The objective of the logistical exercise, even with the choristers, was still, of course, to mobilize fighting effectives in a given place and ideally at a given time. But one will have a richer, truer picture of the life of a medieval siege if one has in mind the cloud of "extras" in the wings of the action. In addition to these were the camp-followers, wives and others, religious mendicants, hawkers and pedlars—possibly, one surmises in exceptional circumstances, washerwomen.

### Laying in supplies

About the year 1390 the citizens of the Bavarian town of Dinkelsbühl, whose medieval walls with their twelfth-century towers are still to be seen, paid a contractor to have the town mill fortified in case of siege. Well-stocked grain stores were of little use if flour could not be produced.

Logistics for an attacking army meant mobilizing transport as well as assembling the supplies at depot points. For the targeted castle or township the job was to fill the warehouses and stores if siege was expected, but to keep them well stocked in peace even if attack was not imminent. Late in 1075, grimly recognizing that his relations with his warlike neighbors, the Norman princes Duke Robert Guiscard of Apulia and others, had soured beyond recall, the universally feared and reviled Lombard prince Gisulf, ruler of Salerno, was preparing his chief city for siege. An order was issued to all householders to lay in provisions for two years; any who failed to satisfy the prince's inspectors would be expelled from the city. In view of what was to come, some may have wished they had risked the option.

The enemy forces arrived with the beginning of summer and Salerno found herself under blockade. The ships of Guiscard and his brother-in-law Richard, prince of Capua, blocked the harbor mouth; their tents carpeted the plain outside the city walls on the landward side. The people of Salerno presumably faced the future with as much confidence as was possible in such circumstances—at least they were, thanks to the prince's prudence and foresight, ready for the long haul. They would soon learn, as others have since, that the "prudence" of government does not necessarily redound to the benefit of the governed. Within days of the siege being laid by the enemies outside the walls, they found that they had a more dangerous threat within. The Lord Gisulf's agents made a circuit of the town demanding a third part of every citizen's supplies for the lord's personal granaries.

To be plundered by the enemy when a siege was lost was to be expected; to be plundered by the home authorities before it had begun was something else. But few complained for, as John Julius Norwich remarks in his *The Normans in the South*, it was "universally known that complaint was punished by blinding . . . or . . . amputation." Not long afterward, the prince's men were round once more, this time to appropriate whatever stores might have survived their first raid. Those citizens prosperous enough to have horses, dogs or even cats ate them; others, less fortunate, faced the onset of famine so much the earlier. Any with the money to do so were obliged, so a contemporary tells us, to buy back from the prince's granary masters, wheat they had themselves acquired at three bezants at more than ten times that price. The death-toll escalated steeply; famished corpses littered the streets; Prince Gisulf picked his way among them carefully but, says our chronicler, quite cheerfully. The city was delivered on December 13, 1176, technically speaking by treachery, since the gates were opened to the Norman troops from within. The garrison surrendered themselves willingly. Gisulf, with his party, fell back on the citadel and held out a further five months (it is not clear why, since the Lombard principality was finished), before being given safe passage through Italy to report his woes to his one remaining friend, Pope Gregory VII in Rome.

### A convoy under siege

Sometimes the logistical exercise of the campaign, the actual movement of the army and its satellite non-military cohorts, or some convoy of provisions, was in itself subject to siege. At the siege of Rome in the sixth century, imperial reinforcements, having offloaded supplies at the Roman port of Ostia, "placed themselves 'in laager' [to use the phrase with which South African warfare has made us familiar] behind their wagons," as historian Thomas Hodgkin wrote in 1896.

In certain specialized instances it is possible to talk of actual "siege on the march." Indeed, for film-goers this type of defensive action used to be a favorite set piece in Hollywood westerns, when the pioneer wagon train was forced to "laager" down, its wagons wheeled round in the form of a circular fortress to see off squadrons of mounted Plains tribesmen, swooping in to the attack. Already a veteran of the Normandy wars, Sir John Fastolf, just turned 50, was involved in just such an action with a convoy en route with supplies for the English forces besieging Orleans in 1429. Attacked by a substantial French force, he halted the convoy in good order, had his men unship the supply barrels from their carry slings and throw together a surprisingly effective barrier. From this improvised stockade they held off, then routed their attackers. How, some two centuries later, William Shakespeare came to adapt Sir John's name as "Falstaff" for his most famous comedy creation is an involved story—had he perhaps heard of the famous "Battle of the Herrings" (so called from the contents of the barrels), an improbably farcical name for an actual engagement? Of course he may have heard that the Sir John of history had also been landlord of the tenements in which the Boar's Head tavern stood—the favorite haunt of the Sir John of his fiction.

## Mobilizing horse power

In June 1359 Edward III of England prepared for the culminating campaign of his challenge to make good his claim to the crown of France. The objective was no less than his coronation in the cathedral of Notre Dame of Reims, the city since the time of Clovis had guarded the holy oil brought down from heaven to St. Rémy. The king and his generals were fully aware of the enormity of the task ahead of them. The route of march, from the English town of Calais, would lie through landscapes denuded of food and supplies of any sort by war, thanks to the recent peasant uprising of the Jacquerie and the orders of the French government. The logistical challenge was to support the army on the march entirely from its own commissariat. The wagon train carried grain and hand mills to grind it as well as field ovens to bake it; falcons and mounted falconers and 120 hounds, not merely for the king's sport of the chase but to bring meat to the field kitchens; and even coracles and portable fishing boats. And all this in addition to the usual stores of weapons, ammunition, siege equipment, clothing and tentage.

The target city, long aware of the English plans, had had time to refurbish and enlarge its defenses and lay in substantial supplies of armaments and victuals. In fact the siege, from December 4, 1359, to January 11, 1360, was a muted, mild-mannered affair, confined to a simple blockade with no attempt to take the place by assault. Technically speaking, if King Edward's claim was good, then the citizens, by refusing to open their gates, were in a state of rebellion and would merit death and destruction if the city were taken.

But Edward wanted willing—not hostile—subjects, and issued orders that the inhabitants of Reims were to be treated with respect. Surrounding towns were ravaged but, despite skirmishing along the lines (the young Geoffrey Chaucer, with the royal army, was captured in obscure circumstances and ransomed with financial help from the king), Reims held firm. English morale dipped, torrential rain made conditions for horses as well as men barely tolerable. During the night of January 11, 1360, the English army withdrew in good order.

The king failed to realize his overambitious objective, yet it had been a great logistical achievement to get the huge force to its destination—an achievement that, like all such feats of transport up to the early twentieth century, depended on horses. Peter Reid, in his enthralling account of England's military in the late Middle Ages, has estimated that approximately 14,000 horses would have been involved. These numbers had to be mustered in England, paid for and shipped across the Channel. They had also to be fed. Reckoning twenty pounds of hay and eight pounds of oats per beast yields a daily total of 175 tons for horse feed alone; allowing for two days on shipboard and providing for an emergency five days establishing the army in hostile country, Reid comes to a grand total of 1,225 tons of stores in addition to the animals. And of course handling equestrian motive power is a good deal more demanding than parking vehicles and storing gasoline or diesel.

### The logistics of armed pilgrimage

For the defenders of a siege to assure their supplies depended on laying in and maintaining stores in time of peace, and in times of war contriving, if possible, delivery. For the attacker, the business of getting men and matériel to the scene of action in battle-ready condition—and maintaining them in place as fit as conditions will allow and for as long as the commanders require—has always been a demanding duty. Given the conditions of terrain, transport and communications for any medieval commissariat it must, at times, have seemed near impossible, and what was achieved against the odds, incredible.

For example, in purely logistical, administrative and military terms, the First Crusade was a triumphant success, despite occasional disasters en route. The bulk of the pilgrim forces traveled overland all the way; but the army, led by Duke Robert of Normandy, a charming, courageous but somewhat negative 40-year-old, took the road late in 1096 down to southern Italy and the domains of his Norman cousin, Roger Guiscard, in Calabria. Rather than risk a winter crossing they lingered among the delights of southern Italian hospitality and only in late March 1097 headed for the port of Brindisi to embark their troops for the crossing of the Adriatic to Dyrrachium (Durrës). Unimpressed by the dilatory nature of the march so far, a number of the pilgrim soldiers had deserted already. More were to follow.

On April 5, the duke's marshals began the embarkation of men, horses, equipment and money at the quayside. But their work was not well done. Stowage of the cumbersome but unwieldy ships of a medieval fleet was a job demanding experience and professionalism (skills even more important in the transshipment of military matériel and personnel). Eventually, the first transport put out to sea. It had barely cleared the port before it capsized. Some 400 men-at-arms were lost, together with many score horses and mules and many coin chests. It was reported that the drowned warrior pilgrims had been recovered with the mark of the cross miraculously imprinted on their shoulders. Thanks to divine intervention, it seemed, these unfortunates would, happily, be deemed to have made their pilgrimage. Others, less than impressed by the expertise of the quartermaster general's staff and cynical of the propaganda, followed the example of the earlier deserters. Nevertheless, most of the thousands still in line on the quays of Brindisi to board the transports held to their pilgrim vows and continued with the army.

And in general the logistical arrangements for the crusade were solidly effective. From the preaching of the expedition in November 1095 to the raising of Christian standards on the walls of Jerusalem in July 1099, a period somewhat under five years, combatants totaling (it has been estimated) some 200,000 men were mobilized into four principal army groups and were then marched through often rugged, sometimes parched and usually hostile terrain a distance of more than 3,000 miles to a theater of war occupied by enemy populations totaling several millions and armies considerably larger than the effective fighting men in the crusader ranks on their arrival. It was a theater, moreover, where warfare was endemic and conducted by often highly professional troops and commanders, according to battlefield tactics unfamiliar to Western European fighting men; techniques that had to be learned and adapted to, often almost literally on the hoof.

Yet the crusading army fought no fewer than five major engagements in the field and took by siege three major cities and a number of lesser ones. Perhaps surprisingly, the tough and brutal northerners proved adaptable to new conditions; in fact such attributes were in part the result of the nature of warfare in Europe and in large part of the fact that siege was the principal activity in that warfare. A successful siege required a head for organization and often the building, or even the devising, on site of specialized engines and equipment. The Western knight, used to combining a diverse range of military skills on his home ground, was mentally attuned to problem-solving in the field. A nickname gives a revealing clue. William of Melun, a man-at-arms of the minor baronage, was renowned for his martial spirit and immense physical strength. More importantly, he was evidently a man with some technical know-how, since he was known throughout the army as the "Carpenter." Even men of knightly class could turn their hands to the building of siege machines and military equipment.

### How a logistical decision liberated Lisbon: the Second Crusade, 1147

Elsewhere (see p. 121) we see how Europe's Second Crusade, preached by St. Bernard of Clairvaux, was humiliated at the siege of Damascus. But yet there was one group of pilgrims, inspired by St. Bernard's appeal, who marked up a triumph, largely as a result of their decision as to how to travel to the theater of war. Rather than join the main expeditions marching overland from various European centers, a contingent of mostly English but also some German, French, Flemish and Frisian warrior crusaders set out from English ports in the late spring of 1147, planning to take the ocean route round Brittany and the Iberian Peninsula.

A number of the Norman baronage of England had joined the royal armies on the Continent; this coastal crusade was headed by men of less exalted rank. As the chronicler Henry of Huntingdon put it, "lesser folk who depended not on great leaders but rather God omnipotent." Apart from the minor noble Saher of Archelle; men of the empire (the German contigent) led by Count Arnold of Aerschot; and Hervey de Glanville (constable of the men of Norfolk and Suffolk), there was: Christian Ghistelles, who headed the Flemings and the men of Boulogne; Simon of Dover, who led the men from Kent; Master Andrew; the men of London; and brothers William and Ralph, the men of Southampton.

Some 164 ships were involved. As always, given the poor condition of roads and the hazards from marauders through the Balkans, it was a matter of weighing the comparative cheapness and convenience of sea travel against the long additional distance traveled. This time, rough summer storms forced the flotilla to weather up in the mouth of the Douro river along the north Portuguese coast. The crusaders

*In this artist's impression, the attackers have had time to construct a planking platform to support the tower. Bowmen in the top stage protect an assault from the fourth stage, while at ground level a team is operating a battering ram to remarkable effect. Archers fire from the protection of pavises (more commonly used by crossbowmen) though one has been felled by a missile from the battlements.* Taylor Library

were unlucky, but to Count Afonso Henriques of Portugal, struggling to assert his independence from the kingdoms of Leon and Castile to the east and the Muslim Almoravid dynasty to the south, it looked as if it might be a godsend.

Progressing with the reconquest of his country against the Muslim power and already adopting the title of "king" he had, in the March of that year, taken the town of Santarem on the north bank of the River Tejo (Tagus) to the north-east of Lisbon and now had that city and its majestic natural harbor in his sights. The fleet's sheltering off his coast might have been designed to aid him in the amphibious operation he had in mind. He approached the pilgrims' leaders. The English contingent opposed getting involved. They argued they had taken their vows of pilgrimage to Jerusalem. The others eagerly accepted the bishop of Oporto's reasoning that their real duty was to fight the infidel wherever he might be found and, here in Portugal, they were on a frontier with Islam and could fulfill their vows on the banks of the Tejo. The count's promise of land and plunder finally won over Constable de Granville, who persuaded his compatriots. The crusader fleet sailed down the coast from Oporto and into the Mar del Palha to beset Lisbon from the water.

The siege of Lisbon opened on June 18 with the formal summons to the governor of the city; it lasted four months. The governor, rejecting the Christians' call to surrender, scorned what he considered the hypocrisy of these pilgrims in the cause of Christ. "It is," he called down from the battlements of the great gate, "nothing but the ambition of the mind that drives you on." He and his fellow Muslims put up a brave resistance. In the end, the walls were overtopped by the great belfry (from which the assault was made on October 24) and attacked at their base thanks to a battering with a roofed mantelet wheeled into place by, we are told, a team from Ipswich; supplies exhausted and no possibility of relief from their co-religionists in Morocco, the citizens and garrison surrendered, on the assurance of their lives and their property. They did not know that Christians rarely honored oaths pledged to unbelievers; most of them were massacred. The English, notes Sir Steven Runciman in his account of the siege, "congratulating themselves on their virtue, played only a minor part." Many of the English did in fact continue their pilgrimage to the Holy Land. Most of the others settled to a new life under southern skies. Among these was one Englishman: the priest Gilbert of Hastings became the first bishop of Lisbon.

### A siege in the war against terrorism: Stirling, 1304

Mounting any but the briefest of campaigning sieges involved major logistical deployment: the siege of Stirling in 1304 was a textbook example. Following a terrorist campaign against the English in Lanark, William Wallace, a disaffected Scottish minor landowner (his name suggests that he was probably of British, i.e., Welsh, extraction) crushed an English force under John de Warrenne, earl of Surrey at Stirling Bridge on September 11, 1297. The defeat was reversed at Falkirk in July the following year when an army led by Wallace was destroyed by an Anglo-Welsh force and Wallace himself fled the field. His reputation as a military leader was destroyed, but his prestige as a terror leader against the English lived on. In 1299 the English garrison of Stirling Castle was betrayed to Scottish patriots and the English king returned across the border in the summer of 1300.

Stirling Castle as we see it today, rising on its massive volcanic outcrop of rock, dates mostly from the fifteenth and sixteenth centuries. Nothing survives of the structure that Edward laid siege to, but it is assumed that it stood on the same rocky eminence. At once we face a problem. Two of the near contemporary chronicles relate that Edward started operations by filling in the moat that surrounded the castle with debris and tree branches but that the defenders foiled this attempt by setting fire to the infill. However, given the nature of the site, it is not clear just where this moat or ditch might have been. The Langtoft chronicle recorded that the place was defended by a garrison of twenty-two with its own stone-thrower—indeed, one great stone felled the horse on which the king was inspecting operations, and so he was dangerously thrown. Given that the "Community of Scotland" had made formal submission to the English king the year before the siege one might ask why he had continued with the siege. The fact was that, though in formal terms the war for Scotland was won, for as long as a handful of fighting men was able to hold the country's major strategic fortress the invaders faced a standing humiliation and the patriots in Stirling Castle offered a rallying point for others. In purely military terms, the place could be neutralized by a small containing force; in terms of the psychology of war it had to be taken. The siege was the spectacle of the year. We are told that an oriel window, that is a projecting window at first-floor level, presumably pierced through the wall of a building in the little town of Stirling, provided a weather-protected viewing platform for Edward's queen, Margaret.

The walls were bombarded by a number of siege-engines with names such as "Segrave," one of the king's officers, and a monster called Warwolf. The construction of the latter required eighteen great beams or "timbers," two "great ropes" with two smaller cords and some sixty carpenters working over several weeks, and ammunition of 784 stones was prepared. This was almost certainly the Ludgar engine (from the French *Loup de guerre*, meaning "wolf of war") mentioned in the Langtoft chronicle; in fact it was not fully ready for service when the garrison offered to surrender. One observer reckoned that the sight of the "high machines" being built persuaded the garrison to abandon resistance. Edward is said to have refused the surrender until his great apparatus was complete so that it could be tested—no doubt the king had been infuriated by the stubborn resistance of the defenders. Earlier, he had paid two archers four shillings (wages for eight man-days) to look for a vulnerable postern gate—they had drawn a blank. His artillery did what was necessary. Apparently it was powerful enough to hurl a stone clean through the major breastwork constructed to protect the gateway. If there had been any doubts in the garrison before, this demonstration of artillery power led the brave hearts to concede. Even before the advent of gunpowder, siege engines could intimidate.

It had been an immense campaign, drawing resources from all over Britain. London sent, among other things, eighty-seven crossbows and the sheriff of Lincoln 236 longbows. Materials were brought from as far afield as Aberdeen and King's Lynn in Norfolk, where pontoons were constructed to be floated up to Scotland for the army crossing of the Firth of Forth, while technical advisers were recruited from the Continent.

Chief among these was Jean de Lamouilly, a native of Bar (border territory between France and the Holy Roman Empire) whose count was an ally of Edward I. Between 1299 and 1312 Lamouilly served with various English garrisons in Scotland and was notable as an expert in state-of-the-art weaponry; he seems to have devised an explosive form of Greek fire for the siege of Stirling. Accounts for the siege show payments totaling £20 made for combustibles, including ingredients that suggest gunpowder as well as, intriguingly, cotton thread; clay pots were also purchased, presumably as canisters for flammable rounds to be hurled by projectile weapons.

One important payment was not honored—de Lamouilly's fee. He made good the loss in the next reign by an ingenious exercise in self-help. In December 1316 King Edward II appointed Aymer de Valence ambassador to the papal court at Avignon to solicit Pope John XXII's support for the English case against the Scots. On his return journey, in May 1317, he was kidnapped by de Lamouilly and carried off to Bar where he was forced to agree to a huge ransom before gaining his release in June. Aymer was saddled with debt for the rest of his life. Even after dividing the proceeds with the count of Bar, de Lamouilly more than made good the back payment of his fees.

Despite the English triumph at the siege of Stirling and the fact that the Scots had no comparable mastery of conventional siege techniques, guerrilla tactics enabled them to take castle after castle in the subsequent decade. The resistance was led by Robert de Bruce, scion of an Anglo-Norman family with remote claims to the Scottish throne, who had had himself crowned at Scone in March 1306. Eight years later, in 1314, Bruce demolished an army marching to the relief of Stirling Castle at the battle of Bannockburn, the most famous—in fact virtually the only—Scottish victory against the English.

### Communications and the logistical causes of the Fourth Crusade, 1204

The shameful sack of the Christian metropolis of Constantinople by the Christian army mobilized by Pope Innocent III had its origins in preliminary decisions as to the transport of the army, its victualing and supply, and in the virtual isolation of the military commanders from their papal sponsor, thanks to the primitive and inadequate communications of the time.

Before the invention of the electric telegraph in 1837, control of a military campaign at any distance from headquarters was a virtual impossibility if the commander on the spot was not in sympathy with the objectives of the high command. The episode known as the Fourth Crusade that set out from Europe in 1202 is a classic instance. Intended by Pope Innocent III to recover the Christian position in the Holy Land from the world of Islam, it encountered no Muslim armies. Instead, even though the place had capitulated on terms, the "crusaders" seized and pillaged the port of Zara (Zarda, in modern Croatia), under the protection of the Catholic king of Hungary, and then went on to plunder the Orthodox Christian capital of Constantinople.

Many factors were to lead to this scandal of Christendom, but the stage was set for catastrophe the moment it was decided that the expedition should travel by sea on shipping provided by the Republic of Venice, rather than overland through the Balkans and onwards across Anatolian territories now in Turkey (but then nominally under the sway of the Byzantine Empire).

The enterprise had started auspiciously in 1199 at a grand tournament at a castle in Champagne, when the 22-year-old Count Thibaut, inspired by the preaching of a fashionable priest "of saintly character" from the Ile de France, had made his crusading vows. Thibaut's sister-in-law was the queen regnant of the kingdom of Jerusalem (where there was no Salic law to ban women from the throne). A number of noblemen followed Thibaut's lead and Geoffrey de Villehardouin, marshal of Champagne, with five other "deputies," was charged with planning the expedition. The decision to travel by sea had much to recommend it. Conditions in the Balkans were unstable; the Byzantine capital was in the throes of a succession crisis, while the borders in Anatolia fluctuated between Byzantine and Turkish rule. Yet, even so, most of the crusaders ended up before the walls of Constantinople and never even saw the minarets and domes of Jerusalem.

What the deputies did not take into account, and probably did not even know when they arrived in Venice to negotiate the terms of the transport, was that thirty years previously the then Byzantine emperor had made an enemy of the Republic when, on the flimsiest of pretexts, he had arrested all Venetian merchants within his domains and confiscated their goods. Relations between the empire and the great merchant city had steadied somewhat, but Venice was still bitterly aware that her immense trade with the East was dependent on the arbitrary goodwill of the emperor. Moreover, the present doge of Venice, 95-year-old Enrico Dandolo, had been personally victimized by the emperor in the aftermath of the 1170s troubles and harbored a burning grudge.

Pope Innocent had called the crusade against the infidel—fearful of possible developments that might endanger his project he had issued express commands against attacking other targets—but it was the man on the spot, Doge Dandolo, who determined the course of events, since it was he who was to be paymaster of the expedition. And there was one more blow to the crusade: its idealistic young leader, Count Thibaut, had died of a mysterious malady. His successor, Count Boniface of Montferrat, had ambitions of his own against the Byzantine emperors. In due course, the pope would receive messengers who reported "his" army's "triumphs" in two of the most profitable, as well as most dishonorable, sieges in the history of European warfare. He could only fume in frustration.

By the terms of the contract agreed in Venice in April 1201 the great expedition was not only to sail in ships supplied by Venice, it was to live off supplies funded by the Republic, and it was committed to sharing any conquests on a fifty-fifty basis. The crusade's leaders had already had to raise a loan of 5,000 silver marks from Venetian bankers before the shipbuilders in the Venetian Arsenal would lay down a single keel. Logistically, the terms probably made sense: the Arsenal was the greatest, most professional, shipbuilding yard in Europe and the Republic, already a center for pilgrim traffic, fully skilled in the business of provisioning on a massive scale.

Politically and, as it would turn out, financially, the terms were a disaster. The entire raison d'être for the expedition would be sabotaged by the logistical arrangements intended to deliver it to its objective. Through their deputies the campaign leaders now agreed to muster their forces at Venice in October 1202, when the balance of the money they owed for shipping and passage was to be handed over.

Many did not make the rendezvous, others made their own arrangements, but the doge insisted on payment in full. He offered a way out. They could discharge their debt if they assisted the Venetians in capturing the port of Zara, which they claimed was in fact a colony that had "defected" to the Hungarian king. Two years earlier the pope had forbidden any attack on Christian territory in set terms.

Now some crusaders refused to agree the Venetian demands and made their own armed pilgrimage. Most, however, took passage aboard ships of the great flotilla, banners snapping in the stiff breeze, priests chanting to the inspiration of the Holy Ghost, drums rolling, trumpets braying, as it set sail from its moorings on the island of St. Nicholas on the Lido. They arrived off Zara on November 10.

They were awe-struck by the beauty of the place, its high walls and lofty towers overlooking the bay, though some were intimidated by the defiance it showed to its Christian attackers with a festoon of what seems to have been tournament shields emblazoned with the sign of the cross. But the battle-hardened Geoffrey de Villehardouin and other veterans like him were well pleased with the resources their quartermasters had at last assembled. These included some 300 pieces of stone-throwing siege artillery and numbers of fine warhorses, which had been safely shipped on specially designed transports and were in good health. Morale was good. For those who cared, the pope, making the best of a bad job, had sent a letter offering conditional absolution to the army for breaching his instructions.

And things went well. The city surrendered after a short siege, on the understanding that the garrison and citizens would be spared. They were militarily outclassed and could expect no help from Hungary. Here were easy pickings for the soldiers of Christ. Zara was systematically pillaged—and then razed to the ground. The pope's demands that the demolition be halted and the king of Hungary compensated were both ignored—money was still owing to the Venetians and the crusaders themselves were virtually destitute. Few episodes in the history of siege warfare reached such depths of dishonor as did the siege of Zara. The city and its garrison had surrendered on terms, and had been comprehensively betrayed.

But now these penniless crusaders, their Venetian creditors still demanding further payments, looked for another profitable target of their holy war—nothing less than Constantinople, the Christian world's eastern bastion against the Islamic enemy.

Some of the crusaders may have persuaded themselves that this too was a legitimate expedition. A pretender to the imperial throne had promised to fund the attack and, after they had established him and his deposed father on the throne there, to propel their campaign to its ultimate objective, the Holy Land. Logistical considerations and funding, instead of facilitating the realization of the original objective, were dictating a change in plan—much to the private satisfaction of Dandolo. But it would be to the dismay of the pope, the supposed commander-in-chief of this maverick force. When he did, finally, get the news of the revised destination (a plan that had long been privately known to the leaders of the army), Innocent sent orders forbidding the attack. Given the communications of the time these could only arrive late; given the determination of the army they would hardly have altered the course of events, even if they had arrived in time.

### Constantinople, 1204: "the greatest booty since the world began . . ."
The Catholic crusaders arrived before the capital of Orthodoxy on June 24. They were intimidated by the sight that stretched before them. "They had never

imagined there could be so rich a city with so many palaces and great churches . . . and there was not a man who did not tremble." The main army, having decided to attack from the landward side, marched up around the Golden Horn where the bulk of the Byzantine fleet could be seen at anchor behind a massive chain or boom; the Venetians made their preparations for an attack from the sea. At length, on July 17, the two forces made a general assault. The Venetians first smashed the harbor chain and then sent in fire-ships to destroy most of the Byzantine shipping. Now the attack on the world's greatest Christian city could begin in earnest. With the final assault in prospect, Doge Dandolo, aged near 100 years yet accoutred in full armor, stationed himself, we are told, in the prow of the leading Venetian war galley, the banner or gonfalon of St. Mark planted before him, and urged his men on to the attack—surely a heroic figure, but fighting for a most ignoble cause.

Constantinople was now at the mercy of what the citizens regarded as a barbarian, heretical horde, which, according to rumor, was going to overthrow the true Orthodox faith for the schismatical creed and practices of Rome. The crusade leaders were demanding that Alexius, the emperor they had installed with his father, pay the money he had pledged, while the citizenry verged on turmoil under rulers forced on them by a Latin army. The emperor begged the Western leaders to pitch camp outside the walls and not to enter with their army while he was negotiating the terms of his return. But only days later he and his father were driven out by another pretender. Outside the walls, the Westerners vowed "to take over the city sword in hand"; install a Latin emperor; and transfer a large section of the imperial domain to the lordship of Venice. The city was to be looted—a small proportion of the proceeds going to the maintenance of the new Roman Catholic ecclesiastical establishment.

On April 13, 1204, Constantinople fell to the Western Christian army. The surrender was unconditional, the rank and file of the soldiery ran amok, but knights, abbots and monks all waded into the mayhem to plunder their full share. Vast booty in conventional treasure was taken: according to Marshal Villehardouin never had so much been taken from a single city since the creation of the world. Even more precious to thoughtful contemporaries were the spiritual treasures of sacred relics associated with the life of Christ and the saints. Not even Rome, at that time, could match the sacred treasure trove, the "halidom," enshrined at the New Rome founded by Constantine, the first Christian emperor.

Stripped from the churches and sanctuaries of the Orthodox metropolis, often by priests, most of the treasure found its way to the churches of France where, in due course, these venerated mementos of faith were to be looted by mobs of the French Revolution and this time destroyed. Many art treasures were lost, of course; many manuscripts, transcriptions of classical Latin texts as well as scriptures, made their way westward; much else was lost track of. Yet when, in 1877, a Geneva publishing house began the publication of a scholarly attempt to describe the sack and enumerate the treasures known to have been pillaged by the Fourth Crusade, the project would take twenty-seven years and require three massive volumes, the last appearing in 1904, 700 years after the desecration.

As for Pope Innocent, he had lost control of his crusade virtually from the outset, thanks to the inadequacies of contemporary communications and the logic of the logistical decisions taken by the army's deputies and the unswerving ambition of the Venetian doge. Innocent had fulminated in vain against the diversion of the enterprise from its proper goal, war against the infidel; he had sought to avert its attacks on Christian targets; and yet, when on May 16, 1204 Count Baldwin of Flanders, elected "emperor" by the crusaders with Venetian support, was to be solemnly crowned in Hagia Sophia, the pope could hardly reject the outcome of the criminally bungled enterprise. The ceremony was conducted by the papal legate. To this day, the four bronze horses awaiting the tourist camera on the façade of St. Mark's Venice provide a memento of the monstrous siege. For some 900 years they had adorned the Hippodrome at Constantinople, but in 1204 they were shipped to the Serene Republic by the order of Dandolo the pirate Doge. Six hundred years on they were looted by that other great pirate, Napoleon Bonaparte, and resided for a decade at Paris.

### Land and water: Nicaea, 1097

The 1204 assault on Constantinople, with two forces under separate commands, crusaders and Venetians, attacking the two targets of land walls and sea walls, was almost a textbook example of an amphibious operation, a not uncommon occurrence in the history of siege warfare. On May 6, 1097 contingents of the First Crusade led by Godfrey of Bouillon and Count Robert of Flanders came in sight of the lake-side city of Nicaea (Iznik, in Turkey), an ancient Christian city where an early Council of the Church had promulgated the Nicene Creed, but now the capital city of Sultan Kilij Arslan. The Westerners had the support and would soon have the concrete help of the Byzantine emperor, Alexius, in the form of a force of 2,000 men. A few days later they were joined by Bohemond of Otranto with welcome supplies of food and after him by Count Raymond of Toulouse. This made a force of some 30,000 surrounding the city by north, south and east. To the west lay the Ascanian lake, skirted by the city wall. Early in June further forces joined them under Duke Robert of Normandy, so that the Turkish garrison was confronted on the land side by a total of some 50,000 fighting men.

Safely lodged behind the four miles and 240 towers of the city's Roman-built Byzantine-maintained fortifications and the lake, the Muslim elite and its garrison, who held the place against the majority Orthodox Christian population, were confident that they could hold out long enough for the sultan to rally a relieving army and scatter the besiegers. But the crusaders acquired a trump card which the Turks learnt about only when it was too late. For not only had Emperor Alexius helped replenish the food supplies of the crusaders and detailed military engineers to help them in the construction of elaborate siege artillery, he now lent them the aid of a powerful flotilla. Up till this point the Western army had been frustrated by the fact that the Turks were supplied by shipments from across the lake. As soon as the crusade leaders requested the emperor to help them, he ordered ships to be transported by overland portage on sledge and roller from the Sea of Marmora to the lake, under the command of his own officer Manuel Butumites.

In her account of her father's reign, his daughter Anna Comnena asserts that Alexius held back until asked so that the crusaders might realize how important his assistance was to their campaign. Be that as it may, when it did come his help was decisive. The Byzantine shipping easily intercepted the supply route across the lake, and the Turkish regime in Nicaea looked for a deal to get themselves out of the city with their lives. On the morning of June 19, just as the crusaders expected to enter the city as conquerors, they discovered that during the night its governing clique had done a deal with Butumites and that imperial mercenaries had entered through the lakeside gates. The Western soldiery had reason to feel aggrieved, having been cheated of the spoils of a sack. They saw the treasures and riches they had expected to loot guarded by imperial troops and the Turkish noble families they had hoped to hold to ransom being escorted by these same troops to the safety of imperial custody. For his part, Emperor Alexius had recovered a city of the empire avoiding the ruination of ritual sacking that accompanied capitulation. The lake route that had saved Turkish Nicaea from immediate capitulation had equally facilitated the deliverance of the city from its expectant conquerors. Anna's account frankly admits to the emperor's double-dealing with the crusaders (this was, after all, an imperial city under Turkish occupation), while Western sources merely report the city was handed over to the emperor.

In England, the "lake fortress" of Kenilworth Castle in Warwickshire in the flood-plains of the midland counties, offered an example of amphibious operations in miniature compared with the drama of Nicaea. Built in the 1120s by the Clinton family, seventy years later it was appropriated by King John. South and west of the castle wound pleasant small streams which, when dammed, produced an artificial lake covering 100 acres. The keep on its mound was more or less inaccessible. Between 1204 and 1215 (the year of Magna Carta) John spent the vast sum of £2,000 on an outer enceinte. Briefly at the mercy of the barons in the months after Magna Carta, he pledged Kenilworth as the guarantee that he would observe the terms of the charter—he did not observe them of course, nor did he hand over the fortress. However, his son Henry III unwisely gave the place to his sister Eleanor, who became the wife of Simon de Montfort, earl of Leicester. Thus, a major royal stronghold was to become a rebel base when Earl Simon emerged as the leader of a new baronial revolt.

The lake, effective against enemies, could also cause problems for the lord of the castle himself. At the end of July 1265, the earl's son, marching up to help his father against the royalist forces, unwisely pitched his camp outside the castle walls so as to be off at first light against the enemy. But Prince Edward, the Crown Prince, making a forced march, caught him by surprise so that young Simon had to swim the lake in his night shirt for the safety of the fortress. Three days later at the battle of Evesham, Edward defeated and killed the elder de Montfort and the following year marched against the remnant of the rebels holding out at Kenilworth. The siege, which has been called the last set piece siege on English soil of the Middle Ages, lasted the best part of nine months. Prince Edward ordered repeated assaults; he had a massive siege-tower—built to hold 200 archers—brought up the causeway to the gate tower, to no avail. Next, having ordered barges to be brought up from Chester forty miles distant, he mounted a waterborne attack across the lake. Given that the preparations presumably entailed the building of dedicated transport vehicles and "navigating" the autumnal roads and trackways of medieval England, the outlay in money and manpower can be imagined. Even so, the attack failed. Terms were offered but still the garrison held out; finally just before Christmas, with only two days' starvation rations left and dysentery rife in their ranks, the defenders surrendered. The de Montfort brothers, expecting little from their father's royal enemy, went into exile.

Fifteen years later Edward, now king, embarked on the building of a cordon of castles with which he aimed to hold down the conquered people of North Wales. Perhaps mindful of the Kenilworth lake, he made sure that all were accessible by water. Most lay near the coast, like Harlech, with its "Gate Next the Sea" in the outer enceinte, Conwy and Caernarfon, though a few, like Rhuddlan on the River Clwyd, were situated on an inland waterway. A site like this posed the attacker an obvious problem. If he did not control the waterway then the beleaguered garrison could reasonably expect to receive supplies, even a relieving force. Indeed, at Rhuddlan the river was actually diverted so that a wharf could be constructed close under the castle wall to ensure that supplies could reach the garrison from the coast in times of unrest. Two centuries later a water route proved the salvation of the French defenders of Orleans, the great city on the Loire river beset by the English army of the boy king Henry VI who claimed the thrones of both England and France.

## The crusade that was flooded out: Egypt, 1218–22

One of the most complex and dramatic episodes of medieval amphibious siege warfare occurred during what is sometimes known as the Fifth Crusade, and was fought out in the Nile delta. The combatants were the army of Ayubite Egypt and a body of Christian warriors drawn from Europe and the kingdom of Jerusalem. This was a motley force under a divided leadership: its original objective had been to establish a base at the still-Christian port of Acre and then march on Jerusalem. At the outset, John of Brienne, the septuagenarian titular king of Jerusalem, considered himself the commander-in-chief, the Hungarians looked to their King Andrew, and the Austrians, who were to prove the most effective contingent, acknowledged only their duke, Leopold VI. The first arrivals disembarked at Acre between August and September 1217 and began in November their campaign toward the Holy City. But the "crusade" now lapsed into a series of *chevauchées*, or raiding forays. King Andrew reckoned he had had a "good crusade" when he had won a number of skirmishes and taken a number of saintly relics, among them the head of St. Stephen (the proto-martyr), his people's patron. He and his army headed homeward, north through Armenia. Hugh, the Christian king of Cyprus, had died meanwhile, and by December Leopold of Austria was the only leader with a significant force still in the field. Nothing had been achieved; the initiative had been lost; and "King John of Jerusalem" still contested the captaincy of the expedition. A comprehensive change in strategy was decided upon.

In the spring of 1218, reinforced by a body of German crusaders, the Christian fleet set sail for the Delta under the command of King John. For the best part of twenty years, advanced military thinking in the West had argued that the basis for long-term success against Islam in Palestine lay in the conquest of Egypt. The aim now was to capture the Egyptian port of Damietta (Dumyat), some two miles upriver from the Mediterranean coast on the Nile and, from this base of operations push on to the capture of Cairo and Lower Egypt.

The siege was to be a protracted and costly affair. The target city was well protected by the salt marsh lake of Manzala and on the sea approach by a heavy chain that stretched across the navigable channel of this branch of the Delta, from the east bank to an anchorage fort on an island near to the west bank. It was backed up by a pontoon bridge of boats lashed together, which could be opened to allow river traffic or closed in time of emergency.

The first attack, against the anchorage fort, was led by the Austrians under Duke Leopold. The place was stormed and captured against stiff resistance in late August. For weeks it had been pounded by a massive "floating siege-engine," presumably a trebuchet, built on a transport barge, apparently at Acre. Evidently an impressive weapon, it was the gift of two wealthy citizens of the ancient German town of Paderborn, who were sailing with the expedition. They saw themselves primarily as "pilgrims" rather than warriors of god, but thanks to their siege-engine this first Christian assault was a tactical triumph. The barrier chain and pontoon bridge were demolished so that the fleet was clear to sail up the channel to Damietta. Had the army pressed forward it could almost certainly have captured the city. Unfortunately, many of the crusading force, considering that by contributing this great victory over the infidels they had fulfilled their pilgrimage vows, sailed for home. While Pope Honorius III had promised a papal support army under the command of Cardinal Pelagius, which did arrive at the Christian camp outside Damietta in September, the all-important impetus had been lost and the Christian army settled down to what would prove a long drawn-out siege.

The camp on the low-lying lands of the Delta was deluged time and again as winter storms offshore whipped up the flood waters; a mystery plague (camp fever or dysentery, one supposes) killed more than one in ten. In February 1219 news came that al-Kamil, sultan of Egypt, having been warned of a plot on his life, had abandoned his camp blocking the approach to Damietta; yet even so the Christians, weakened and dispirited, failed to storm the city. Next the sultan made an offer that if the Christians would lift the siege and leave the city in Egyptian hands they should have Jerusalem, Bethlehem and Nazareth, then within his sultanate. These were astonishing terms. King John and the barons of the kingdom were delighted, and the pilgrim knights from England, France and the German lands were eager to accept. But the papal envoy indignantly rejected the very idea of bargaining the fate of the Holy City with the infidel. The Italian city-states who provided much of the shipping agreed with him—though on commercial rather than religious terms. If Damietta should be taken they could establish trading stations there. In November 1219 the city finally succumbed, its defenders starved out and riddled with disease; the enemy army walked in unopposed. Had they then marched on to Cairo it is conceivable that they might have taken it too (ignorant optimists in the Christian camp even talked of the end of the religion of Islam). As it was, a short-lived rededication of the great mosque at Damietta as a cathedral was the summit of the crusade's success.

Throughout 1220 then, a sizeable Christian force was encamped on Egyptian soil around its principal port. But only in the summer of June 1221, despite advice that the best of the campaigning season was over and the Nile flood imminent, did the cardinal commander, rejecting further surrender terms from the sultan, order the march on Cairo. In late July the army was held by the Egyptians at a junction of the river with a man-made waterway. The Nile water duly rose. The Christian forces were marooned in hostile territory inaccessible to any back-up supply operation. Egyptian reinforcements were able to sail down the channel and cut off Christian shipping. The Christian camp itself was now in danger of being besieged. Logistically speaking, Pelagius had marched his people off the map. At length, he had to agree on a general withdrawal. But the moment when this could be achieved in orderly manner was long past. And now the Egyptians opened flood control sluice gates. The besieged army became a rabble as retreat degenerated into slow-motion panic in mud and flood waters. In September 1221 the army had to admit terms of defeat. Damietta, which had been gained so laboriously, was evacuated. The soldier pilgrims embarked for home with nothing more than the promise of an eight-year truce.

### Logistics dictate the target of a siege: Prague, 1420

For wiser commanders than Cardinal Pelagius, contact with a logistical network was a top priority. Some did their best to assure their supply lines before embarking on a campaign. In the summer of 1420, the Holy Roman Emperor presumptive, the Roman Catholic King Sigismund of Hungary, at the head of a mostly German multinational army some 80,000 strong, was expecting to receive the surrender of Prague, the Bohemian capital.

Its heretical population of Hussites, so called from their devotion to the teachings of Jan Hus, were, however, determined to defend themselves, their beliefs and their national identity against the empire, allied to the spiritual sanctions wielded by the Church. So would begin a long-running conflict known improbably enough by churchmen as the Hussite Crusade. For their part, the Czech heretic nationalists lacked, as yet, any recognizable military establishment.

Bounded on the one side by the curve of the River Vltava and on the other by walls embracing both the old and new towns, Prague was menaced from across the river by the great castle on the Hradčany and to the south by the smaller Vyšehrad Castle, both held for the royalists. Sigismund demanded the citizens surrender their arms, dismantle their fortifications and submit unconditionally. The reply was outright defiance. The king prepared to lay siege to the place, confident in rapid success.

Central to his preparations was the capture of the Vitkov hill. This natural vantage point fortified by orders of the Hussite commander Jan Žižka, controlled the main route to rich agricultural regions to the east. So long as it was in rebel hands, so ran the reasoning, Prague could withstand siege. For Sigismund "the capture of the Vitkov, in itself a limited military enterprise, would be the easiest way to ensure a complete and effective blockade." With the hill in his hands, he planned an immediate follow-up assault, anticipating a quick capitulation by the demoralized city. Battle was joined on July 14. Sigismund's Germans soon won the upper hand, but a surprise flank attack ordered by Žižka turned the scales. With "the fugitives from the field fighting with each other to lead the flight" the Germans were in rout. Sigismund led his army back to their encampment "in fury, disgust, grief and bitterness." The Praguers fell on their knees "to render thanks to God in singing the Te deum." They expected Sigismund to resume his attack the following day. That he did not may have been in part due to persuasion by the Bohemian Catholic nobles in his army, fearful for their future in the event of the triumph of the German majority. But the fact remains that the siege was called off before it properly began following defeat in a preliminary engagement determined by logistical considerations. Dissident Bohemia remained an independent entity within the empire for much of the fifteenth century.

### Siege on the move: "tanks" and the logistics of siege artillery
Jan Žižka, "the Blind" (a disability he shared with the Bohemian king, John of Luxembourg, killed in the French line at Crécy, in 1346), who was to lead the Hussites to many a victory, was also the pioneer of mobile warfare in the West. His troops were largely untrained townsmen and peasants, but under Žižka they defeated trained foot-soldiers and cavalry. His great innovation was the Hussite war wagon. Nearer in capability as a military vehicle to a twentieth-century tank than an ancient war chariot, it was a four-wheeled farm cart, modified to produce a fighting vehicle. A heavy board was slung on one side of the cart to provide protection for the vehicle's crew of eighteen armed men. Other boards could be slung out over the wheels to protect the vehicle and between the wheels beneath the wagon as stabilizers. On the march, the wagons carried army supplies. With the approach of an enemy in open country the crews maneuvered their vehicles to form a compound where infantrymen could shelter. This could be further reinforced, if the army was under prolonged attack, by closing the gaps between the wagons with dedicated heavy shield boards. Sited on rising ground and further defended by a ditch, such a wagon laager became a near impregnable fortress. Žižka may have got the germ of the idea from campaigning experience in Russia where transport wagons were sometimes thrown into a defensive laager known as a *goliaigorod*. The Hussite armies seem to have been the first to deploy the fully developed idea on a Western battlefield. Within minutes the enemy who thought he was engaging a bellicose rabble of under-trained civilians found himself confronted with a well-defended fortress.

Žižka experimented with the concept. He mounted artillery pieces in the wagons—"those snakes with which they destroy walls," wrote a contemporary. Then he equipped the crews with handguns. There is evidence that he deployed the war wagons in action on the move. In one battle, we are told, "they advanced

*A section of a Hussite war wagon fortress laager. The chalice banner proclaims their cause, the right of the laity as well as the clergy to take the wine at communion. Occasional gaps, guarded by heavy pavise shields, might have been left between wagons to provide sally ports. The wagons could be maneuvered almost like battle tanks (light field guns could be mounted through the ports).* Gordon Monaghan

and, by shooting at the enemy with their guns, drove the king and his whole army from the positions that they held." At the Battle of Malesov in June 1424 he anticipated tank tactics, using his wagons to break an enemy formation. Holding a hilltop, he positioned a line of rock-filled supply wagons flanked by cavalry troopers. "When half of the enemy force had crossed the bottom of the valley . . . he ordered the battle wagons be rolled down the slope and thus broke up the enemy ranks." His own horsemen were then able to scatter their opponents with comparative ease.

The new war wagons, adaptable to attack or defense, became the hallmark of Hussite armies and probably influenced military development elsewhere. For them to be effective, chain-of-command discipline, far from standard in the average medieval army, was essential. Maintaining them in running order, deploying them efficiently on the move and finally working them in battle conditions meant division of labor among the eighteen-man crew, rigidly enforced in action.

By the mid-1400s at the latest, the logistics of artillery deployment, an essential element of a siege campaign, made such discipline imperative in a major department of all Western armies. A siege train of twenty-five guns was quite normal and each battery of four guns required a minimum of twenty-two wagons with four horses per wagon. The gun-barrel and gun-cradle each had their own vehicle; cannon-balls took up another; then there was the powder wagon (probably still with the ingredients stowed separately to be mixed on site). In addition, transport would be needed for the cranes, one to each battery, and a fully equipped forge. And of course the entire gun convoy was accompanied by its trained gunners and defended by infantry.

### Some conclusions

In this chapter, I have aimed to demonstrate how all-pervasive logistical considerations were in medieval siege warfare. From the laying in of supplies to the sending in of replacements, as Sir John Fastolf discovered, a man might find himself under siege when running a convoy. Essentially logistical decisions, such as the choice of route by which to gain the theater of war or strategical preparations for back-up provisions or to deny the enemy reinforcements, could decisively affect the outcome of an entire war. Amphibious campaigns presented their own problems, but water access could prove a valuable asset in the siting of a fortress. Above all, the quartermaster's department—the marshall or master of horse—was responsible for the mobilization and transportation of massive numbers of men and horses. Often, as in the Fourth Crusade, an entire fleet of transports had to be commissioned and laid down in the shipyards; they could include ships specially designed for the transport of stone-throwing siege artillery, or high-mettled warhorses. Overland, it has been estimated that the transport of an army of 30,000 men with equipment (the pavise shields of the crossbowmen would probably need carts in addition) complete with artillery corps would take up at least four miles of road. The team who had to organize and supervise all this were vital professionals if hostilities were to be initiated at all, let alone brought to a victorious conclusion.

CHAPTER NINE

# War Games, Psychology and Morale

*"Greater watchfulness must be employed when the enemy has withdrawn ..."*
Vegetius

W riting on the ethos of the British army during the First World War, Gordon Corrigan observes in *Mud, Blood and Poppycock* (2003) that British officers "had it drummed into them that the welfare of their men was one of their major responsibilities" and that, as part of the business of maintaining company morale, "they kept in close touch with their men's off duty activities." The general principle seems to have been well understood by Sir John Radcliffe, lieutenant of Calais in the 1430s. No doubt priding himself as something of a wag, he also knew that, in times of peace, garrison service could be boring and aimed to keep the men on their toes. *The Brut*, or the *Chronicles of England* tells us that in the early afternoon of April 23, 1436, "Saynt George Day," and without first alerting the soldiers of the garrison, he sent a note to the town watch dayshift, to "rynge out the larom bell." And so there was a great commotion but, at length, the "sawdioures (*sic*) were in thaire harneys" believing that enemy raiders had come to round up the animals wandering the streets. But there was no enemy. Sir John had done it "for sport," because it was St. George's Day and because he wanted to see "how his saudioures (*sic*) wold bokkell and dresse them to their armour." Presumably for the next few weeks at least, they buckled to quickly enough.

In his companion to medieval warfare David Nicolle comments on the "great use of stratagems, treachery and surprise attacks" in siege warfare in the later Middle Ages. This chapter explores an aspect of our subject which was frequently decisive in the outcome of a siege and also reveals the inventive, sometimes almost playful, ploys that were resorted to in the combat of wits to demoralize or quite simply to trick a surrender out of the enemy.

About the year 1370 the Bascot de Mauléon, a swashbuckling Gascon and ruffianly soldier of fortune, having lost his castle of Tuzaget, decided he had to do something to "bring in some money"; there had been times recently when he had not even a horse to his name. He could still rally a following among the soldiery in the country around Albi, mercenaries who remembered his reputation in the good times, and he sent a party to "prospect" the town and castle of

*Siege operations from the sea. More often, it seems, as at La Rochelle, naval forces were used to blockade a port under siege from military deployed on the landward side.* Taylor Library

Thurie, "a day's ride through woods and heathland" from his temporary base. They returned to report that the hay harvest had just been brought in and that the townswomen had a morning routine of fetching the day's water supply from an "excellent spring outside the town." De Mauléon saw his way "to have the place."

Having acquired a few water-pitchers and sets of women's clothing, he recruited fifty companions and rode to the woods outside Thurie. Leaving most of his men in ambush he went forward with five others in their cross-dressed disguise, hiding in a haystack till morning. The town gates duly opened and the townswomen, pitchers in hand, began coming out to the spring. To their surprise they encountered a small group, kerchiefs masking their faces presumably against the rising heat of the sun, who had already filled their pitchers. "By the Blessed Virgin you're early"; "Yes, aren't we?" came the reply in fluting falsettos and the local patois. And that was the nearest de Mauléon and company came to a challenge. There was no guard on the gate, only a cobbler setting up his stall. Out of sight, one of the troopers blew the horn signal for the men in ambush. The cobbler, deciding it must be Master Francis the priest riding out for his morning hare chase, paid no more attention. The raiding party galloped into the town and the place yielded without a single man, citizen or garrison soldier "prepared to put hand to sword" in its defense. And so by an impudent ruse de guerre (trick of war) de Mauléon got his castle, a money machine that brought in a good 100,000 francs over the next few years, what with plunder, protection money, the occasional ransom and the like.

### Double-cross in the Hundred Years' War: La Rochelle, 1372

Recognized as English in the 1360 Treaty of Brétigny following England's victory near Poitiers in 1356, twelve years later the port city of La Rochelle, like a number of other places, was looking to switch allegiance to France as the Breton commander Bertrand du Guesclin began to swing the wars back to the French cause. The citizens were in secret negotiations with the constable of France but could do little while the castle garrison held for England. Its commander, Sir John Devereux, had marched with half his strength to help his opposite number in Poitiers, also under French attack. He arrived too late; the town had fallen. But in any case the decision to leave La Rochelle had been unwise. First, the man he left as deputy, the courageous, debonair but illiterate and, as it turned out, gullible squire, Philippot Mansel, was a lightweight for such crucial responsibility; secondly, the city and its strategic harbor were under blockade from a Castilian fleet allied with France. The Rochellais were in secret dealings with the high command and their mayor, Jean Caudourier, a man adept at stratagems, was determined to liberate his city from English lordship.

Having first got the support for his plans from other leading citizens, he hosted a banquet with Deputy Commander Mansel as the guest of honor. Before they sat down at table, he informed him that only the day before, he, as chief civil functionary of the town, had received a message from "our dear lord the king of England" and would like to show it to him and have it read out to him "as of course it should be." Mansel, who we are told was a man utterly without guile, welcomed the suggestion; the mayor duly went over to a documents chest and produced an open letter relating to other business but with the royal seal attached and offered it for Mansel's inspection. Unable to read, the squire could certainly recognize the great seal of England and asked for the letter to be read to him. At Caudourier's request his secretary, having already memorized the mayor's fake message, duly "read it out." It turned out that the king wished the mayor to arrange a full parade of the town's fighting men and also of the castle garrison in the town square, so that he and the commander might make an accurate count of the numbers to report back to the king by the bearer of the letter. Mansel was happy to comply with these royal orders, the more so as the mayor had apparently been told, in another letter, to pay the soldiers' arrears of wages from the town coffers. After an excellent dinner Philippot returned to garrison headquarters, announced the good news and left the troopers enthusiastically polishing up their kit in anticipation of the morning's pay-day parade. Needless to say, when they poured out of the castle the next day, leaving the castle gates unguarded, expecting to return soon, they were rounded up by an armed ambush of city militia and the castle taken by the mayor at the head of another contingent. The city was lost to the English.

The king of England had been double-crossed. Now it was the French king's turn. A deputation of twelve leading citizens was sent to Paris where, before he received the fealty of his good people of La Rochelle, King Charles V had to agree to demolish the castle; to authorize the city mint to issue coinage to the same quality and value as the Paris mint; to exempt the town from arbitrary taxation; and finally to defray the costs of a papal dispensation for its infringement of its oath of fealty to Edward III. Only then would the place open its gates to the French.

### Keep the opposition guessing

Given that morale and sound intelligence were as important in the siege as in any other aspect of warfare, the shrewd commander might even gain a decisive advantage, without loss of life, merely by playing games with the opposition.

Following the capture of Jerusalem by Saladin in 1187 the Muslim forces under his command recovered most of the territory lost to the crusader kingdom during the previous ninety years. A major gain was the port of Acre. In fact, it was here that a great Christian counterattack began. In August 1189, forces under Guy de Lusignan, the king of Jerusalem defeated at Hattin, rallied the rump of the shattered army and, along with other supporters, established a siege line round the landward side of Acre, backed up by ships guarding the entrance to the port. The Muslim defenders were soon on short rations and supply presented a major headache for their friends outside. Even so, a ship from Beirut up the coast broke through the cordon carrying 400 sacks of grain, wheels of cheese, onions and joints of lamb among other provisions. No doubt using Christian prisoners and slaves for the job, the commander also loaded a few pigs on to the upper fore deck. He knew that one thing a Christian knew about Islam was that a Muslim would not eat pork and considered the pig an unclean animal. He calculated that a ship approaching with pigs on board would be taken for a Christian vessel. To heighten the deception he and a number of his officers shaved their beards in the Frankish manner and put on Frankish clothes.

As they sailed up to the Frankish boats patrolling the harbor entrance the guards shouted up to ask why they, a Christian boat, were heading for the city. The disguised Arab captain shouted back, as if in surprise, "Haven't you taken the place yet!?," "No," came the reply. "Then I suppose we'd best head for the troops on the beaches," shouted the captain and then went on. "But there's another ship following us in on the same wind and you'd best warn them of the situation." There actually was a real Frankish vessel some way out to sea and the patrol boats headed off to warn it. Meanwhile, the Muslim slipped the blockade and his supplies were eagerly unloaded into the city's warehouses— all except the pigs of course.

### Games for fun

Sometimes the "games" were just that, most famously the soccer match between British and German troops on the Western Front in 1914. And the stalemate between the entrenched opposing armies might entitle much of that conflict to be dubbed a "siege."

Something similar had happened eight centuries before on the battlelines between crusaders and Muslim forces at the siege of Acre. In the early days of the campaign, the Muslim defenders were unconcerned by what seemed a paltry Christian presence before their walls. There were episodes of fraternization. Indeed, the fighting might be halted for an hour or so while the emirs of the garrison and the crusader knights exchanged news and views. A tournament-like atmosphere could develop, so that on one occasion a mock battle was arranged between two boys from the city and two from the besieging army, to relieve the tedium. One of the Muslim youths threw his opponent to the ground and claimed him as a prisoner—a Christian knight solemnly ransomed him for two dinars. The "friendly" was over and hostilities resumed.

With Saladin this kind of relaxed good nature during hostilities helped account for his reputation for chivalry among the Franks. The siege of al-Karak in November 1183 was classic. At this time under the command of Saladin's arch-enemy among the Christians, Raynald or Reginald of Chatillon, the castle was hosting the most brilliant wedding of the season between Count Humphrey of Toron and his child bride, the 11-year-old Isabella of the royal house of Jerusalem. Great hopes were pinned on the marriage both for the dynastic and political destiny of the kingdom. As well as the wedding guests, entertainers and jugglers had flocked to the castle from all parts of Frankish Palestine. By the middle of November the party was in full swing, even as Saladin and his allied army from Egypt converged to mount the siege. They overran the little township below the castle walls but failed to storm the fortress. Saladin now set up his siege-engines and opened a heavy bombardment. Within the walls the festivities went defiantly on; but, we are told, the bridegroom's mother had dishes specially prepared from the banqueting to be sent out to the chivalrous Saladin. He responded with typical gallantry, asking on which stretch of the walls the couple's bridal chamber was situated so that his artillery men might direct the fire elsewhere. In the end, the Christian army came up from Jerusalem and the sultan decided to withdraw. Saladin's exact intentions at al-Karak are not clear—it was one of the strongest of the Christian castles and eventually fell to a year-long siege five years later. It seems probable that his aim in 1183 was to mask the passage of a rich caravan up from Egypt to Damascus from harassment by Raynald and the Christian forces. Whatever his military intention, his conduct of the siege could only enhance his reputation for urbane humanity as a commander.

### One to one: Rennes, 1356–7

Sometimes commanders would issue a challenge to their rival opposite number to decide the issue in single combat. And very occasionally such duels did take place. During the siege of Rennes in Brittany in 1356–7 the Breton commander, Bertrand du Guesclin, fought with the English commander, Sir Thomas Canterbury. Rennes witnessed another chivalric, almost romantic combat between the English esquire John Bolton and the French gentleman Olivier de Mannay. Out hunting with his hawks during a lull in the hostilities, Bolton brought down no fewer than three brace of partridge. Riding up to the walls he shouted up that he would sell them to feed the ladies of the town. Olivier scorned the offer, proposing to duel with the Englishman to win them for the ladies' table. The governor refused to open the gate for such folly, so de Mannay swam across the moat. He won the contest and returned, though wounded, with his prize.

Game-playing, in the sense of mockery and deception, was a common part of the psychology of siege. In the early stages of the siege of Bari on the southern Adriatic coast of Italy in the late summer of 1068, when the dour and ruthless Norman adventurer Robert Guiscard was battling to take the place from the rule of the Byzantine Empire, the prosperous Greek citizenry derided his pretensions. They were, in fact, so confident in their defenses that they paraded the walls of the city, brandishing their treasures—gold and silver candelabra and tableware, coronets and cloth of gold garments—to taunt and tantalize the ruffianly soldiery below, dazzling their eyes with glare of sunlight reflected from great silver salvers. Guiscard, the greediest man in Italy they yelled, had a fight on his hands if he reckoned that he and his army of brigands could defeat the imperial might of Constantinople. The Norman, quite unfazed, shouted back his thanks to them for looking after what he called his property and assured them they would not be troubled with the responsibility much longer. When, the best part of four years later, the Norman army duly entered as conquerors, the citizens expected the place would be sacked and laid waste. But Guiscard was working to found a prosperous principality for himself. He took his loot and rewarded his army handsomely, but a massacre of merchants and the smoking ruins of one of the great commercial centers of Italy was no part of his plan.

### Under siege

The first thing to strike a time-traveler through medieval continental Europe would be the open landscapes and the sparse signs of human occupancy in the underpopulated countryside—isolated villages and hamlets scattered among woodland and open fields, their houses mostly of wood or wattle and daub and just one or two stone buildings, church and manor house; the looming towers of a royal or baronial castle or the occasional great abbey complex enclosed by high walls.

In fact, walls would surely be the second thing to arrest the attention. Every town of any importance would be girdled with its ring of fortifications; at a few places like Avila in Spain they are still to be seen, guarding and enclosing the throbbing town life within. Each night the gates were shut, whether in wartime or peacetime, for even in peace there were liable to be bandits or footloose soldiery left over from some war or another and roaming the countryside on the lookout for opportunities of loot or plunder. In our terms, normal life in a medieval town could seem claustrophobic and oppressive. Not so for the people of the time. The German tag *Stadtluft macht frei* (town air makes one free, or "means freedom") referred to the fact that a runaway serf who could maintain himself in a town for a year and a day without coming to the attention of the authorities could be deemed to have broken from his serf status. So, for the townspeople, walls were seen not as a restrictive but as a protective feature of life. If there was trouble abroad and the gates had to be closed and guarded day as well as night, so much the better. One was secure.

This feeling of security would hold good, no doubt, for the first few weeks in the event of a siege. But as food began to run short, as fire-arrows or trebuchet fire-bombs caught houses on fire, as boulders hurled from outside the walls killed one's neighbors, those walls of safety must surely have come to seem more like the walls of a prison. Press-ganged into military duty on the parapets as the situation deteriorated and the garrison numbers became depleted, soon one would begin to call to mind stories one had heard of other towns where the commander had refused to accept terms and the enemy soldiers had been let loose to savor the delights of legitimate sack and pillage. Then the walls must have loomed more and more as the palisades of a slaughter house, inescapable and menacing.

During the Ostrogoths' siege of Rome in 537–8, in which they aimed to prevent the capital returning to its allegiance to the emperor now in Constantinople, shepherd boys on the neighboring slopes of the Apennine hills had a game in which two of them were set to wrestle to decide which side would win, one representing Witigis (the Gothic king) the other Belisarius (the imperial commander). On one occasion when "Belisarius" won, "Witigis" was condemned to a mock hanging. He was duly strung up but, tragically, a mountain wolf, charging down on the flock, scattered his terrified companions before they could cut him down. The mock execution had turned out for real and the news of the death of the shepherd "Witigis" spread like a summer fire storm across the region.

The Ostrogoths' siege strengthened by the day, and even such a brilliant omen did little to boost Roman morale, brought to its nadir by a breach in the aqueducts that brought the water to Rome from the hills around the city. Food was strictly rationed; for the average citizen water was doled out only for drinking and that from the brackish flow of the Tiber; for everybody the daily pleasures and hygiene of the baths were a fading memory. It was decades since Rome had been under a Caesar and most citizens had become used to Gothic rule. Now, hungry, thirsty, uncharacteristically dirty and tired from broken nights on the 24/7 roster to man the walls (bands of musicians played at intervals to boost morale but also to keep them awake), many were beginning to grumble that such discomforts and sacrifices of their familiar lifestyle were not worth the dubious honors of a restored imperial administration and imperial taxation. In any case, despite the death of the shepherd "Witigis," it seemed highly improbable that the city, with its quite inadequate imperial garrison, could hold out. Surely the bands of soldiery that could be seen from the city walls looting and burning the villas of the rich or trashing the countryside walks all around the city must soon be within its walls.

These medieval Romans would not be the last city population to wonder whether a quiet life was not to be preferred if it could be had on reasonable terms. The Gothic king sent a deputation to offer terms in the open Senate. Belisarius admitted them, but he held firm and a reluctant city followed him. In the event, thanks in part to incompetence of the Gothic leader in siege warfare and illness (possibly dysentery) among his troops, Witigis raised the siege in its 374th day on March 12, 538. Even then, despite his small forces, Belisarius harried them as they marched north so that the one-time besiegers, now themselves utterly demoralized, could be seen fighting one another to gain a foothold on the Milvian Bridge that carried the road, the Flaminian Way, across the Tiber away from the city.

### Garrisons under pressure

For a castle garrison under siege the considerations were somewhat different; whether mercenaries or knights of the feudal levée doing castle guard, they were there to do a job and should, at least in theory, have been better able to weather the stress and pressures. Confronting the enemy beyond the walls and across no man's land, they were presumably trained in the basic skills and precautions of castle warfare.

First and foremost, as with all soldiers, it was a basic principle to keep one's weapons and equipment in trim. Second, and equally obvious, to keep out of the line of fire—ducking where possible below parapets when moving from the protection of one merlon to the next; if an archer, to fire from cover as far as possible—ideally from within an arrow loop—and, if hurling missiles, to expose oneself for as short a time as possible. The number of illuminated illustrations that depict a soldier transfixed by an arrow, sometimes through the breastplate, while raising a rock to deposit on an escalading enemy, suggests either that medieval troops could be very silly or that illustrators liked to inject drama into their depictions. It is true that missile weapons, notably the siege crossbow, delivered a considerable punch; it must also be admitted that to hurl a rock over a battlement without exposing oneself at all would be virtually impossible.

One hazard of garrison duty required special precautions, the presence of prisoners from the opposition within the precincts. The castellan would probably be expected to treat any such captives of knightly status with due regard in times of truce, but during active hostilities all privileges would have to be withdrawn and strict security enforced. There seems to have been some relaxation of discipline at Dover Castle in the summer of 1265. The castle had been surrendered to the rebel earl of Leicester, Simon de Montfort, while fourteen royalist knights had been incarcerated in the keep. Earl Simon had gone north in his wars with the king, and his wife, the Countess Eleanor, with her 3-year-old daughter and a group of supporters took up residence in the castle to hold it in his name. But on August 4, disaster struck. At Evesham, in Warwickshire, the Lord Edward, heir to the crown, defeated and killed Earl Simon and the Leicesters' eldest son, Henry. The baronial cause was lost from that day forward. But in Dover, the widowed Countess Eleanor hired a group of archers and prepared to hold out in the hopeless cause.

The Dover garrison now had divided loyalties, while the royalist prisoners, getting wind of the news, decided to take their chance. Helped by garrison members, perhaps some of the mercenaries, they took over the keep and its stores and barricaded the doors. The royalists also managed to get news to the Lord Edward, who rapidly assembled an army and laid siege to the castle. Lady Leicester and her party were soon under attack on two fronts, the prisoners in the keep from within and the royalist army from without. She had to abandon the quite unequal fight and, as sister to King Henry and so aunt to her captor Prince Edward, she was treated with courtesy, though required to go into exile.

### Enemies within

The history of siege warfare leads to the conclusion that the concept of the "impregnable" is delusory. Even the formidable defenses of the Tower of London were penetrated in the turbulent days of the Peasants' Revolt of 1381, when the Lord Chancellor of England (and Archbishop of Canterbury) was seized and beheaded and the ladies of the court were transfixed in terror at what might happen to them. Many another "invincible" stronghold fell, whether to superior generalship or to ingenuity on the part of the besiegers, to an unlucky chance, to outright treachery or to fifth columnists.

When the army of the First Crusade arrived outside the walls of Antioch in the year 1098, the city, formally part of the Byzantine Christian empire, had been in Muslim hands for about 400 years. But there were still many Christians in the Middle Eastern lands conquered by the armies of the Prophet and a fair percentage of the population of Antioch was Christian. Among them was an Armenian, a senior man in the military, who commanded one of the towers in the city's defenses. A career soldier, permitted like other non-Muslims to practice his religion on the payment of prescribed taxes, he had had no problems as to his religious loyalties before; but the arrival of a Christian army dedicated to recovering the Holy Land for the True Faith changed all his priorities. He managed to get a message to the crusading force. If a company of men at arms could reach the foot of the wall below his window in the tower he would make sure the coast was clear for them. He also suggested the army strike camp as if preparing to raise the siege and march away in frustration.

Late the next afternoon, watchmen on Antioch's city walls and gate towers saw enemy troops being marched off from their positions. The secret was so well kept that not even the crusading soldiery knew their maneuver was merely a ruse. About midnight, the companies involved were ordered to face about. They were back in position outside the city before daybreak. With the Armenian's help the advance party accessed the city; the guards on one of the gates, fooled by the enemy's withdrawal the night before, were easily overpowered. Some 500 Frankish troops quietly entered through the captured gate. As dawn broke and the night-watch was being changed along the rest of the walls, "the Franks sounded their trumpets." The surprise was almost total; the city fell; the Christians set about plundering. However, though the city had fallen there was still the castle within the city held by a well-supplied and determined garrison—but that is another story.

Surprisingly, given what we are led to suppose about the Ages of Faith, the sanctions of religion were rarely deployed, perhaps because they rarely had much impact on a determined defending force. At the siege of Kenilworth, Prince Edward had summoned up the Archbishop of Canterbury with two attendant bishops to threaten the garrison with excommunication. Not only were the churchmen defied but when they actually carried through the ceremony they were mortified to observe a soldier mount the battlements, blasphemously clad in the white vestments of a priest, to deride them and their royal commander. As we have seen, Kenilworth did eventually capitulate but only because it was starved out.

In the end, even the legendary Krak des Chevaliers, held for the Christian faith by the Knights Hospitaller of St. John from 1142 to 1271, capitulated to the armies of Allah, and did so long before its reserves of food were exhausted and while the enemy was still battering at the walls. This time, it was not a case of treachery so much as a failure of morale. By the spring of 1271 Krak was one of the very few strong points in Palestine still being held for the crusaders' cause. Its defenders were pledged to hold to the last, but when Baibars, sultan of Egypt, marched north determined on its capture and at the head of a huge army, the world knew that the case of the garrison was hopeless. Even so, when, after a month's fighting and at great loss of life, the Egyptian attackers took the first wall in the defenses only to find another, there were many who began to doubt whether the legendary fortress could be taken. Eventually of course, any place would fall once all its defenders had died of starvation—but beyond that?

Baibars gambled on the morale of the garrison and its commander. After all, virtually alone in Christian Palestine and with no sign of significant help from the Byzantines or from Christian Europe, they had nothing but capitulation to look forward to. He decided on trickery to bring the matter to a quick solution. One day, with the siege in its sixth week a carrier pigeon was seen to fly over the walls of Krak. It carried a message for the garrison commander and was, apparently, from his superior, the head of the Order of St. John. It ordered the knights to seek honorable surrender terms with the Egyptians. Thankfully, they prepared to do so. In fact the message was a forgery written by a Christian clerk with the army of the sultan. Probably the castellan suspected as much; but he was not about to reject a formula that would put a brave face on defeat. Baibars played his part, and the garrison was allowed to march out with their possessions.

### Trickery and deception

More than one commander found he had to trick his own people if their spirits were faltering. During the protracted siege of Parma in 1247, with citizen morale at a low ebb as food supplies seemed to be running out, the cardinal commander Gregory of Montelongo organized a banquet for the local notables and his senior knights. Evidently the stores were better stocked than rumor had reported. Moreover, it was thought that an important announcement was to be made. In fact, the proceedings were rudely interrupted by a hammering at the door of the dining hall. A travel-stained courier forced his way in to deliver a dispatch direct to the cardinal at the head of the table. Rather ostentatiously surprised, Gregory ordered the man be taken to the kitchens for a square meal. Opening the parchment (which he himself had dictated the evening before in his study), the commander's face lit up and he reported to the cheering company that relief was on the way. The distinguished guests hurried back to their homes spreading the news as they went. Luckily for Montelongo unexpected help did in fact arrive not long after.

Following the Fourth Crusade's seizure of Constantinople in 1204, the French conquerors spread into Byzantine territories in Greece. Their leader, Sir Geoffroy de Villehardouin, facing stubborn resistance at the siege of Nikli (near ancient Tegea), let fall some apparently chance remarks which, as reported by the Byzantine Chronicler, very much suggest a calculated ruse. Villehardouin knew full well that there were Byzantine Greeks in the ranks of his army with relatives in the garrison. The chronicler tells us that "Sir Geoffroy swore an oath" that if he were forced to take the town by assault "he would massacre all the inhabitants." By Western European conventions of siege warfare he could argue he had the right; rules in the Byzantine world, that is the Eastern Roman Empire, as the Byzantines termed their state, seem to have been less barbarous. At all events, we are told that "when the Romans who were with the Franks and who had relatives inside the castle heard this, they shouted to their relations . . . and the castle was then yielded."

One stronghold, the island castle of Monemvasia, had stood firm against Villehardouin; its capture by his descendant William was a model of what one might term "siege by patient diplomacy." Standing in the sea off the south-east coast of the Peloponnese, Monemvasia (the name means "the place with only one entrance") was William's first objective on becoming ruler of Achaia in 1246. Now best remembered as the center for Malmsey wine, the mile-long island rock, approached by a causeway, rises 600 feet; atop the cliffs can still be seen the ruins of the castle. The "Gibraltar of Greece" was governed by three families, one of them surviving into the twentieth century. They had been privileged by the Byzantine emperors and considered their fortress impregnable.

William prepared his campaign thoroughly. First he summoned to his aid the vassals of his principality, among them the French duke of Athens and the duke of Naxos and the count of Cephalonia, both Italian and both omitted from the French accounts of the siege. Next he obtained the assistance of four Venetian galleys and then he began the investment of the rock fortress by land and sea. It was to last three years and its defenders, "like nightingales in their cages" wrote the chronicler of the besieged rock indeed noted for the birds, did not consider surrender until the very cats and mice had been eaten. William was prepared to wait it out. Even then the surrender was not unconditional: those who remained were to be made free of all feudal services that could be demanded by a Western lord. The three commanders or archons now advanced along the causeway to William's camp, where they surrendered up the keys of the fortress town. "The conqueror received them with the respect of one brave man to another, loaded them with costly gifts [perhaps, be it said, negotiated beforehand] and gave them fiefs [in his principality]." It was a notable conquest, though at great cost and of short duration. Thirteen years later Monemvasia returned to Greek control.

We find still more determined resistance at Malta, toward the end of our period, during the great Turkish siege of the Knights of St. John in 1565. At first, it seemed that the fate of the island could depend on the survival of Mdina, the central city in Christian hands. It was the inland support base for the Christian defenders of the coastal fortresses, St. Elmo and St. Angelo, guarding the great bay later to be known as the Grand Harbor. It was built on a highly defensible site, but the walls had long been in need of strengthening and general rehabilitation; the garrison was hopelessly undermanned; and the governor was handicapped by having to feed hundreds of civilians who had sought refuge from the Turkish armies marauding in the island. According to received military wisdom these were "useless" mouths consuming resources but of no benefit to the defense. However, if it was short of trained manpower Mdina was overstocked with armor and equipment. By a stroke of imagination Don Mesquita, the governor, perceived a use for those useless mouths. The peasants and their wives were ordered to change into military gear and on the approach of enemy forces parade the walls bearing the weapons from the armory.

Similar ruses had long been part of the practice of war. In preparation for the Battle of Pelagonia, in western Macedonia, in 1259 the Byzantine commander, Theodore Ducas Sebastocrator, deceived his Frankish opponent, William Prince of Achaia, as to the size of his army by persuading peasants from surrounding villages to ride into his camp on their packhorses; before the invention of the telescope, to an observer in the distant enemy camp such movement could well look like the late arrival of reinforcements. The general used other fairly standard devices, such as having his troops light hundreds of extra night-watch fires and sending "deserters" across the lines to report the poor morale of his army and other negative rumors.

Three months in Malta with nothing to show for the immense expenditure of lives and ammunition thanks to the determined resistance of the forts on the great harbor, Mustafa Pasha, whose spies had told him that Mdina was weakly defended, decided that he could pick up an easy conquest to impress his master, the aging but imperious Sultan Suleiman the Magnificent. But as the leading columns of the assault force he had sent inland toiled up the long slopes toward the old city they saw that the spies had got it wrong. The walls bristled with defenders and even before they were within proper range, the city's artillery opened fire. The commanders called a halt and sent scouts round to the farther side where steep ravines defended the site. But even here the battlements were packed with troops and still the guns fired.

Don Mesquita in fact was as short of powder and shot as he was of trained soldiers, but the ruse carried the day. Mustafa Pasha came up from the coast to satisfy himself that things were as his juniors had reported. Convinced that here was no easy victory he ordered a withdrawal. Had he pushed on with the attack, Mdina, a valuable support base for the Christian cause, would have fallen and very possibly the coastal garrisons would have been forced to capitulate.

### War games for real: Damascus, 1148 and 1154
In conflicts between Christian and Muslim, religion was always a major motivating force. The siege of Damascus of 1148 was a climacteric in the struggle triggered by the First Crusaders (1099). Incited by the triumph of the Muslim hero Zengi in overrunning the Christian state of Edessa in 1144, a Second Crusade—this time led by monarchs, Louis King of France and Conrad Holy Roman Emperor—marched to the Holy Land determined on vengeance.

The leaders knew nothing of the complex world of faith and politics they were entering; the rank and file cared less—they had come to fight Muslims and make the pilgrimage to Jerusalem. The crusader states, led by the king of Jerusalem, had to keep their footing in the treacherous sands of regional politics. The burgeoning power of Aleppo was in the hands of Zengi's ambitious son and successor, Nur-ad-Din, a dynastic hero of reputed piety but with designs on the territory of his southern neighbor, Unur of Damascus. That nervous ruler, dearly wanting a deal with the infidel kings, was putting out feelers—even though his public opinion saw such politicking as a betrayal of the Faith. Seen from Jerusalem, some kind of agreement with Damascus also made sound political sense; a military coalition, with the powerful army from Europe on side, might have stood the chance of strangling the growing power of Aleppo at birth. But religious correctness ruled such thinking out of court among the Westerners. They knew little about Aleppo and cared less whereas Damascus, renowned in the Acts of the Apostles as the city where St. Paul had pledged himself to

Christianity, was a proper target for liberation from Islam. Strategically, too, the capture of the city could be justified. In Christian hands it would block communications between Muslim Egypt and the Muslims of northern Syria and Iraq; politically, however, to attack it would be disastrous. Nevertheless, the Christians threw Unur's overtures back in his teeth. Instead, led by the warrior pilgrims from the West, they announced their determination to march against Damascus, and so forced its ruler to appeal for help to the man he feared most.

The siege of this beautiful city, set like a second paradise among gardens and orchards, was a saga of mismanaged heroism on the Christian side and stalwart, heroic resistance by the Damascenes. Setting up camp on the edge of the garden areas on the south side of the city on Saturday, July 24, the army of Jerusalem scored important early successes.

According to strict principles of siege warfare, the gardens and orchards around the city should have been cleared before the enemy arrived so as to deny them cover on the approaches to the walls. In fact Unur, taken totally off guard, had had little time to prepare his defenses beyond dispatching horsemen to the governors of neighboring towns requiring whatever troops they could spare. In the meantime the Christian infidels drove the defenders back behind their walls: for a time it seemed that guerrilla fighters posted in the orchards might, paradoxically, redeem the mistake of leaving the trees standing and harass the Christians to withdraw. In fact, they too were driven back and the wooded terrain cleared for the continuing Christian advance.

Thanks to the heroism of Conrad they were soon established close to the city walls and preparing for a final assault. Now it was the enemy that cut down the trees, but only to build barricades so as to secure advance positions. To watchful and experienced citizens their home seemed doomed and they started to raise barricades in the streets. But then the Muslim reinforcements began to arrive, marching in through the north gate. With barely time to rest after their march, they were directed against the enemy in the south. Wave after wave went in over the next two days and skirmishers infiltrated back into the woods. Now the Christian force was on the defensive. King Baldwin of Jerusalem and his allies, Louis of France and Emperor Conrad, decided to withdraw in the face of this harassment and relocate in open terrain to the east of the city. But they had not reconnoitred the territory; there was no adequate water supply; they were now confronting the strongest part of the city walls; and sorties from Damascus were still able to skirmish on their flanks.

In military terms, the decision was so crass that angry muttering in the ranks charged that the leaders had been bribed by Unur to make the deployment. But the leaders were arguing about who was to be the Christian lord of the city once it had fallen to them. The barons of Jerusalem assumed it would be incorporated into the kingdom; the count of Flanders, with the crusading army, was manoeuvring to have the place awarded to him as a feudal fief. Unur seems to have played on these divisions by offering well-calculated bribes. Meantime, everybody knew that the army of Aleppo was approaching inexorably from the north. Its progress was calculated and dilatory; Nur-ad-Din was relying on a political game as much as actual hostilities to win himself a strengthened position in Damascus. In fact, on Wednesday, July 28, after only five days of besieging Damascus, the crusading army struck camp and fell back toward Galilee. Unur ordered unrelenting harassment.

The average citizen of Damascus celebrated a day of glory; now, despite the reluctance of the ruler, he could fight his part in the swelling Holy War alongside the army. It was a day of legend. In later years men told how, when the general came up with the aged lawyer al-Findalawi marching to the battle, he accosted him: "Sir, do not trouble your age with fighting, it is its own dispensation from the battle. I will concern myself with the defense of Islam this day, I beg you retire." But he would not and, alluding to a passage in the Qu'ran, replied: "I offered my self for sale and God has bought me; I do not ask that the contract be annulled." And he went on to fight the Franks and was killed that day not far from the walls of the city.

Such stories would build into the swelling tradition of the jihadi teaching. The fact that the Franks withdrew on news that Nur-ad-Din was at last marching down from Aleppo was enough to convince the average Damascene that the lord of Aleppo had saved their city even though he played no part in the battle. He had, however, played his hand with consummate skill. And the fact that their ruler relapsed into his old friendly contacts with the Frankish kingdom when the Westerners had left Palestine only heightened their bitterness and strengthened their determination. Thus the failure before the walls of Damascus was more than the failure of a siege; it was the failure of a policy and a boost to enemy morale, as the sympathies of the people of Damascus turned decisively toward Aleppo.

Six years later Nur-ad-Din played the siege card again. In 1154 the new ruler of Damascus agreed to a renewed annual tribute to the kingdom of Jerusalem. Public opinion was outraged. For six years the ruler of Aleppo had been trumpeting his own triumphs in battle against the infidel. Now his agents fomented the discontent in Damascus. Its ruler tightened security measures against what seemed the looming attack of his powerful neighbor to the north. A poor harvest meant there were food shortages and relief was expected from Aleppo. Rumors were spread that the looming famine was the result of the ruler's incompetence and Nur-ad-Din halted the relief convoys. His army was all the time making a slow approach to the embattled city. On April 25, thanks to treachery, the gates were opened to his generals and the troops marched in to jubilant demonstrations. The takeover was bloodless; looting was forbidden, and, when soon after the delayed convoys miraculously made their appearance, praise for Nur-ad-Din the deliverer was instant—at least among the more naive sections of the population.

The art of the spin doctor is generally despised, but, if we are honest, "keeping the troops happy" whether in war or in politics, needs attention and expertise. A moment's reflection tells us that there is no reason to trust the intentions or the abilities of those who take the lead in public affairs; while in times of war, when trust is at a premium, maintaining confidence in the high command is a prerequisite. By contrast, if that confidence can be undermined or manipulated, so much the better for the interests of an enemy. In this chapter we have seen how from the simplest of deceptions—from a forged letter to the most cynical of stratagems, such as the covert subversion of a subordinate by Nur-ad-Din—triumphs can be manufactured and submissions induced with comparatively little effusion of blood or loss of matériel.

# Chapter Ten

# Women at War

*". . . the Frankish women . . . behaved in a more masculine manner than even the Amazons."*

Byzantine historian

On the morning of June 27, 1472 the advance guard of the army of Duke Charles of Burgundy appeared unexpectedly before the gates of the great market town of Beauvais in northern France. The choir of its cathedral of St. Pierre, still the loftiest such structure in Christendom, proclaimed its wealth; its walls, sturdy and in good repair, a determination to repel attackers. Burgundy, as we have seen, was the leading figure in that confederacy of great nobles calling themselves the League for the Public Weal (*La Ligue du Bien Publique*), who, in a protracted civil war, were demanding reforms from King Louis XI for the benefit of the commonwealth of the French people—and of course a large share in the government for themselves. The king was at length able to outmaneuver them because of their divisions, but his cause was in a parlous state and the loss of the greatest town in Picardy would be grievous.

In terms of its fortifications Beauvais was well equipped to withstand a siege, but it was without artillery and its garrison consisted not of professional mercenaries but a handful of knights of the old-fashioned feudal levy. It was up to the citizenry to hold the place for the king. De Crèvecoeur, the Burgundian general, summoned the place to surrender in due form and was perhaps surprised to be met with defiance. He ordered simultaneous attacks on the two main gates and, although one was badly holed by artillery fire, his men were fought back by citizen defenders supported by women and even children, bringing up arrows and crossbow bolts and flaming torches to hurl in the faces of the attackers. Many women in fact plunged into the bloody hand-to-hand mêlée, hurling torches on their own account and helping ensure that the enemy could not force entry through the damaged gate that was now an inferno.

Duke Charles, observing the battle that afternoon, reckoned that once the flames at the gate had died down his soldiers would be able to force the breach and take the town. But, as dusk fell, troopers from the neighboring garrison town of Noyon were able to enter Beauvais by another gate and in the following days their numbers were swelled by further reinforcements, while wagonloads of vital supplies and engineering equipment were brought in from Paris and Rouen. The resistance must have been truly heroic because the Burgundian artillery, advantageously emplaced along the high ground surrounding the city, seem to have kept up a 24/7 barrage. Houses and fortification were smashed, and after two weeks, King Louis heard, 25 percent of the walls lay in rubble. Yet assault after assault was thrown back by the defenders; the relieving soldiery was still backed up by the improvised citizen militia; the women of Beauvais still fought in the ranks. On July 22, Duke Charles ordered the siege be raised.

Beauvais had inflicted a humiliation on Duke Charles and the Burgundian army; and as the army fell back toward Normandy, they wreaked their vengeance on the countryside leaving fields and villages in flames. Beauvais had also won a charter for a municipal corporation from the king and exemption from taxes. Above all, the women of the town who, along with their children, "had not spared themselves, even unto death," received a special honor. At a time when sumptuary legislation regulated dress according to social rank, any citizeness of Beauvais might wear what she pleased; and the annual procession inaugurated to commemorate the victory was to be led by the women. In their fore was Jeanne Laisné, the axe-wielding heroine of Beauvais remembered as Jeanne Hachette for having seized a Burgundian banner from the hands of its standard bearer—a classic feat of arms. No doubt there were those who remembered that forty years ago it was the bishop of Beauvais who had arranged the hand-over of another warlike Jeanne, Jeanne d'Arc, to Burgundy's then allies, the hated English. "Joan of Beauvais" had surely vindicated the honor of her city.

## Women fighters

The notion of female inferiority seems to have been deeply ingrained, even in the most unlikely people. Writing to the German king, Conrad III, the nun Hildegard of Bingen warned him that "the time in which you are living is an effeminate one, weak like a woman." The widowed Ermengarde, viscountess of Narbonne, a great landowner, recruited an army from her domains for the crusade of reconquest against the Muslim states of Spain and led it in person to the siege of Tortosa. We do not know whether she actually engaged with the enemy, but, according to the chronicler Orderic Vitalis, Helwise, countess of Evreux (in Normandy), "rode as a knight among knights and showed no less courage."

Of course, women's role in the support functions of war, such as nursing, weapons and ammunition manufacture, bringing supplies up to front-line fighters, has always been crucial. In modern armies they are also enlisted in the fighting ranks. In the medieval period the sources record comparatively rare instances of women fighters, from which we can infer that they were more frequently active though never formally enrolled in the lists of war. In at least one case, womanpower seems to have contributed to the operation of a traction trebuchet—to judge from a somewhat crudely drawn manuscript illustration of the siege of Toulouse in 1217.

Plundering the battlefield Christian dead of their weapons and armor following one of his great victories, troopers in Saladin's army were more than once astounded to find themselves stripping the valuable mailshirt from a woman's body.

## Camp-followers and others

Even before they reached the Holy Land, the women camp-followers with the army of the First Crusade had been active in the more traditional roles of women in battle. At the Battle of Dorylaeum of July 1097, when the army stood siege against the relentless and surging attacks of the Turkish horsemen of Kilij Arslan, and the non-combatants huddled "like terrified sheep in a fold," some, anticipating defeat, were seen to be prettying themselves up hoping to be spared their lives by the lustful victors—preparing, as it were, for "a fate worse than death," so as to avoid being killed. Others, more warlike and practical, were acting as water-carriers for the fighters in the front lines.

Once established in Palestine, the army of the kingdom of Jerusalem would surprise their Muslim enemies in their attitude to women at war. Saladin's secretary expressed amazement at reports that the crusaders' high command had arranged for women of pleasure to be shipped down to entertain the army at the siege of Acre. For him the conflict in the Holy Land was a holy war and should be treated as such. Sexual services to the soldiery were hardly the proper concern of the commissariat. If we are to accept the account of Imad-ad-din-al-Isfahani, a varied menu was on offer:

A shipload of 300 lovely Frankish women full of youth and beauty . . . glowing with ardor for carnal intercourse . . . licentious harlots, proud and scornful . . . singers and coquettes . . . tinted and painted . . . versatile and cunning . . . pink-faced and unblushing . . . each walking proudly with a cross at her breast, they set themselves up each in a pavilion or tent erected for her use, and opened the gates of pleasure . . . dedicating as a holy offering what they kept between their thighs to the soldiers who were far from homes and without wives.

This was presumably exceptional even in Christian campaigning at the time of the crusades, but any medieval army had its camp-followers. From time to time we find a nobleman on crusade accompanied by his wife. Sometimes great ladies would venture themselves in the cause, leading divisions recruited from their own estates. A noblewoman, a queen in her own land, we are told by a Muslim source, arrived accompanied by 500 knights with their horses and money, pages and valets, paying all their expenses out of her own wealth. They rode out when she rode out, charged when she charged, flung themselves into the fray at her side, their ranks unwavering as long as she stood firm.

There were indeed Frankish women who rode into battle with cuirasses and helmets, dressed in men's clothes; who rode into the thick of the fray thinking to gain heavenly rewards by their acts. The behavior of Frankish women settlers and travelers in the Middle East provoked wonderment verging on dismay to both Greek and Muslim observers. The Byzantine historian Nicetas Choniates tells us that when the army of the Second Crusade entered Constantinople women were seen riding mounted in the ranks of the knights and men-at-arms—not, like the ladies of the East, in closed litters, not even on modest pacing horses or palfreys, but on fine warhorses "boldly sitting their saddles astride after the manner of men . . . dressed in armor just like men." In fact, with their "warlike looks" and the pennants streaming from their steel tipped lances "they behaved in a more masculine fashion than even the Amazons."

The English chronicler Gervaise of Canterbury says that Isabella of Anjou rode armed to war, but it is not clear that she wielded a weapon in anger. The dowager margravine Ida of Austria, reputedly a great beauty as a young woman, had joined William IX, the troubadour duke of Aquitaine, on his doomed expedition of 1101. Whether she was merely in quest of the thrills to be had from pious play-acting, we do not know. We do know she did not return and was probably killed—though rumor reported a sighting in a Turkish harem. Even then, harem life would have seemed an outrage to a Western noble woman. At home she might suffer severe legal disabilities, could expect to be subject to her husband and even have to submit to beatings at his will, but she was not confined to the house.

### Ladies of Outremer

There were women in the first crusading expeditions and among them were wives. They must have noticed important differences between the status the women of Outremer (meaning literally, "oversea") enjoyed, when compared to that of their stay-at-home sisters. In the early days, for example, it seems that women even of noble family were allowed to marry as they pleased. Such permissiveness did not, however, apply where a landholding was linked with military service; in Outremer military service was a condition of the very survival of the state. Here, an aristocratic heiress who followed her heart rather than her duty might cause real problems of security—a handsome minstrel or wealthy young merchant was no substitute in the armed levy of the kingdom for a knight expert in the arduous profession of mounted armed combat.

Even so, where a woman held title to land by the rights of a widow, or as an heiress through the death of her father, she could be required to marry only if the estate was a fief carrying an obligation of military services from the fiefholder, services that a woman could not discharge. In this case marriage, and in the case of widows remarriage, was virtually obligatory—a woman who refused could legally be deprived of her fief. But here again compromise was possible. According to one legal opinion, a woman over the age of 60 could not be obliged to marry. Not only would such compulsion be "contrary to God's will and to the dictates of reason" it would be out of line with the regulations for male fiefholders "in the usage and custom of the kingdom of Jerusalem and of Cyprus." They were excused military service after the age of 60 so the women should receive the same concession. "Thus," comments historian James Brundage, "the ladies of the Latin kingdom, in the view of one of the kingdom's most eminent jurists, constituted a branch of the kingdom's army."

### Ladies of note

Some women of Outremer merited such an estimate in their own right. For example, Beatrice, countess of Edessa, proved a stalwart castellan to her second husband, the hapless Count Joscelin. Under him the once great county had been reduced to a paltry collection of lands centerd upon the town of Turbessel. When in 1150 the count was captured and blinded by the Muslim champion Nur-ad-Din Lord of Aleppo, the situation seemed hopeless. That summer the Turks laid siege to Turbessel. However, thanks to Beatrice, the inevitable was postponed for twelve months. Under her command the city put up so spirited a defense that Nur-ad-Din withdrew, abandoning the attempt for that campaigning season. A year later, however, in July 1151, Beatrice surrendered the city with honor and was permitted to retire to the crusader capital of Jerusalem with her children Joscelin and Agnes. Her husband paid the penalty for his failure and died in captivity eight years later, in 1159.

Another lady, Eschiva of Bures, the courageous princess of Galilee, was known as a capable chatelaine and would probably have won distinction as a siege commander had she been permitted to. But she had brought her second husband Raymond of St. Gilles, count of Tripoli and lord of Tiberias, four stepsons, and according to one account this fact contributed to the downfall of the crusader kingdom of Jerusalem in its year of destiny, 1187.

That summer, as the armies of Saladin maneuvered in the hope of bringing about a decisive engagement with the Christian forces, Eschiva had been deputed by Count Raymond to the command of the garrison at Tiberias. He, with the four boys we are told, was with the main army of the kingdom, under the leadership of King Guy of Lusignan, in its well-defended and well-watered base near the coastal port of Acre, some seventeen miles away. Between lay a barren waterless plateau, arid and scorching at this time of year. Saladin's target was the city of Jerusalem; his principal obstacle the army of the kingdom, now fully mobilized and a formidable fighting force; walled cities like Tiberias were its important fall-back points, but the first priority, for the survival of the kingdom itself, was to hold the army intact until the end of the campaigning season. At that point the emirs that made up the motley Muslim army, each with his own division, tended to melt away, returning to attend to the domestic politics in their autonomous city territories. If Eschiva could hold on in Tiberias for the summer months the thriving stronghold could be counted on for the Christian cause for another season. Raymond, who knew his wife's capabilities, was confident she could do the job.

### Heroine of a siege

For two decades, Saladin had been preparing his final assault on the Christians in the Holy Land, holy to Muslims as well as Christians and Jews. This year, having forced unity on the various Muslim states of the region, he was going to go for the kill. His aim was to lure the crusader army out to fight against his coalition of forces, confident that on a battle site of his own choosing he could destroy his enemy. As the penultimate move in his grand strategy he sent a force to take Tiberias. He calculated that King Guy would be forced to lead his army to the relief of this important Christian city, and that the voice of Count Raymond, a senior figure in the council of war, would force the issue. Accordingly he laid siege to Tiberias city. Eschiva, as the local commander, sent word to the army at Acre and fell back with her garrison force into the well-fortified castle or citadel within the city walls, content to hold the place for the duration.

So far, things were going according to the book. The Muslim force prepared to besiege the castle, well-fortified and well-provisioned. In the army council of war, Raymond, fully confident that Tiberias was safe in his wife's capable hands, implored King Guy not to fall for the ploy prepared by Saladin, not to lead the army across those arid uplands to relieve the city. Should the march across the exposed uplands falter, the kingdom's sole protecting force would be at the mercy of its enemies with an unpredictable outcome. His honorable and disinterested counsel was dismissed by his political enemies as the words of a coward, willing to surrender his wife rather than face the infidel. His stepsons, with tears in their eyes we are told, begged the council to go to their mother's aid. As to the princess herself, beyond reporting the fact of the Muslim attack, as was her military duty, she seems to have made no application for help— knowing as well as Saladin the dangers that such a rescue march could bring to the Christian cause. But the warmongers won the day in council.

On the morning of Friday, July 3, King Guy ordered the march for Tiberias. That evening the army was forced to bivouac on the exposed hills over the landmark known as the Horns of Hattin. The following day the army of the kingdom was demolished and the fate of the city of Jerusalem sealed. At Tiberias, the garrison and its warlike commander were still holding out. But now Princess Eschiva, realizing that further resistance was pointless, surrendered the citadel. Saladin treated her with honor and allowed her to go with all her household to Tripoli.

## Women under challenge

In earlier days the warlike conditions of the Christian intruder state in a Muslim world could infect internal politics. Following the excruciating three-day death of her husband Amalric in a horrible hunting accident, Queen Melisende of Jerusalem assumed full control of the government as regent for her 13-year-old son, Baldwin III—indeed the Patriarch of Jerusalem had crowned the two as joint rulers. But Melisende continued to exercise power well after Baldwin attained the legal age of majority. For a time, mother and son ran rival administrations, hers operating from her stronghold in Jerusalem's Tower of David until, in the end, the young king decided to enforce his mother's submission by the military expedient of laying siege to her. Such unchivalrous behavior was not unknown in Europe. At about the same time, the 15-year-old Duke Arthur of Brittany was laying siege to his grandmother, the renowned Eleanor of Aquitaine, fifty years before the famous warrior queen of the Second Crusade.

Determined women of rank and style could force their own equality in a man's world, but women of all ranks had, in the last resort, to submit to any injustice coming their way. The plight of a woman prisoner of war in the crusader states depended entirely on her husband's indulgence. In 1132 the wife of Renier Brus, lord of Banyas, was taken captive during the siege of his castle of Subeibe. When, two years later, she recovered her liberty, her husband refused to take her back and she was obliged to retire into a convent in Jerusalem.

It is possible that Renier had heard rumors about his wife's behavior during her captivity that might have excused his unchivalrous treatment of her. The rights accorded to husbands did not sit easily with the mounting cult of chivalry. In the Muslim world, husbands enjoyed still great authority over the women of their household. This was the real world, but Arabic poets and mystics of the tenth and eleventh centuries were evolving conventions of love that required devotion and respect for the lover and an honored position for the woman; the troubadours of southern France may have been influenced by this in their development of the conventions of courtly love which ultimately laid the foundations of the elevated position accorded to women in the world of chivalry.

### Siege by courtesy: Oreja, 1139

Saladin's chivalry was the theme of many anecdotes: Within twenty years of his death there were noble families in Europe boasting, on no evidence of any even plausible kind, that one line could trace itself back to a clandestine affair between of their female ancestors and the great Muslim warrior. He certainly had an eye for romantic detail, even during a critical campaign, as we have seen at the siege of al-Karak during the wedding festivities of Humphrey of Toron late in 1183. In the autumn of that year Saladin's target was the massive castle and the destruction of its lord, Raynald of Chatillon, a continual threat to Muslim trade routes through Syria. Even so, the sultan had a care for the wedding couple. In November he arrived before the walls of the little town below the castle with a combined force drawn from Syria and Egypt. The Christian peasant farmers of the district had taken refuge there with their flocks. It seems that Reynald, with a small body of knights, was there too, but he was able to make good his escape back into the citadel across the bailey bridge, which was then destroyed. Saladin prepared for the duration.

Another demonstration of such Arab chivalry occurred during the wars of the Spanish Reconquista, thanks to the wily exploitation of her gender by Queen Berengaria of Castile, wife of King Alphonso VIII. In 1139, the king was besieging the Muslim city of Oreja at the head of a massive army and Wali, ruler of Muslim Cordova, decided that before going to the relief of the town he must induce Alphonso to divide his forces. Accordingly he marched on Toledo, held by a small force under the command of Queen Berengaria, and made formal declaration of siege. The script called for King Alphonso, on hearing of his wife's danger, to come to her aid.

Unfortunately for the cause of Islam, Wali was vane of the reputation for chivalry he enjoyed on both sides of the religious divide. Berengaria decided to play on it. She sent a herald to the enemy camp with a message, "If you really intend to fight the Christian army, you will find it encamped before the gates of Oreja. Here at Toledo I a mere woman hold the command and it is surely not honorable for a brave and worthy knight to make war on women." The queen must surely have been astonished when the ruse worked. In due course a Muslim herald presented himself, begging pardon on his master's behalf for unchivalrous conduct and requesting permission to salute her with due honors before leaving her in peace. One of the classic pageants of siege warfare now followed. The queen attended by the court clad in all their finest robes, came up on to the battlements, while the emirs and captains of the Cordovan army filed past, banners flying and drums beating. At about the same time, we are told, King Alphonso, his colors flying too, was entering Oreja as its conqueror.

### Women commanders

The crusader kingdom of Jerusalem provided the stage of action for many noble women of the twelfth century, and at least one lady may have owed her warlike genes to her crusader connections. Matilda of Boulogne not only claimed descent from Charlemagne, she was also niece to Godfrey and Baldwin, the two first sovereigns of the crusader state. Her marriage to Stephen of Blois, subsequently king of England, opened the way for her to display her obvious talents for the military life. They would be needed as Stephen fought with the supporters of Matilda, daughter of his predecessor King Henry I and the widow of German Emperor Henry V. At first it was as the Lady of Boulogne, at that time the dominant Channel power thanks to its port of Wissant, that his queen proved her importance to his position.

When the port of Dover declared for Matilda "the Empress," it seemed that Robert of Gloucester, her half-brother and chief supporter then in Normandy, would have untroubled access to England. This was to reckon without that other Matilda. For Stephen's queen blockaded Dover by land and sea—her ships from Boulogne proving invaluable—and forced it to submit to her. Thwarted, the earl of Gloucester remained ineffectually in Normandy for sixteen months.

In 1141 the empress succeeded in establishing herself in London, where she was well placed to win the citizens to her cause. Again her rival proved her match, both diplomatic and military. Where King Stephen had recognized London's claim to be a self-governing "commune," and his allies flatteringly addressed the city guild as "the glorious senators . . . of the *commune concordie* of London," the empress insisted on the payment of a large levy and even expected the proud aldermen to do humiliating homage to her after the custom in the imperial court—and she had not yet been crowned queen.

Using the limited resources available to her, Matilda the Queen turned the situation around. With an army of Flemish mercenaries at her back, she marched up from Kent to London's Thamesside and there proceeded to pillage and lay waste the properties of the leading Londoners. In contemporary terms it was a standard use of military force for punitive purposes. It worked like a charm. The Londoners regretted their desertion of King Stephen and saw that his rival was unable to defend their interests; eager to maintain the commune they pealed the church bells in the call to arms familiar in the communes on the Continent. Next they made a mass attack on the royal complex in Westminster where the empress and her supporters were about to sit down to a banquet to celebrate her coming coronation. They were forced to flee the capital, never to return. The sequence of events showed Matilda the Queen as a commander capable of decisive and timely action. As at Dover, by making herself mistress of a vital strong point, she had ensured the triumph of her husband's cause.

Queen Matilda had the power of command and the strategist's eye for a key pressure point. The career of Nicholaa de la Haye, spanning the turn of the century, revealed talents for the steady application of military expertise. During the 1190s Prince John, acting, he claimed, with the approval of his absent brother, Richard the Lionheart, was contesting the regency with his brother's chancellor, William Longchamp, bishop of Ely. The chancellor demanded the surrender of the vital castle of Lincoln, then commanded by the sheriff, Gerard of Camville and his wife, Nicholaa de la Haye, daughter of the hereditary castellan. The official sought protection at the prince's court, leaving his wife Nicholaa in command of the castle's defenses.

They were in good hands. Nicholaa clearly had a penchant for her father's profession and had learnt the trade well; she was well respected for her courage and competence and held Lincoln's castle against a major investment. The records show that Longchamp assembled a force of some thirty knights, twenty mounted men-at-arms and 300 infantry; in addition he engaged a force of forty miners to attack the walls. But he was pitted against a woman well able to match the challenge. Prince John took advantage of the breathing-space Nicholaa's stand brought him, to seize the important Midland castles of Nottingham and Tickhill. Longchamp decided to seek terms.

### Domestic violence with a difference

During the troubled decades of the English fifteenth century commonly known as the Wars of the Roses, an English family's home might, literally, be their castle. As we have seen (page 28), the Paston family of Norfolk regularly found themselves beset by the armed retainers of the local gentry, on occasion the duke of Norfolk himself. The family residence often had to be defended, usually under the command of the redoubtable Mistress Margaret Paston, the menfolk being in London on business and occasionally doing the shopping to her orders. Among the hundreds of Paston letters to have survived is a somewhat unusual shopping list. "I beg you," Margaret writes to her husband John, "to get some crossbows and quarrels . . . as our house is so low that no man can shoot out from the windows with a longbow, no matter how great the danger." In addition she needs two or three poleaxes to hold in reserve indoors and a supply of "stiff jacks," that is, padded leather jackets worn as body armor against arrows and swords.

Here was a family where the woman's place was most certainly in the home—if she had not been there the place would have been overrun by the armed thugs of the local big man—but as well as being the military mind behind the defense of the household Margaret was mistress, too, of the usual arts of the housewife. She rounded off her shopping list with somewhat more conventional supplies, among them almonds, sugar and lengths of Friesian cloth for the children's gowns, which she herself would make up when she had time. A friend had told her that the best cloth as to price and choice was to be had at Hayes's shop.

During those same troubled times Southampton, 150 miles to the south-west of the Paston's Norfolk home, was in the grip of a protection racket run by a local boss called Thomas Payne. His modus operandi was simple enough; he ordered a householder to hand over his property and, if refused, sent in his bully boys. John Nymithalf was one victim. He handed over his house, obviously a pretty substantial property, and moved out. However, his wife, Christina, was less easily intimidated. She locked herself and her two children in the first-floor bedroom and prepared to stand siege. Payne's men at once moved in and, hoping to cut off the embattled family from outside help, "violently nailed up the door of the house and kept her in the said chamber." But Christina did obtain help, from a brave sister who came round to the back of the house after dark with food, which she stuffed into a bag Christina let down on a rope. The weather was bitterly cold; mother and children kept warm for a few days by burning the bed boards and straw mattress, but their situation was of course desperate. Eventually a few neighbors rallied and tried to break into the house and free the family.

It was no good. So far as Payne was concerned this was war. He actually had a gun mounted in a nearby house and forced the relieving party back. Christina eventually had to capitulate; but she had proved resourceful, first securing her defenses and then organizing supplies—given the freezing weather, icicles from the eaves no doubt provided some drinking-water.

### Heretic, saint and warrior: Orleans, 1429–30

History's most famous female soldier may, it now seems likely, have played little part in her most famous victory. Recent historians have contested whether Joan of Arc so much as wielded a sword in anger at the siege of Orleans, but this sort of remark tends to be the kind of rather perverse conclusion of historians. For Joan herself it was certainly the banner that she bore with its depiction of Christ in Judgement and the name of Jesus that embodied her mystic powers, the banner that she grasped as she stood by Charles the Dauphin at the altar during his coronation as King Charles VII of France at the Reims Cathedral.

The coronation and consecration at Reims, by authenticating beyond question Charles's claim to the crown of France, assured the triumph of his cause and the ultimate expulsion of the English armies from France. It was the insistence of Joan of Arc that had persuaded the king and his advisers to march on Reims for that coronation; it was the raising of the English siege of Orleans that had so changed the political landscape in France so as to make that decision possible; and, whatever her martial activities during the siege, it was her presence that inspired the French soldiery and seems to have intimidated the English and so ensured French success and made possible the French victory in the field at the Battle of Patay five weeks later.

It was on October 12, 1428 that the English armies, campaigning to make good the claims of their king to be rightful king of France, inaugurated the siege of the great city on the River Loire. In fact, the city was so large and the English forces so comparatively small that they were unable to invest it completely. Even if they had, the broad stream of the Loire offered a channel along which supplies could be forced through to the defenders. In any case, the Orleanais had long been anticipating the English attack; they had built up provisions for twelve months and their defense was provided by a force of 5,000 men equipped with no fewer than seventy-one pieces of artillery.

The decision to take Orleans was made by Thomas de Montacute, earl of Salisbury and England's finest soldier and commander-in-chief; the decision was

*Joan of Arc in action, according to a modern illustrator. It does seem clear that her banner was the only "weapon" that she brandished, though there is no record of her actually leading an assault up a scaling-ladder. However, legendary heroes and heroines have their own iconography.* Taylor Library

opposed from the outset by John, duke of Bedford, uncle to the boy king Henry VI and his regent in France. Nevertheless, the English drew first blood when Salisbury seized the bridge over the Loire and drove the French troops defending it back into the town. A commander of genius, Salisbury might have brought the siege to a successful conclusion but, on October 27, he was mortally wounded by a chance artillery round and died, in agony, five days later. His was the first recorded fatality from artillery fire—his death a disaster for the English. They erected a series of wooden forts around Orleans, connected by tunnels and trenches, but lacked the manpower to seal the place off.

In the meantime the 16-year-old peasant girl Jeanne d'Arc, from the village of Domrémy now in the *département* of Bar, had begun her remarkable career. Inspired by mystic voices that her destiny was to see Charles the Dauphin crowned at Reims, she made her way, partly through English-occupied territory, to the Dauphin's court at the château de Chinon, near Tours. After investigation by the prince's advisers, she persuaded the demoralized Charles that the way to recover the military initiative from the English was to raise the siege of Orleans. There were those who doubted the wisdom of the strategy, but the project was distinctly possible and her arch-enemy, the earl of Bedford, now in command at Orleans, would have been forced to approve Joan's military intuition. She had a letter of defiance sent to him in her own name, and on April 27, with a force of 100 men commanded by La Hire, she set out from Blois for Orleans. Two days later she and La Hire entered the city with supplies. On May 4, on a divine impulse she claimed, she made her first intervention against the enemy, inspiring a French attack on one of the English forts. Over the next three days Joan's inspiring presence with her banner in the heat of the action proved decisive. It is possible the superstitious English soldiers believed they were battling against a witch; it is certain that on Sunday, May 8 they were seen quitting their lines and retreating from Orleans.

The siege of Orleans lasted from October 17, 1428 to May 8 the following year. It had been a strange kind of siege, thanks in part to the water access afforded by the River Loire that the English never fully closed off. The city walls were never breached; the place had never been completely surrounded; at the end the forces inside Orleans were larger, probably twice as large, as at the start; and even after six months the citizens had hardly begun to feel any real shortage. In fact, a week before the end of the siege, covered by a diversionary action by the French relieving force that she had brought to the scene, Joan herself was able to enter the city with a supply convoy.

Some eighteen months later, in September 1430, Joan was taken by Burgundian and English forces as she led a sortie from the siege of Compiègne. In due course she came to trial, condemned for heresy by a court headed by the bishop of Beauvais in a trial counselled by theologians from the University of Paris. The English held her for a heretic, the Church held for a heretic, while the king of France did nothing to ransom her. The successful process for her canonization began only 400 years after her death when France, humiliated in the Franco-German war of 1870, looked back upon her as champion of the nation against the foreign enemy. During the First World War French postcards depicted her cradling wounded British Tommies on battlefields, where England was the ally of France. Her canonization was promulgated in May 1920.

## The woman's place

It is of course true that, compared with the armed forces of our own day when women are regularly recruited to all ranks whether combatant or non-combatant, the military role of women in the Middle Ages was very restricted. On the other hand, if we compare them with warfare in the intervening centuries they seem to have been more active, performing not only the support role of camp-follower and soldier's wife but also, from time to time, the role of commander and even combatant. At a time when a noblewoman was expected to share her husband's life as castellan she might well find herself deputizing as his lieutenant on active service, directing siege defenses and maintaining discipline among a garrison during his absence. Likewise, when adventurous or devout women could follow the armies of the crusaders as pilgrims, the brave among them might evade scrutiny and find their way to fight for the faith in person. In time of siege the citizeness could find herself pressed into service in the front lines. In many ways, it seems that "the woman's place" and certainly the place of women in the higher ranks of society, was not so circumscribed in these early centuries as was to become later.

## CHAPTER ELEVEN

# Rules of Engagement

*"The kings of England are better served when they consult parliament in matters of war . . ."*

Philippe de Commines

Given that so much hung on the outcome of a siege—it could decide a campaign, it could spell death to thousands of civilians as well as soldiers—it was subject to prescribed formalities. First there came a fanfare of trumpets from the heralds of the attacking army, followed by the call upon the garrison to surrender and to signify this by admitting the envoy into the town in his master's name. At this point the garrison of a fortress or the citizens of a town were also given warning of the consequences of any refusal.

The pageantry was no doubt colorful: it was also deadly serious and could sometimes go wrong. At Rouen in 1417 the duke of Exeter, acting as emissary from King Henry V, "unfurled his many banners and sent his heralds forward to warn the citizens on pain of death to receive our king in peace." The whole basis of Henry's warlike presence in France being his claim to be its true king, according to the laws of war at the time, it was the duty of the Rouenais to open the gates to the army of their liege lord. In fact they responded with a fusillade of shots and a cavalry sortie against the duke's parleying party. These retired at speed.

*Once the siege is set . . .*

In fact, one more formality was needed after the summons to surrender for a siege to be deemed to have begun. That was the discharge of the first missile from the besiegers' artillery. Once this had happened both sides were committed, the attackers as much as the defenders. Indeed, if the attacking force was commanded by its king or prince in person he was in honor bound to force the place into submission; to withdraw on any other conditions would be an admission of defeat and a severe humiliation. Once, when Duke Charles of Burgundy withdrew from positions he had taken up before a rebellions town he hastened to rebut any imputations of dishonor that might be leveled against him. In a letter to an ally he explained that, although he had led his army against the town, he had not laid siege to the place since not a single shot had been fired from his siege-guns. Maybe Charles had in mind the protestations made by his father, Duke Philip the Good, some thirty years before, when he too had withdrawn from Calais and had been charged with having abandoned a siege. He refuted the accusation in a letter to Charles, duke of Bourbon: "we were there only by way of temporary lodging (*manière de logis*) and not by way of siege as is said, we did not establish ourselves there (*ne y feismes asseoir*) nor cause any guns (*bombardes*) to be fired. . . ."

Once that shot had been fired, a garrison was in a state that could have grim implications. It was entirely at the discretion of the commander of the besieging army whether terms should be offered or accepted. Until he made that decision the rule, unwritten but fixed by convention, was war to the death and no quarter to be given. Indeed, "anyone seeking to enter the place or give aid to those within is worthy of death, *according to the laws of war*" (emphasis added). Such at least was the situation in Italy, according to the French Burgundian chronicler and diplomat Philippe de Commynes (d. 1511), though he claimed it was not "normal" in France. The practice certainly was known in France, as Commynes, who began his professional career in the service of Duke Charles, must have known. In the early stage of his siege of Nancy (the Old Town) in 1477, Charles ordered the hanging, by way of example, of an otherwise innocent man who had attempted to get into the city. Worse befell the messenger of Philip of Navarre who was intercepted while attempting a surreptitious entry to the town of Pont Audemer under siege in 1356: he was beheaded and quartered, and hanged in front of the castle.

Once the siege had been laid, the attackers had to win to maintain their honor; meanwhile, the defenders could be subject to the full rigors of those "laws of war." People were shocked when undisciplined soldiery ran amok in Chartres in 1431, pillaging and raping and perpetrating other extraordinary conduct "as if in a conquered city according to the customs of war (*"selon les coutumes de la guerre"*).

Of course, rape, pillage and plunder were not automatic on the termination of a siege. In July 1420 Henry V arrived with his army before the gates of Melun, one of the Armagnac strongholds he had been pledged to take by the terms of the Treaty of Troyes, signed the previous month, which recognized his title as king of France. (An intriguing footnote to that event was proffered in 1994 by the French historian Jean François Chappe, who observed that, since the title was acknowledged by international treaty signed by the queen of France who declared her own son and heir a bastard, and finally ratified by the Estates General of France, the Parlement de Paris and the University of Paris, few kings have had better title to the throne of France than Henry of Lancaster, king of England.)

Melun's small garrison put up a stalwart defense against a large besieging force that included not only the king but also 800 men-at-arms and 2,000 archers brought by Henry's brother, John, duke of Bedford, and 700 men recruited, at the king's cost, by his brother-in-law, Count Ludwig of the Rhineland Palatinate. Yet despite an artillery train of large caliber guns and despite the fact that every night "the king of England had a great number of trumpets and clairons blown with a great *beubant* that resounded through the woods and across the meadows" the Anglo-Burgundian allies made little impact on the defenders.

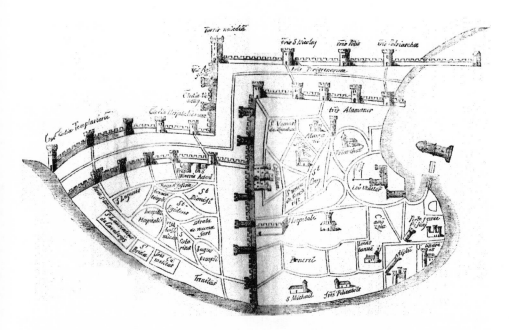

*A plan of the city of Acre in 1291, when it was taken by the Sultan Baibars, the last of the crusader holdings in Palestine. It depicts the towers and wards assigned to such bodies as the Knights Templar or commemorating the benefactors who paid for their construction, like the English Tower, funded by King Edward I. The tower protecting the harbor was known as the Tower of Flies.* Taylor Library

But by mid-October, with the specter of famine looming, the town decided to surrender unless relieved by the army of Charles the Dauphin. On November 17, accordingly, Melun opened its gates with the guarantee that the citizens and combatants too, having first deposited their arms in the castle, would be spared and released once ransoms had been paid. Only a twenty-strong company of Scottish mercenaries was excluded; but they too would have been spared had they begged for mercy. The Scottish king, James I, being in the Tower of London at the time (not the first such monarch to have been lodged at an English majesty's pleasure over the centuries), Henry had him brought over to appeal to them to surrender. They refused, and were hanged for this disobedience to their own sovereign.

### Capitulation, compromise, catastrophe

Whatever the rules of engagement, whatever the conventions of surrender, whatever the terms agreed, after weeks of combat the lust for blood and booty was bound to be up and the commanders on both sides who hoped for a peaceful handover knew that the balance between compromise and catastrophe was a delicate one.

So it was in 1291 during the last days of Acre, which for a century since the fall of Jerusalem in 1187 had been the opulent capital of Frankish Outremer. The crisis that dislodged the last foothold of the Christian rule in medieval Palestine began in the summer of 1290. Pope Nicholas IV, appealing for a new European crusade, received no official response but fired the enthusiasm of the rural and urban poor of Lombardy and Tuscany. He appointed the bishop of Tripoli, a refugee in Rome, as "leader" of the thousands of would-be soldiers of God together with the twenty Venetian galleys to carry them. They reached Acre in August. There was a truce with the sultan in Cairo and the markets of Acre were thriving. But the "crusaders" had come to kill infidels and by September their murderous rioting had caused the deaths of hundreds of Muslim traders: this ended the truce and determined Cairo to end the Christian nuisance and win the great entrepot back for Islam.

Early in April 1291, a huge army encamped before the walls. Arab estimates ran as high as 220,000 men—however exaggerated the estimate, the reality would far have outstripped the number of defenders. To the 14,000 foot-soldiers, among them the untrained Italian pilgrims, 1,000 men-at-arms and mounted sergeants, we can add a civilian population of some 30,000. The Egyptians had 100 siege-engines specially constructed in Egyptian workshops and at Damascus. Top of the range were the "black oxen" mangonels, noted it would seem for accuracy and speed of fire; most destructive were the two mammoth "catapults," the "Victorious," brought down from Krak, and the "Furious."

The walls of the city, a double line guarded by towers such as the English Tower, the Templars' Ward and the Tower of King Henry of Cyprus, were in good repair. In fact the defenders were regularly replenished with food from Cyprus and though they were desperately short of armaments and ammunition, King Henry himself was to sail over with troop reinforcements. Furthermore, the city kept control of its port and indeed a ship-mounted catapult did great damage in the camp of Sultan al-Ashraf.

From April 6, the enemy's bombardment was unrelenting, and soon his miners were moving against the towers; rumor had it that 1,000 miners were assigned to each. The defenders fought stubbornly against fearful odds, but by May 15, despite heroic resistance by the Templars and the Hospitalers, five of the towers were out of action and on May 18, al-Ashraf ordered an all-out assault. It was obvious that nothing could save the city; those who could fought for places on the galleys that were putting out from the harbor. By the end of the day Acre was in Egyptian hands, all except the Templars' stronghold. After eight more days al-Ashraf offered the commander, Peter de Sevrey, marshal of the Orders, terms by which he and all the people in the fortress should be allowed free passage, with their possessions, on condition the place were yielded up to the Egyptians. The terms were accepted and 100 Mameluke soldiers under the command of an emir were admitted to supervise the evacuation, while a Muslim flag was hauled up above the citadel. But the terms did not hold; the delicate balance tipped. Tempers were high; the Mamelukes began molesting Christian women and boys and they were slaughtered to a man. The flag was torn down. The next day, the sultan ordered the attack renewed and by May 30 the fortress as well as the city was in his power.

### Honor, contracts and loot

A commander of a city or fortress held the place for his lord or king. If he should surrender it when there was still chance of resistance, his personal honor and his life were at stake. In 1377 William de Weston was charged before parliament with having traitorously surrendered the castle of Outhrewyk to the Scots. In his own defense he said, truthfully, that he had withstood the enemy's cannonade; but it was shown that money had changed hands at the surrender which had included a payment for the supplies still in the castle at the time. Clearly, he had surrendered when there was still the chance of defending the place. William was condemned to death and was lucky to escape with a pardon. In the same year Richard Annesley charged Thomas Catrington in the Court of Chivalry that he had sold the English king's town of St. Sauveur le Vicomte to the French. The English king himself was not involved since the case was between two individual knights, the one charging the other with a breach of chivalric honor. The charge was proved against Catrington in trial by combat, when Annesley killed him in a duel.

Honor could be saved in a businesslike way if one had a contract drawn up. In 1385 Sir Henry Percy, then aged 21 (to be immortalized as Hotspur in Shakespeare's play *Henry IV*, Part I), drew up an indenture with the government of King Richard II for the captaincy of the border town of Berwick-upon-Tweed against the Scots. It stipulated that if the enemy should lay siege to the town and the king should send no relieving army within seven weeks of being petitioned, Percy should be free to make terms without dishonoring himself. Some fifty years later just such conditions are to be found in a French contract of captaincy. The concept of knightly honor, though somewhat demeaned by such legalistic terms and often no doubt betrayed, was still the most powerful sanction recognized among contemporaries. Nothing was more likely to ensure the proper defense of a fort, town or castle than the threat of personal dishonor and a traitor's death for the captain who surrendered.

There were recognized patterns for terms of surrender that made surrender a permissible act. Most important was the case where the warring parties agreed to a cessation of hostilities for a specified period at the end of which time the commander might surrender if no relieving army had come from his side. In such a case, where the indentures mention a specific period after which the commander may surrender without blame or dishonor, it is likely that we are dealing with what was considered a siege of high standing, a *siège de prince*. Such a situation was held to exist at the siege of Sens in 1420 where, according to an English participant, "it was worthily beset, there being present two kings, two queens and four dukes." However, if when the agreed period expired without aid arriving, and the commander was considered to have discharged his obligations of honor to his liege lord, he should still hold out against the besieger, then the town could be put to the sack. Since loot was a major inducement to soldiering in the later Middle Ages, when the old feudal levy had been almost completely replaced by paid, mercenary armies, to forego a sack was to risk trouble among the soldiery.

The rewards could be immense. In May 1268 the city of Antioch fell to the army of Baibars, sultan of Egypt. For 171 years the city had been the wealthiest city of the crusader states of Palestine; the Franks had mostly left by this time but the native Christians were to be punished for their dealings with the Mongol armies threatening Islam from central Asia. Even Muslim chroniclers were shocked at the slaughter of the inhabitants that followed. By orders of the sultan's emirs the city gates were shut and locked. Citizens found in the streets were killed outright; those found cowering in their houses were tortured for the whereabouts of their wealth, then sold into slavery—or simply killed. Those who had fled for refuge in the great citadel were mostly spared death but sent, too, into slavery. It was said that every soldier in the sultan's army left the siege with at least one slave—and so the price, even of pretty girls, plummeted. When, on May 19, following the sultan's order, the booty was collected for distribution, some side-streets were blocked by the piles of gold and silver valuables while gold coins were distributed, uncounted, by the basinful. Of recent decades the fortunes of the Christian Levant had much declined, yet even so, in the words of Sir Steven Runciman, "[Antioch's] accumulated treasures were stupendous."

### Catastrophe averted: Calais, 1347–8

In the year 1886, Auguste Rodin, whom many still consider the greatest sculptor in the Western tradition since Michelangelo, completed a monumental group statue, *The Burghers of Calais*; it would be hard to think of a more profound or evocative monument on public display in the Europe of his day. But the mayor and city fathers of Calais, who had commissioned the work, far from congratulating themselves as the fortunate sponsors of a great creative achievement, were outraged. They had expected their commission to produce a testament to the heroic defiance by their forebears to the conquering King Edward III of England at his capture of the city in 1346: what they got was a life-size study of suffering in defeat. In the event, Edward's surrender terms to Calais were perfectly within the conventions of fourteenth-century warfare, while his eventual settlement with the townspeople, pitiless to a modern liberal observer, was reasonable.

The story of the Calais burghers is well known. Following his great victory over the armies of King Philip VI of France at Crécy on August 26, 1346, Edward marched north toward the port, arriving in the morning of September 4. It was his natural point of embarkation for England and, according to the rhetoric of his claim to the French crown (the reason he had given for going to war in the first place), like all the towns of France, it was "his" town. He demanded it open its gates. Jean de Vienne, its capable commander, loyal to Philip of France, refused. The town might be small but at that time it lay among sand dunes and salt marshes that de Vienne knew provided strong natural defenses. Edward's military judgement agreed. He decided the place could not be stormed by assault and settled down to a blockade.

As 1346 dragged into 1347, still the people of Calais defied Edward's calls to surrender. Given his claim to be king of France as well as England this made them traitors in his eyes. Since Philip of France to whom they claimed allegiance, failed to relieve the siege, Edward was confident the place would fall eventually. (After ten months Philip led an army as far as Sangatte but judged the English position impregnable and so withdrew.) By this time, Edward had succeeded in blocking the harbor mouth, thereby stopping the trickle of supplies that had come in by sea. The town had to fall to him: Calais attached to the English crown would be a huge advantage in future campaigning in northern France, making the English independent of French ports in landing invasion forces.

Edward never once left the siege. Even news that the Scots had raided south into England at the request of the French king left him unmoved. Before crossing into France he had been careful not to recruit from the northern counties, and left Borders' defense to the Percy and Neville families, aided by the archbishop of York. Led by King David II, in October the oval spear rings of the Scottish schiltrons were cut to pieces at Neville's Cross near Durham city and the Scottish king taken prisoner to the Tower of London, where he remained for the next ten years.

The courage of the people of Calais delayed Edward's plans but eventually they were starved into submission. They surrendered unconditionally. As traitors, those Calaisien(ne)s who could not ransom themselves were liable to the loss of their lives. Edward was determined to act with the full rigor that the conventions of war permitted him. In fact his advisers, led by Sir Walter Manny, managed to persuade him to a degree of mercy. Edward agreed to spare the people's lives, on condition that six leading citizens come to him, dressed in rags, with nooses around their necks and bearing the keys. Once they had surrendered the keys they were to be executed. A meeting of citizens was convened and the terms put. At once, we are told, Eustache de St. Pierre, one of the town's richest men, stepped forward to offer his life. Men and women flung themselves at his feet in gratitude; amid emotional scenes five other volunteers came forward. With crowds of the stumbling, starving population at their heels they walked out through the gates and knelt before the king.

A near-contemporary illustration shows Edward receiving them, the royal wand of office in his right hand. The courtier chronicler Jean Froissart tells how, kneeling in supplication, Edward's queen, Philippa of Hainault, begged for their lives. Her husband relented—all were spared. In fact, the entire citizenry was allowed to go free, on condition they quit the town. They had their lives but had lost everything else. Calais was repopulated with English settlers and remained in English hands for more than 200 years. Very few victories have proved more consequential than this siege. Though it is estimated to have cost the royal exchequer £150,000 at time when the royal income can have totalled little more than £80,000, for the next two centuries England now held a port of entry to the territory of her traditional enemy.

Philippa's presence at the siege was no coincidence. For the best part of a year, the army's camp had been home to the royal court. Dukes and earls and great men of every kind pitched tents across the sand dunes and the links along the coast. Luxury pavilions, banners flying in the wind, flanked temporary timber accommodations lined up in veritable streets housing the families and retainers of the great. Markets were held on Wednesdays and Saturdays, while Flemish merchants flooded in from the surrounding hinterland to set up their shops in this "Brave New Town" (Villeneuf-le-Hardi they called it) clinging to the shore.

Before Edward's unyielding act of clemency, the people of Calais had been in deadly danger. Once the order was given to license the sack of a town, the soldiery was entitled to kill and to loot at will. A general might try to impose conditions, for example, setting church buildings out of bounds; but such conditions had to be rigorously policed by officers and lieutenants if they were to hold. If the place had fallen to an assault by an army that had fought its way in, in hot blood, there was virtually no hope of restraining the killing. In fact, a prince or commander might set up a systematic, almost a disciplined, sack. With the place secured, the noble or royal commander might make a ceremonial entry with his entourage and then proceed to the chief church to give thanks. During these proceedings the army stood to arms, lining the processional route. Once the solemnities were over they were let loose to plunder and murder and torture citizens reluctant to disclose the whereabouts of their treasures.

In theory such horrors could be averted if a town or its garrison commander was able to negotiate an agreement, essentially a contract of surrender, with the enemy. By its terms a place was handed over and the attacker's claims acknowledged. It was the fact that Calais had come to no such understanding with Edward of England that had made its position so precarious. Now, as then, those who commit the counter-atrocities feel fully justified. The injunction to "love thine enemies," even when not dismissed as absurd, has yet to find practical expression in time of war.

### Bastides and vignerons at risk

So far as a medieval army was concerned, the opportunities offered by a sack were among the principal reasons for going to war. King Henry V, campaigning in France, kept remarkably tight discipline among his troops on the march—his reasoning was that since he was at war to recover the allegiance of his true French subjects, restraint on the soldiery was a way, perhaps, to win hearts and minds. But then, thanks to parliamentary grants made in England and later to taxation levied in occupied Normandy, he was a comparatively rare phenomenon on the medieval battlefield, a commander able to pay his army. His rival, Charles the Crown Prince and would-be king as Charles VII of France, is said to have promised recruits the chance of sacking Paris itself, then loyal to the English king, to raise an army.

Even so, a general who never permitted a sack could expect discontent in the ranks. Plunder could make a man rich and, with armies increasingly recruited from professional fighting men, that was a serious factor. In 1451, two years before the English were finally expelled from the region round Bordeaux, there was outrage among the ranks of the French army laying siege to the fortified township or *bastide* of Fronsac when it was learnt that the English garrison had reached an *agrément* with the French command. No doubt the malcontents surmised, and no doubt rightly, that their officers had been handsomely bribed to make an arrangement that would spare the population, particularly the more prosperous bourgeois, the kind of pillage that would profit the common soldiery. Together with the neighboring *bastide* of Libourne (founded about 1270 by Sir Roger Leybourne, friend of Edward I and his lieutenant in Gascony), Fronsac offered control of the lower reaches of the Dordogne river, just as Bourg and Blaye were the keys to the Gironde and the vital communication between Bordeaux and England. With names now venerated by lovers of the wines of Bordeaux, in the thirteenth century too these were noted centers among the vinous monoculture of the region, but with the added importance in the English strategic hold on that region.

For three centuries this region of France had been under the lordship of the kings of England and the men of Guyenne by now regarded the French as even more foreign than the English. In 1406–07 another French army had been marauding here, but the *bastides* held firm and the people of Libourne had written to the *jurade* of Bordeaux pledging their determination to defend themselves "by the grace of God, the Virgin Mary and Monsieur St. George" and with the aid of the expert sent from the regional capital to manage their "engines" or war machines.

Now, in June 1451, forty-five years later, the end of English rule was in sight and the English commander of the highly defensible castle at Fronsac had promised to surrender if he did not receive aid from his masters within ten days. While he awaited the surrender, the French commander Dunois, the Bastard of Orleans and former brother-in-arms of Joan of Arc, sent a detachment of men to take Libourne and St.-Emilion while another French force threatened to roll up the whole of the Entre-deux-Mers. It seems the French soldiery believed the agrément covered the bastide as well as the castle. Evidently, feeling cheated of their fair booty, they staged a mock assault. While the officers were at supper they heard the rival battle cries of "St. Denis" (for France) and "St. George," and dashing out found their troops running amok in the narrow streets. They had broken through the defenses, they said, in pursuit of a party of English who had made a sortie under cover of darkness into the French lines. This "English attack," which had breached the *agrément* and so legitimated the seizure of the town by assault, was revealed after a few enquiries to have been a put-up job by the French troops. Fortunately there was little killing, but no doubt many a prosperous *vigneron* was plundered that night.

### Parades and small-arms' fire: Neuss, 1474–5

From June 1474 to June 1475 Charles of Burgundy laid siege to the German city of Neuss, situated on the west bank of the Rhine, across the river from Düsseldorf. Charles's life was dedicated to winning the status of kingdom for his duchy; he was a devotee of the elaborate code and rituals of fashionable courtly chivalry; connoisseurs of the code reckoned this siege to be "a school of honor, there were so many knightly combats." As the months dragged by, local merchants set up stalls to supply the wants of the noblemen and their retinues; luxurious pavilions, proclaimed by heraldic banners and blazons, gave the camp the aspect of "a pleasant little town," and when jousts were in progress it must have seemed to Arthurian enthusiasts a latter-day Camelot. According to Olivier de la Marche, court chamberlain and connoisseur of all things chivalrous, it was the most magnificent siege for a hundred years. It was clearly a great event; equally clearly, one feels the classic military principle of "economy of force" was far from the mind of the duke at the planning stage.

The siege was formally opened by a grand parade round the city's walls in which the noblemen, accoutred in their finest gear and bearing their pennoned lances, hurled challenges at the defenders to come out on to the plain and fight in single combat. Nobody took this very seriously, but the professional siege experts in the duke's army could size up the defenses and decide on the placement for their artillery pieces.

The serious work was already beginning when the young bloods came laughing and shouting back to camp to see to the arrangements for their accommodation. They were to "take pleasure" in arranging their tents like so many castles with galleries and gardens round about. These besiegers, commented Olivier, "lacked nothing. There were taverns and tennis-courts and wine shops." And then the tournaments began. Fashionable young aristocrats made a point of attending the siege of Neuss for a few weeks as though it were a date in their social calendar. As always, the tournament as well as a school of honor was considered a training ground for the arts of war. The tournament had begun life as a "war game" in the sense of a mock engagement to test participants' readiness for real war and train them for it (in fact, more than one participant lost his life in the frenzied atmosphere of these hostile encounters). The dashing engagement of rival knights at the siege of Lincoln during the civil brawls under King John of England was sometimes called the "Fair of Lincoln"—since jousts could be scheduled at fair times. At Neuss, the tournaments attracted their own fair.

For all his own love of the joust, Duke Charles relied on skilled soldiering: almost half his force of 22,000 men were paid Italian professionals, many of them expert in siege warfare, who could invent new equipment on site. But Neuss and its fighting men proved a match for them. According to one Burgundian chronicler even the citizens of Neuss were half-man, half-soldier. "They had been brought up in fire, iron and blood; they had had saltpeter for baby food and the shouting of soldiery over the crash of guns for their childhood lullabies. They were so expert with firearms that a man was dead if he showed his head as much as two fingers above the breastwork."

By the 1470s, small-arms manufacture had advanced so that weapons such as the arquebus, already in use in Spain for about twenty years at the time of Neuss, were sufficiently accurate up to 220 yards to provide the art of the sniper with a deadly new tool. After six months Charles was getting worried. The town still had huge stocks of food; back-up supplies were ferried up the Rhine from nearby Cologne and barges coming up to supply his army were sunk by the citizens there; and the brilliant inventions of his siege-engineers produced little by way of results—even a massive crane-like contraption designed to hoist 300 soldiers at a time over the walls failed to deliver. When it became clear that the siege would run into a second year, Duke Charles abandoned operations.

True to his reputation for largesse, he held a great banquet for his allies before withdrawing his battered army from the walls of the defiant city.

## Chivalry underground

There were by now conventions for every department of war, even for the usually squalid and brutal hand-to-hand encounters underground, when countermine broke through into mine. Whether the conventions were observed was another matter; but when they were, the result could be what one might term a bout of chivalrous blood-letting encounters. At the siege of Limoges in 1370, John of Gaunt, second duke of Lancaster, fighting back French attackers countermining against the mine that he had initiated, found himself hand-to-hand with a worthy opponent. "Art thou count or baron?" "Neither," came the reply, "I am but a poor knight." (In fact it was the garrison commander, Jehan de Vinemeur.) "Even so," responded the duke, "I beg that you tell me your name for it may be that I shall find honor in trying conclusions with you, whoever you may be." When his adversary complied, Gaunt said, "Monseigneur Jehan de Vinemeur, it gives me great joy to have proved my self against so fine a chevalier as you are. Know then that I am the duke of Lancaster."

It is worth pausing for a moment on this exchange. Of course it conformed perfectly with the behavior that the knightly class loved to read in the romances of Arthur and the Knights of the Round Table. The notion that, whatever his social standing, a knight was the equal of any other in the rankings of chivalry was central to the cult. Edward III's foundation of the Order of the Garter was, among other things, a brilliant attempt to bind this concept of knightly brotherhood into political society.

When the knightly class spoke of warfare in terms of "honor" they were not necessarily canting hypocrites. In July 1357, after besieging the Breton city of Rennes for some nine months, that "epitome of the chivalric knight" Henry of Grosmont, the first duke of Lancaster and Gaunt's father-in-law, having sworn his oath that he would not quit the siege before he had planted his personal standard on the battlements, refused to withdraw on the instant, even when ordered to by his friend and sovereign King Edward III—and even though he had been pledged a total of 100,000 crowns in compensation for the costs of the siege (60,000 from the city and 40,000 in prisoner ransoms). Over the months there had been a good deal of jousting and courtesy visits between the town and the besieging force. Now, the recently promoted garrison commander, the renowned Bertrand du Guesclin, agreed to allow Lancaster privileged entry to the town along with an honorary escort of ten knights, that he might hold the keys of the city for a few hours and briefly raise his standard there and so fulfill his vow. It might have been a technicality, but honor was saved.

Of course, profits did come from campaigning. Grosmont himself is said to have built the Savoy, his palatial London residence, at a total cost of £35,000, on the proceeds of his campaigns in Aquitaine. But for lesser gentry, warfare as a profession involved considerable outlay on weapons, armor and other equipment; a warhorse might cost a knight a year's income, and though its loss could attract compensation from the royal treasury, that was only for the first such loss. It also, of course, involved considerable hazards to life and limb. Lancaster's failed attempt to take the little town of Bray-sur-Somme in a later campaign involved his men wading shoulder-deep through the moat to the foot of the walls, while under attack from the rear. To quote Andrew Ayton (*History Today*, March 1992, p. 38), "The proposition that the English gentry's military adventures were prompted primarily by the profit motive must be treated with caution."

Evidently the actual conditions of John of Gaunt's Limoges combat—gritty, muddy, sweaty and foul-smelling—would hardly suit a tapestry backdrop in the great hall, but the event in question does not seem to have been merely a flight of archival fantasy—Gaunt was in fact injured when a pit-prop was dislodged. Records of the 1420 siege of Melun tell of jousts actually held by the light of flares and torches in the mine galleries, in which King Henry V himself was among the knights taking part. Foot jousts were a recognized feature of tournament play, though at Melun, we are invited to believe, some of the combats were on horseback.

We do not know what the professional miners who had constructed the galleries thought of such goings on. (Henry generally employed miners from Gloucestershire's Forest of Dean, traditionally a highly independent-minded body of men.) But it seems that such underground bouts of chivalry could be highly rated among the military caste. Some fifty years earlier, at the siege of Verteuil, in central France, Castellan Regnault de Montferrand was stunned when his antagonist raised the face-guard of his helmet to reveal himself as no less a personage than Louis, duke of Bourbon. Commander of the enemy forces, Duke Louis was also a member of the royal family; the records show that Regnault was so flattered that he offered to surrender the castle there and then—on condition Duke Louis knighted him.

### The Italian way: Montecchio, 1338

Warfare and siege warfare in Italy, where the city-states came to rely more or less exclusively on mercenary forces, had its own rules. In 1338, during the war between Verona and the allied mercenary forces of Venice and Florence, a Veronese army was besieging the Venetian castle of Montecchio. Venice promised her German mercenaries the bonus of a month's salary if they raised the siege. In fact, they did not reach the place until late in the day on July 17, when the Venetian garrison was preparing to make its surrender to the army from Verona. Then, just two hours before sunset, the Venetian force loomed into view, taking the besiegers completely by surprise. They made no attempt to fend off the attack but instead abandoned their camp and all their supplies and fled headlong as if in rout. The castle garrison was spared the shame of surrender; their castle had been liberated without the German soldiers having to draw their swords; the Council of Venice argued, in effect, that no fight meant no bonus and refused to pay out on their pledge. The German mercenaries went on strike, refusing to take the field for several weeks against any force or territory of Verona.

Given the cessation of hostilities, the Veronese were able to bring in the harvest, replenish their empty grain stores and prepare to withstand a resumption of the siege by the alliance. It would have been wiser for Venice to concede that the appearance of the German troops, even though they had not actually fought the besieging army, may have contributed to the garrison's surrender, as their spokesmen argued. Penny-pinching accountancy had in fact contrived a substantial military setback for the alliance.

The dispute was referred to the arbitration of Emperor Ludwig IV, himself a Bavarian, and the Germans consented to return to duty pending his decision. However, according to a twentieth-century historian of Verona, the incident had given the Venetians "an uneasy sense that their mercenaries could not be relied on." When the emperor's decision went in favor of the mercenaries and the allied republics had to pay up, the Florentines refused at first to meet their obligations. The Venetians were disgusted. Thus a dispute over a technicality in a siege of a minor fortress threatened the stability of a major alliance.

In conclusion, it may be worth pointing out that in the next century, when the calculating business of the mercenary captain was at its height, the Venetians' suspicions would probably be justified. Jacopo Piccinino, mercenary commander for the displaced Angevin dynasty of the kingdom of Naples, remonstrated with the loyalist general for Alfonso of Aragon who had conquered this place in 1422 and whose triumph is still commemorated over the gates of the Castel Nuovo, "Why are you trying to defeat me? I am the source of your present wealth. Without me to fight you would be idling your time away unprofitably at home. . . . Our policy should be . . . to prolong the war. Its end will mean the end of our gains."

# CHAPTER TWELVE

# The Horrors of Total War

*"It is better to subdue the enemy by starvation, surprise or terror than by battle; for here fortune or chance more generally decide the issue."* Vegetius

Horror at Hiroshima was the logical culmination of the carpet bombing of German cities by the Allied Air Forces in the Second World War: it was demonstrable progress in military technology. The twin objectives, terror and death among the civilian population and demolition of residential, commercial and industrial property, were achieved in a single raid by a single aircrew in place of scores of sorties by hundreds of bombers over several weeks—and achieved completely. More recent developments such as cluster weapons and indiscriminate minelaying have taken the horrors of total warfare one stage further, if that were possible, seeding peaceful landscapes with the intent of bloodthirsty mayhem against non-participants, chiefly children, for decades into the future. In Iraq, thousands of Kurds were killed by chemical weapons when a government declared war on its own population. Medieval warfare had nothing to offer on this scale. It lacked the technology. But it is a mistake to suppose that total warfare as such is a modern invention. By definition, the siege of a city was a declaration of hostilities against a civil population.

## Marienburg / Marlborg, 1410

Often, a city could be implicated in a siege even if it was not being directly targeted. In 1410, following their crushing defeat by Polish and Lithuanian forces commanded by King Władisław II of Poland at the Battle of Tannenberg Grünwald, the German crusader knights of the Teutonic Order fell back upon their great fortress of Marienburg (known in Polish as "Marlborg," some fifty miles south-east of modern Gdansk). This was, in itself, so elaborate and extensive in its administrative and residential quarters as to be effectively the "capital city" of the Ordensland, as the Order's territories were known, but over the years a beautiful township had grown up outside its walls. With their sway stretching across Prussia as well as parts of modern Poland and Lithuania, the knights had been the preponderant power in the region for some 200 years; now their hegemony seemed about to collapse.

Heinrich Reuss von Plauen, a regional commander of the Order's at the head of an estimated 3,000 men who had survived the slaughter on the battlefield, rode hell for leather for their capital fortress. First, however, before withdrawing within its walls, and so as to deprive the anticipated besieging force of all possible cover, they razed the prosperous town of Marienburg by fire. The name declared the place, like the castle that loomed over it, as dedicated to the Virgin Mary, but in what the crusader knights clearly considered a just war even the Mother of Jesus had to yield before the exigencies of defense.

Unfortunately, the knights were not able to haul the town cannons within the fortress walls before the city was surrounded by the teeming host of the Polish army. These were to do considerable damage to the fortifications but, due in the main to the determination of von Plauen, the defenders held out and the Polish king raised the siege after just two months. In the First Treaty of Thorn (Torun) that followed in 1411, the Order's territorial losses were comparatively slight. Von Plauen's military deployments, which included the demolition of a flourishing merchant city, had been justified by success for the Order. For the once prosperous citizenry the case was, presumably, different.

In the years that followed, however, the fortunes of fortress and city reversed. The one was relinquished to the Poles and then the Bohemians, and in the 1450s, the city had recovered sufficiently to offer a fortified place for the rump of the Order to brave another siege. After three years of heroic and doomed resistance during which time the Polish army occupied the citadel, the loyal city surrendered and its burgomaster, Bartholomaeus Blumen, was beheaded. Over the centuries the Marienburg castle lapsed into ruins until restoration work in the nineteenth century. During the Second World War, again in German hands, it served as Stalag XXII prison camp; severely damaged by the advancing Red Army it was to be once more restored, this time by the Polish government, and is today a notable tourist attraction on the Baltic coast.

### The wrath of a king: Rouen, 1418–19

While the people of Marienburg town had been powerless to halt their town's destruction in the 1410s, those of Rouen, anticipating a siege from the English army of King Henry V in the same decade, took a willing hand in preparing their city for the coming conflict. Following his famous victory at Agincourt in 1415 Henry embarked on a campaign across Normandy as a first step to making his French subjects recognize his claim to the French crown. The French royal garrison in the city of Rouen, the capital of "his" duchy of Normandy, prepared with terrible determination to resist the city's "lord and king." Chroniclers record how they started by destroying all the houses in the suburbs of that "beautiful city," cutting down the trees and hedges of their gardens and burning what remained. Six fine churches "without the walls" were leveled, so that "neither stick nor stone was left standing"—even before the English army arrived the terrain surrounding the city was as bare of cover for the attackers "as the palm of a man's hand."

Things were set to get very much worse. Confident in a promise of relief from the duke of Burgundy, the city's commander was to hold out long after he should have capitulated. The classic horrors of a protracted siege ensued. Soon the poorer citizens were to be seen hunting through the garbage heaps in search of decaying vegetables or rotting meat scraps; the leftovers from the butchers' shambles on the town markets were scavenged for their putrid debris.

Even in the best of times these sites, where the livestock was slaughtered for sale, were a standing health hazard. A decade earlier, the parishioners of St. John's Peterborough had decided to erect their new church on the site of the old shambles by the town market. The entire area was so blood sodden that it was excavated to a depth of a meter and the spoil deposited out of town before building began. To this day, the floor of St. John's, built on these sunken foundations, is about 20 inches below street level.

At Rouen, blockaded by the English army, people were ready to feed off the rotting carcases of horses, while the rich, insisting on freshly killed meat, had to content themselves with that of dogs, cats and even rats. Stubbornly the constable of the city held out. To conserve food for the garrison he decided to expel all useless mouths—the poor, the weak, the old, the very young. Forced out of the gates they stumbled terrified toward the English lines. A few soldiers took pity and gave them bread "although they had fought against us so bitterly." But King Henry would not allow them to pass through the lines. Maybe he feared there were spies among them, planted by the enemy commander; more probably, like King Philip at the siege of Château Gaillard two centuries earlier, he hoped to shame the city to accept them back and so stretch their own resources. It was standard practice.

The poor victims lived and died in the dry moat that surrounded the walls. Henry relented at Christmas time and sent supplies to the starving civilians; but after the modest "feast" the siege went on as before. In fact the plight of these refugees helped decide the issue. It seems that their able-bodied relations, allowed to remain in the city to help with the defense, forced the constable to sue for terms. In any case, the situation was becoming intolerable even for the richer Rouenais.

Negotiations were agreed upon and two pavilions were set up in the no man's land in the moat. There envoys from the army met a deputation of prosperous burghers, warmly clothed and, if a little slimmed down, far from emaciated, to settle the surrender. Their discussions were punctuated by the cries of starving skeletal figures held well back from the tents by the soldiery. The moat was like a battlefield, though no fighting had taken place there. The survivors, "thin as dried twigs" we are told, stood or kneeled among a sea of bodies, ten or twelve dead for every one living. King Henry had recovered "his" city—and achieved the deaths of hundreds of its citizens in the process.

### The barbarities of princes and potentates

Such scenes were repeated at many another siege. It is important to realize that, in the last resort, when a sovereign or great prince laid a siege he was, effectively, a totally independent agent and sole arbiter of the conduct of hostilities. Early in 1476, Charles the Bold of Burgundy forced the Swiss garrison of the fortress of Granson at the borders of Swiss territory to capitulate. Like much of the warfare of this larger-than-life prince, the siege was part of a lifelong plan aimed at expanding his territories to the status of a kingdom. Accordingly he had "surrounded himself with great pomp in his army . . . so as to impress ambassadors from Italy and Germany." The 800-man garrison surrendered unconditionally. In a bloodthirsty gesture of power, Charles, in the bleak words of historian Philippe de Commynes, "had them all killed." In fact, hundreds of the defenders were hanged from the branches of the walnut trees surrounding the town and hundreds more drowned in the waters of Lake Neufchâtel.

When the Turkish army moved against the fortress of Corfu on the island of that name, which by then was a Venetian colony, in late August 1538, the victims were the inhabitants of the suburb outside the walls known as "the Mart." It was quickly overrun and its inhabitants, finding themselves barred retreat within the town walls by its governor, were forced to crouch under the castle ramparts on the rocky promontory that projected toward the shoreline or behind the breakwater. Without food and deprived of shelter, the poor wretches huddled together on the narrow rock shelf suffering from off-target missiles, stones hurled down by the garrison against the besiegers, and lashed by the sporadic storms of rain common at that time of year. The Venetian governor banned the readmission of any of these unfortunates, callously determined to conserve the dwindling stocks of food for the garrison; but some, able to convince defenders on the walls that they could pay bribe money, were hauled up by ropes, leaving their companions to perish of cold or hunger. Inevitably, the governor next ordered the expulsion of children and the old and infirm; inevitably, the Turkish field commander refused their pleas for food. Many of the men were veterans with scars to prove their service in the armies of Venice in earlier times; even their pleas were ignored. Wandering about distractedly between the walls and the besiegers, their eyes blasted by the fires started in the suburbs by the Turks, they could only lay themselves down to die in the shadow of the walls that had once been their safe haven against disaster.

But at least the traumatized Corfiotes who survived could boast of victory. The Turkish force on the island eventually withdrew. Virtually every man-made structure outside the town walls was razed to the ground; farm animals were slaughtered and the best part of 20,000 inhabitants driven off into slavery—some twenty years later it was estimated that the population had still not recovered its numbers before the siege. And yet the island remained Venetian territory until the Serene Republic was abolished by Napoleon and, in 1807, Corfu was absorbed by France. In 1815 it became a British protectorate until 1864 when it was assigned to Greece.

When Byzantine Emperor Manuel II came to the throne in the 1391 the citizenry of the Eastern Christian Roman Empire had been under Turkish attack for the best part of three centuries. Not strong enough in siegecraft to take cities by conventional methods, these Seljuk Turks, nomadic horsemen from the Asian steppes, devised a method as demoralizing as it was inexorable. Each year they waited for crops in a city's fields to ripen and then surrounded the place, pitching their camp in the vicinity while the peasants and citizens took in the harvest. That done, the raiders rode away with the bulk of the grain leaving the locals a residue to eke out a livelihood over the winter months. Come seed time, a new crop was planted and come harvest the predatory horsemen returned. The pattern was repeated until eventually, in despair, the population would abandon their city, trekking as refugees to another more remote from the empire's frontier. This strategy, added to conventional campaigns and classic razzias or plundering raids, meant that the lands held by the Christian empire in the East continually shrank.

Of course, warfare on civilians was not confined to Muslim strategists. An admiring contemporary described the mode of war favored by Duke William of Normandy, future king of England. The duke waged campaigns of unrelenting devastation, "so as to sow terror in his neighbors' lands by frequent and lengthy invasions and by inflicting an incessant toll of calamities. Vineyards, fields and estates with their houses and dwellings were systematically laid to waste."

## Circumvallation of misery: Gaillard, 1204

Records of the final stages of the siege of Château Gaillard in 1204 illustrate the depths of suffering that might be inflicted on the non-combatants during the course of a medieval siege. The famous fortress (gaillard, the nickname given by Richard, means "lively" or "saucy"), one of the most complex examples of medieval military architecture, stands in a break in the wide sweeping chalk cliffs on the right bank of the Seine, some miles above its junction with the River Eure. Built upon a plateau some 600 feet long and about 200 feet at its widest point, atop a massive rocky outcrop surrounded by steep ravines, it dominated the fortified town of Les Andelys, hub for a network of dams and canals aimed to protect the river approaches—at the time a flood plain, fed by the little tributary river, Gambon.

Richard the Lionheart, king of England and duke of Normandy, and contemporary Europe's finest military mind, began the building of this great fortress in 1196 after his delayed return from the Third Crusade, where he and his rival King Philip II Augustus of France had vied for leadership. Philip had returned to Europe some four years earlier aiming to destabilize the vast French possessions of Richard. The English king was determined to secure them. The castle's modified "concentric" plan showed obvious affinities with the crusader castle of Krak des Chevaliers. Richard's aim was to secure the eastern approaches of his duchy against attack from Paris. He had chosen a magnificent site; the huge structure, together with its river outworks, took barely three years to complete; it was, however, situated in the lands of Walter of Coutances, archbishop of Rouen. Richard ordered building to begin nevertheless; the archbishop placed the duchy under interdict of the Church; and divine displeasure was manifested in a rainfall of blood, we are told. Richard apparently vowed that even should an angel descend and bid him stay his hand he would meet it with a curse. When his castle was safely built he placated the spirit world by the payment of handsome compensation to the archbishop.

In the summer of 1203 Philip of France resolved to take the castle as the first essential stage in conquering the duchy of Normandy from its dukes, who since 1066 had also been kings of England. Thanks to the contemporary account left by the chronicler William of Brittany we can trace the campaign in great detail. The fortress was held for Richard's successor, King John, by a loyal and capable commander, Roger de Lacy, formerly constable of Chester; the garrison, sufficient to defend the castle though not the outworks, was predominantly English and was well provisioned to withstand a long siege. John considered

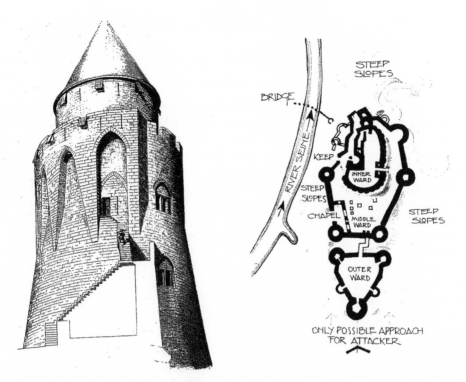

*A dramatic visualization (left) of the inner side of the donjon at Château Gaillard, though the upper works no longer exist. It is supposed that the huge inverted buttresses were intended to support machicolations as shown here. The outer wall of the donjon pierced the wall of the middle bailey (see plan) and was effectively protected by the precipitous cliff face. Sketch plan (right) of Château Gaillard.* Taylor Library / Gordon Monaghan

he had time to return to England and recruit reinforcements for the defense of the duchy. It was a reasonable calculation; on the other hand his brother, a hands-on soldier, would hardly have left a vital theater of war at such a time. The French king himself directed operations from the start, and while he visited other parts of his domains during the eight-month-long siege he returned at crucial moments.

In August he attacked the town of Les Andelys and the defense works along the river. De Lacy, to conserve his resources, conceded the position in mid-September. He withdrew to the fortress on the hill with some 1,500 townsfolk—liege people of a rebellious duke, they could look to little consideration from King Philip. As it was, many of them were to suffer horribly in the course of the operations. In its basic plan the castle comprised three baileys, the keep or donjon being built at the most inaccessible point of the third bailey: an attacker could only assault the donjon, the final fall-back point for the garrison when he had taken each of the baileys in turn. The French now moved against the castle proper and Philip ordered the construction of elaborate works of circumvallation to prevent any sortie or attempt at breakout. The peninsula formed by the two rivers, on which Gaillard stood, was cut by a double trench controlled by walls and wooden towers and drawbridges. The besiegers were at this point out of range of the defenders, who were condemned to frustrating inactivity. As winter advanced garrison morale was bound to suffer while the French jeered at the eagles' eyrie "crowded with fledglings that will be forced to try their wings come the spring."

Crowded the place was, for in addition to the 300 men of the garrison Constable de Lacy had admitted the refugee civilians from Les Andelys. As the weeks dragged on these "useless mouths" made serious inroads into provisions laid in to sustain a fighting garrison rather than provide social handouts—Gaillard had been designed as a military unit, not as a welfare facility. After two months, de Lacy decided to relieve the pressure on his supplies. Some 500 of the oldest and weakest were expelled from the fortress; a few days later another 500 followed and they too were let through the French lines. A third party of expellees was condemned to a fearful fate. King Philip gave orders that they were to be driven back; from the French point of view these were, after all subjects rebellious to the king and the responsibility of their English lords.

But now, the gates were barred against them. De Lacy could no longer afford the luxury of compassion. For the best part of three months these hapless people, the innocent victims of total war, found what shelter they could from the winter conditions by digging holes in the ravines between the castle walls and the besiegers counterworks. Anything that might be considered food, roots, straggling vegetation and the rotting carcasses of starved wildlife, was scavenged and devoured. But long before the end those who had not died of exposure or succumbed to stray missiles in the crossfire between the contestants resorted to cannibalism, to the fascinated horror of onlookers from the castle walls. Returning to the siege from a survey of his campaign elsewhere in the duchy, King Philip ordered that these skeletal figures be admitted to the lines of the besieging force and fed. Most of the unfortunates who had survived thus far died as their weakened digestions succumbed to a substantial meal after months of starvation.

At the end of February, the French king decided to abandon this starvation policy for systematic attack. Artillery pieces were trained on the south-east wall of the outer bailey, and sappers set to work on the corner tower. On its collapse the garrison troops withdrew across the next moat or fosse by the connecting bridge to the middle bailey. The bridge was of course down, but the ditch had to be crossed. After five months the French had reached only the second line of defense. A resourceful soldier, nicknamed Peter the Snubnose, now spotted a possible access through a new building abutting the outer wall. He and a posse of friends climbed up through a latrine discharge point and broke into a room through an unbarred window, where they hammered on the locked door hoping no doubt to be mistaken for garrison members. Instead of opening up, the defenders fired the wooden structure, only to find the flames swept across the middle bailey by an unexpected change in the wind. And now the intruders, breaking out of the inferno, managed to open the gate of the middle bailey to their comrades. Even now the defenders, reduced to fewer than 200, holed up in the citadel tower, defended by the walls of the inner bailey, in a last desperate hope of relief. They were betrayed by the one weakness in the castle's design: the bridge leading to the gate of the bailey connected with a tongue of solid rock, which gave the attackers a firm base for their next operation—to sap the masonry of the gate under the protection of a mobile penthouse or cat. Professional soldiers, the defenders countermined and forced the attacking party back. But the gatehouse tower, undermined and attacked by petrariae, finally collapsed and the situation was no longer defensible. Still the 36 knight and 120 soldiers under de Lacy's command refused to make formal surrender and were taken into captivity.

It had been a model of professional soldiering on both sides, though no doubt costing terrible pains among the fighting men. Of course, the civilians' plight must have been worse. This was not their battle but they, as the French say, suffered their own calvary nevertheless. King Philip's humanitarian gesture had been only a brief respite. Gaillard's castellan, a steely-hearted professional soldier, had not allowed himself such sentiments; he did not have the food to feed "useless mouths" and defend his fortifications at the same time. Philip's subordinate commanders, although they had the food, reverted to their master's original decision, perhaps to shame the castellan into readmitting the starving victims behind the walls there to share the dwindling supplies and so to sap his combat capabilities, perhaps as a warning to other civilian populations not to support the English king's castellans.

### The pitilessness of power
There are numerous cases of pitilessness in the medieval record. At the siege of Brescia in July 1238 both sides hardened their hearts to the utmost brutality. Finding that his mobile siege-towers were taking heavy punishment from the defenders' ballistae, Emperor Frederick II had Italian prisoners of war strapped to the front of the structures in the hope that the Brescians would stop firing to spare their countrymen; for their part, the citizens suspended prisoners they had taken from the imperial forces in sorties in front of the besiegers' battering-rams that were pounding their walls.

During the Italian wars of the 1440s the ruthlessness of power was visited in all its horror on the people of Piacenza when, threatened by domination from Milan, they barred their gates to the army of its mercenary captain, Francesco Sforza. Piacenza had state-of-the-art fortifications and its stores were well filled; the citizens were courageous and determined and many thought the place impregnable. After a prolonged and bitterly fought siege, Sforza and his mercenaries won their victory—many considered it a triumph of the military art. The sequel was unimaginable horror. As was his right according to the laws of war, Sforza gave the city over to his soldiery to sack and pillage at will for a period of forty days. Such license was unprecedented and the more startling as Sforza was generally considered a merciful victor by the standards of his day. For some six weeks, if we are to belief the sources, women young and old were being raped in their homes or in the streets; churches plundered of their sacred treasures, mansions of their luxurious fittings, tapestries and furniture, people robbed of money and jewels and tortured until they yielded their hiding-places or until their tormentors had had sufficient entertainment. Thousands were killed out of hand. And all this had been licensed by "the ablest and most loved and admired general of his time" at the height of the age of humanism.

But if Sforza suffered little opprobrium for the atrocity and his later reputation was barely dented, such was not the case with Edward III's son, Edward Prince of Wales, who to many of his contemporaries was a paragon of chivalry, following the horrors that ensued on the sack of Limoges in September 1370. Up until August the city had been one of the principal towns of English Aquitaine, but on the 24th its bishop, Jean de Cros, had handed it over to the duc de Berri and admitted a French garrison. As duke of Aquitaine Edward was incensed at this betrayal and vowed that he would retake the place and have the lives of everyone who dwelt in that "city of traitors." In fact, dying of the disease that would kill him, the prince had to leave the conduct of operations in the hands of his brother, John of Gaunt, duke of Lancaster.

Having installed a garrison under the command of Jean de Villemur and provided it with artillery, Berri left the city. Over the ensuing weeks he was to make no response to its desperate pleas that he raise the siege. The English also had artillery but made little use of it, relying on mining operations, directed by Lancaster in person, to achieve one of the few instances in the Hundred Years' War of a successful attack on a walled city. It took a month to excavate and prepare the mine. One French account reports that the garrison drove a countermine but failed to stop the English advance. At length, on the order given, the combustibles at the mine head were fired and, we are told, 100 feet of rampart and masonry came down. The first assault was beaten back but the second succeeded and Limoges fell to the fate vowed by the prince. For once Froissart, whose Chronicle, we know, rarely dwells on the bloody consequences for "poor folk" of chivalry in action, is shaken. "Men, women and children fell on their knees and begged 'Please, good sirs, have mercy!' But they were so inflamed with hatred that none listened. . . . More than 3,000 persons were murdered that day. God receive their souls for they truly were martyrs."

Commenting on this quite legitimate atrocity, Michael Prestwich has observed that the pressure of French campaigning against the English rule in France was by this time so intense that the desertion of the bishop and people of Limoges from their allegiance provoked a reprisal from the prince "suggestive of desperation." While this may be so, one would like to think that a paragon of chivalry such as the Black Prince (so named by later generations from the color of his favorite armor) would comport himself better than a mercenary captain like Sforza.

### "The greatest siege in history": Malta, 1565

One of the most horrific of all sieges in premodern times, the siege of Malta has also been called "the greatest siege in history." It should have been over in four weeks; it lasted four months; the sufferings on both sides were extreme and protracted; of the emaciated and decimated defending population barely one was free of some disfiguring wound or wracking sickness when relief belatedly arrived. As to the defeated attackers, when they sailed back to their imperial capital it was in the knowledge that they faced a lifetime of disgrace.

On May 18, 1565, lookouts posted along the fortifications manned by the Knights Hospitaller on their island stronghold of Malta counted a fleet of almost 200 ships sailing steadily onwards, banners fluttering in the breeze and, as they came nearer, with the flash of sunlight on armor, sword blades, helmets, guns and here and there the gilded glint of an emir's diadem or head circlet. A year in the preparation, this was the fleet vowed by the septuagenarian Sultan Suleiman the Magnificent of Constantinople to the destruction of "those sons of dogs," the Knights of St. John, who had been harassing Turkish shipping first from Rhodes then from Malta, ever since their expulsion from their headquarters at Acre in the Holy Land some 270 years before.

The sultan's distant opponent, the Grand Master of the Hospitallers, Jean Parisot de la Valette (whose name was to be immortalized in the new fortified city built after the siege) was also in his seventies. For months, under his direction, the island and its two chief forts of St. Elmo and St. Angelo had been reinforced and stocked with weaponry and provisions; his iron will and heroic courage were to inspire all. On the morning of May 29 the enemy troopers, 30,000 of them, began to debouch onto the beaches from their transports. Malta was thinly populated, its chief town, Mdina under-garrisoned (see page 120). There were two fine harbors, but their defenders amounted to less than 10,000 men and of these fewer than 550 were fully equipped men-at-arms. The two forts, for all their recent reinforcements, were old-fashioned.

The Turkish army commander's brief was to capture the island for Islam so that it could serve as a base for Muslim conquests into Spain and southern Italy. He was assured of yet more ships and 10,000 more regular soldiers in the near future. His plan was to occupy the entire island and then force the forts to surrender by starving them out. Time was on his side. But the final decision did not rest with Mustafa Pasha. He shared the command with Commander of the Fleet Admiral Piali, who was fearful of the sultan's rage should he lose valuable ships in freak storms. The general agreed to deal first with the forts guarding the harbors to assure safe havens for the shipping. It was an historic mistake. Against all the probabilities the forts held out for months.

The Turks brought the finest guns in the European theater to bear on the defenses of St. Elmo. A man at the center of the fort looked up at the rampart and straight into their black mouths. They threw shot weighing up to 176 pounds; their gunners were the world's most expert. Thousands of superbly trained infantrymen stood ready to storm the walls. They, like their Christian opponents, were certain they had God on their side. Both believed that death in this battle assured them instant entry into heaven, and that all their sins would be forgiven.

As May moved into June the sun burned like a furnace. Screams rose from both sides for water. Every day St. Elmo, pounded by up to 6,000 rounds, "erupted like a volcano spouting fire and smoke"; every night the dead and dying were replaced by reinforcements ferried across the harbor from the garrison of St. Angelo that could barely spare the men. Those in St. Elmo were not classed as wounded if they could still walk or crawl; too weak to fight they humped platters of bread soaked in wine or water to the front line. On June 23, the enemy at last overran the rubble heaps that had once been the defenses. The commanders, too badly wounded to stand, had had themselves lashed into chairs anchored in the breach in the wall, now flailed as best they could at the enemy tide with their massive two-handed swords.

Mustafa Pasha had lost a quarter of his men but he still outnumbered the enemy four to one. He turned his attention to the castle of St. Angelo. One feels that reason no longer determined his tactics; no longer was it a matter of winning havens for the admiral's ships. The honor of the commander, of the sultan even, of Islam, was now mortgaged to the capture of the Christian fortifications. For three more months a storm of fire and shot raged down on the castle. The roar of the guns could sometimes be heard in Sicily, seventy miles away.

For the Maltese population this conflict, of little consequence to them, brought total war. Women and children joined the battle, hurling stones and fireballs down on the attackers. Their menfolk formed companies of swimmers that battled with Turkish assault troops in bloody hand-to-hand fighting in the shallows and on the beaches. Many civilians suffered horrible casualties, many died from starvation, mothers giving birth under horrible stress lost their babies, men and women both would only survive the inferno as maimed and disfigured cripples. Yet, whether for good or ill, the island emerged triumphant from its ordeal. In mid-September a Spanish relief fleet finally arrived with men and supplies. By that time, however, the Turks had abandoned their campaign, beating for home waters before the advent of winter storms.

### A way of life: a way of death

"Martyrdoms" like those of the people of Limoges and agonies like those of the defenders of Malta litter the history of siege warfare. As one reflects on the hecatombs of dead in the "collateral damage" of modern warfare it is sometimes tempting to suppose that in some earlier age civilians were less involved. It may once have been so, but that earlier age is not to be found in medieval Europe where the conduct of siege operations time and again implicated, when it did not directly target, the non-combatant population.

Since the theme of this book has been siege as an act of war prosecuted by men of war for their own, often inscrutable purposes, it seems proper to conclude with them in the frame rather than those millions of innocent souls implicated in the hostilities, bitter and unjust as their fates undoubtedly were. Sometimes the points at issue between combatants were, to our eyes, petty, sometimes entirely unjust, but on a few occasions they were matters of high principles and agreed to be so by their contemporaries. On such occasions though, the sufferings of civilian non-combatants were terrible; but the fate of the combatants themselves was harsh indeed when the cause was lost.

When, in December 1522, their defense of Rhodes was heading inexorably to the bitterness of defeat, the defenders, some barely strong enough to lift themselves from the ground, were living like foxes, with holes in the earth their only retreat from the snow and sleet of that harsh winter. Over the previous six months the once brave citadels and towers, together with the communal buildings of the Order and churches and houses of the citizenry, had been reduced to hillocks of rubble punctuated with decaying corpses and body parts. In that landscape of bleak horror, breathed over by the stench of death and putrefaction, these heroic victims of defeat had time to muse over their misery and beg for relief from their pain. There was perhaps some solace for them not only in the thought that they had died in the course of duty but also in the fact that the lives that they had to look back on would have been marked in memory by days of glory as well as days of horror.

# Appendix

## Vegetius, the Medieval Textbook of Warfare

These notes are based on the edition and translation of *Epitoma rei militaris* by Leo F. Stelten (New York, 1990).

The text known as the *Rei militaris instituta or Epitoma Rei Militaris* ("The Handbook of Military Matters") among other titles, probably written about the year AD 400, survives in various medieval manuscripts of various dates, with slight variations of title. The author, "the illustrious Flavius Vegetius Renatus," is concerned with the decline, as he saw it, of the imperial Roman army and his recipes for reform of the military structure to be based on a revival of the legion. However, he surveyed all aspects of warfare, tactics and strategy and siege.

"Vegetius," as he is commonly known, also provided the basis for other writers on warfare notably Egidio (Aegidia) Colonna (d. 1316); Christine de Pisan, the celebrated French writer on numerous topics; and even Machiavelli (d. 1527) who drew heavily on Vegetius for his own *Arte della Guerra*.

The *Epitoma*, or at least a version of it, first appeared in English published by William Caxton in 1486 as *The Booke of Fayttes of Arms and Chivalrye*, a translation of de Pisan's famous work *Le Livre des Faits d'Armes et de Chevalerie*.

Vegetius' text also provided the inspiration for a number of sets of illustrations, in fact artist's impressions or attempted reconstructions based on the author's not always clear descriptions of machines of war he either knew of from personal experience or had heard reports of. These illustrations, some fanciful, all speculative, provided the basis of various theories or assertions about Roman military apparatus.

This appendix notes principal points made by Vegetius on siege warfare and other observations on warfare in general.

### Book I

*Chapter 12*: concerning the initial attack on a fortress or city. The attacker can expect the greater losses; accordingly, he aims to intimidate by display of arms and martial trumpet calls and then moves the scaling ladders against the walls. Inexperienced defenders may well surrender, but if the assault is repelled by an experienced garrison then the morale of the populace will be increased.

*Chapter 14*: concerning a testudo. Vegetius describes here a wooden structure covered with leather and goats' fleeces (soaked in water, presumably) so as to be proof against fire lances and arrows. Inside is a beam which may be fitted with an iron hook with which to loosen the masonry or shod with iron and called a ram because it swings back and forth in the manner of a battering-ram. But it takes its name from the tortoise, because just as that beast retracts its head within its shell and then thrusts forward, so the machine vibrates its head back and forth against the stonework.

*Chapter 16*: describes *musculi*, which according to the description are protective wheeled sheds (the "cats" of medieval military men), better termed "pilot fish" if we are to retain the marine imagery because they advanced ahead of the siege-tower, like pilot fish ahead of a whale) protecting work parties detailed to fill in the moat.

*Chapter 17*: *De turribus ambulatoriis* (mobile towers). According to Vegetius in earlier Roman times these structures could be from 30 to 50 square ft. at the base and so high as to overtop not just the walls but even the turrets above them. They had several levels and might have bridges protected by tunnel-like structures of twigs and branches. The topmost stage of the tower would be manned by bowmen and troops called *contati* (contact men, probably) armed with pikes with which they cleared the defenders from the wall by direct contact.

*Chapter 18*: ways to destroy such towers include sortie by a fire detail; the use of fire darts hurled by missile throwers; by commando troops let down on ropes from the city walls at night with covered lanterns to set fire to the structure.

*Chapter 19*: defenders may raise the height of the wall at the point where the siege-tower is aimed. Vegetius' answer to this was to construct a siege-tower with a telescopic stage, which is sunk within the tower until the last moment when it is hauled up by ropes and pulleys to overtop the wall or its height extension. Whether such "telescopic" towers ever were actually deployed is doubtful.

*Chapter 20*: describes a defense against a siege-tower by tunneling out from the walls once it was clear along which route the tower was to be advanced; when it reached the head of the tunnel it would sink under its own weight.

*Chapter 21*: deals with the hazards of troops on scaling-ladders and attributes the invention of this mode of assault to Capaneus, an obscure hero from ancient Greek mythology whose name would have meant very little to a medieval commander. It also describes a swing bridge attachment to a siege-tower which is lowered onto the enemy wall by pulleys at the last moment and another type of bridge thrust out from the tower.

*Chapter 22*: describes the *ballista*, a type of mounted crossbow strung with ropes made of animal sinews and which requires specially trained operatives, and the *onager*. The Latin means "wild ass" and this machine, also powered by multiple sinew cordage, Vegetius reckons the most powerful of the stone-throwers. Vegetius says nothing about how the thing actually worked; perhaps it was powered by the torsion of the twisted sinews being suddenly released.

*Chapter 24*: describes two types of mining operation (alluding again to the mining industry of the Thracians, presumably the Bessi, a people of north-eastern Thrace, a region known for its mine workings): First, the piercing of tunnels under the walls through which assault parties may penetrate the town; second, the incendiary mine beneath the foundation of the walls to collapse them.

*Chapter 26*: describes the maneuver of faked retirement by the besieging force. The ruse was used at Antioch in 1198 and on numerous other occasions.

*Chapter 30*: how to arrive at the specifications for scaling-ladders and siege-towers. One method of measuring the height was to fire an arrow, with string attached, to the top of the battlements (presumably from as near the base of the wall as possible). A second method was to measure the length of the shadow cast by the wall and compare it with shadow cast at the same time by a rod of known length.

Vegetius ends this part of his summary of machines and maneuvers in land warfare by re-emphasizing that no amount of skill or apparatus can save a fortress that has not been properly provisioned.

### Book II
*Chapter 11*: a legion had carpenters and other artisans in wood working as well as masons and blacksmiths, who could be employed in building winter quarters or making machines of war and wooden (siege-) towers. They even had miners skilled like the Bessi (Henry V of England, one remembers, used professional miners from the Forest of Dean for tunneling operations against the walls of Harfleur).

*Chapter 19*: Vegetius recommends that some soldiers be skilled in note-taking, chiefly for maintaining the weapons inventory. Sire Daviot de Poix was consulted by the commission drawing up the inventory for Philip the Good of Burgundy's proposed crusade of 1454—a very comprehensive document. It seems that a clerk did attend the Burgundian artillery train as record-keeper.

*Chapter 22*: deals with three types of bandsmen to accompany the army. Trumpeters (*tubicen*; tuba, the straight trumpet) had the duty of sounding attack or retreat for the infantry; "horn or cornet" (*cornu*) players gave signals for the maneuvers of standard-bearers; and players of the curved trumpet (*bucinatores*) sounded the special trumpet call (the *classicum*), to signal the presence of the emperor. There are many records of trumpeters with medieval armies, though commanders hardly needed book learning to specify this item of equipment.

*Chapter 25*: this chapter deals with "iron weapons" and the machines of the legion including the *carrobalista*, a missile-throwing weapon hauled by mules; fifty-five such weapons are specified for each legion. There should also be small boats (hollowed-out logs) and ropes for preparing pontoon bridges.

### Book III
*Chapter 7*: casks can be used for pontoons.

*Chapter 8*: deals with laying out and preparing a camp.

*Chapter 24*: speaks of sickle-bearing chariots and elephants in battle; the use of *tribulos* (caltrops) against cavalry and of *carroballistae* that shoot arrows.

### Book IV

*Chapter 2*: on defensive walls. These should be angled, not straight, so that the attackers find themselves surrounded as if in a bay.

*Chapter 3*: two walls should be built about 20 feet apart and the space between, packed with earth from the ditch, solidly rammed down. Outer walls should be successively lower so as to give the innermost defenders a commanding view of the enemy's approach.

*Chapter 4*: gates should be protected by an outer bulwark and the wall above them should have openings through which water can be poured to extinguish any fire started by the enemy.

*Chapter 6*: speaks of *metellas*, apparently "trip" baskets filled with stone to be tipped down onto assault troops.

*Chapter 7*: exclude useless mouths, the old, women and children, from the start.

*Chapter 8*: maintain a store of bitumen, sulphur, liquid pitch and "the oil which men call incendiary" *(oleum quod incendiarum vocant*; presumably petroleum) to be used for burning the machines of the enemy. Also store round stones from river beds because these are heavier in proportion to their density; keep the larger for stone-throwing machines and the largest for rolling down from the ramparts. Oppose war machines with war machines; and keep stores of iron nails, beams and planks for raising the height of your wall in emergency.

*Chapter 9*: hold a supply of sinews for the *ballistae*, otherwise they are useless. Horsehair can be used and even the hair of women in emergency. He refers to an attack on the capitol at Rome when the *ballistae* were failing through wear and tear and the supply of sinews were failing; how the women cut off their long tresses because they preferred "to live in freedom with their husbands" with the temporary disgrace of shorn heads rather than as the servants of the enemy.

# Glossary of Technical Terms

Since the accounts of medieval military engagements were, in general, written by clerics with little experience of warfare or of the apparatus and maneuvers they were recording, terminology is not always precise or reliable.

* indicates a cross-reference with another glossary term.

*agrément*—a truce agreed between defenders and attackers that a castle or town should be surrendered if certain conditions were met.

*arbalet*—an improved type of *crossbow, fitted with a cranked mechanism to help increase the pull on the string.

*arrow loops* (French, *archères*)—slits in the walls of a fortress through which the bowmen of the garrison could fire from protected positions. On the inward side the slit splayed out, allowing the archer to move from one side to the other so as to command a wide arc of fire. On the same principle, a gun loop comprised a small circular aperture with, behind it, a splayed platform to mount a light artillery piece within the castle wall.

*bailey*—an area, or ward, of a castle enclosed with a *curtain-wall or palisade; in it might be outbuildings such as stables or residential quarters, or possibly, in a royal castle, a banqueting hall. A large castle might have two baileys, one enclosing the other, or even three as at Château Gaillard, where an outer bailey guarded the *moat entrance to the main fortress which could only be approached across a bridge from this outer bailey.

*ballista*—artillery weapon operating on the principle of a giant *crossbow mounted on a frame. But the term (like *petraria*) seems often to be used of stone-throwing artillery in general.

*barbican*—masonry outwork built to protect the approach to a castle gate.

*bastide*—fortified market township, notably in south-western France, established by the policy both of the French and English governments to plant trade on a firm footing in bandit country and later against the armies of rival jurisdictions. Many of the market towns in the region of the Dordogne today, then part of English Gascony, received their foundation charters from English kings, notably Edward I.

*bastion*—an outwork tower projecting from a rampart or curtain-wall. The word apparently derived from medieval French *bastir*, "to build."

*batter*—the downward widening of the lower part of an outward facing castle wall toward its base. This would make it less vulnerable to sapping. Toward the end of the medieval period, in the event his castle did not have this feature, a commander might order that the lower courses of masonry of a wall or *bastion be protected with *gabions, stacked sandbag-fashion in front of it, in anticipation of the attack.

*battlement*—a defensive feature atop a wall in which *merlon alternates with *embrasure to provide openings in a parapet from which soldiers can fire missile weapons or dump missiles on men below and rapidly retreat for cover.

*belfry* (French, *befroi*)—a moveable *siege-tower. In this case, it was often fitted with a pivoted ramp at the top, to be swung down on to the enemy *rampart once the tower was in place so that the attackers could fight their way on to it. It may derive, as does the German *Berchfrit*, from an Old Teutonic word meaning "place of shelter."

*berquil*—a large outer reservoir within the *curtain-wall. It was a feature of some crusader and Arab castles (classically, Krak des Chevaliers) and provided an additional defense against attackers who had penetrated the outer walls.

*black powder*—the earliest form of gunpowder, now displaced by smokeless powders in ammunition for fire arms though still used for fireworks, signal maroons and other devices. The mixture, of salt petre (potassium nitrate), sulphur and charcoal, which must be ignited by fire or heat, burns out rapidly, yielding about two fifths of explosive gaseous products and the rest in solid particles appearing as smoke.

*bolt*—another name for the quarrel, the short heavy missile fired from a *crossbow. In Froissart it may denote an iron missile fired from a cannon.

*bore*—a device, as the name implies, for "drilling" a hole through masonry. It seems to have comprised a massive cylindrical beam shod with an iron point like an arrowhead, and to have been rotated by means of a giant bow drill. Necessarily the operating team worked under a protective roofing, *cat or *mantelet.

*brattice*—a wooden gallery or hoarding, particularly one constructed to overhang the base of the walls so that defenders could harass attackers working to undermine the foundations or raise *scaling-ladders, without themselves coming under fire.

*casemate*—a vaulted chamber built in the thickness of a castle's ramparts.

*castellan*—the governor of a castle and commander of its garrison.

*castellation* also *crenellation*—the addition of intermittent rising masonry members on the parapet atop a fortress wall ("the battlements"), to provide cover to bowmen or handgunners firing from the wall.

*cat*—see "mantelet."

*chevet*—a semicircular or polygonal east end of a church, which in the chapel of a fortress might project beyond the circuit of the walls.

*circumvallation*—literally the building of a wall around a castle so as to seal it off from any potential relieving force, or to prevent the garrison from making sorties to forage for supplies.

*concentric castle*—term for a style of castle design from the mid-twelfth to late-fourteenth centuries; the basic layout is of a central stronghold or keep ringed by circuits of outer walls. Sometimes a fortress acquired a concentric configuration as the result of additions and modifications over time—the classic instance of this is the Tower of London. More often this type of castle was so designed from the start, for example Beaumaris in Anglesey or Château Gaillard in Normandy.

*constable*—the commander of a town or of the troops in a garrison.

*cranequin*—a rack and pinion device to help brace the string of a crossbow.

*crenellation*—an alternative term for the familiar *battlements atop a castle wall. The term seems to have been adopted in the nineteenth century in England; in medieval French the word was *crénelage*, both deriving ultimately from the French *créneau* or *crénel*, meaning a niche or gap. The first edition of the *Oxford English Dictionary* cites as its earliest usage a book on domestic architecture of 1852: "Laurence de Ludlow had license to crenellate his mansion of Stoke Say." In his *Complete Guide to Heraldry* of 1929 A.C. Fox Davies describes one line of partition on an heraldic shield as "embattled" but notes that "the term *crenelé* is used almost equally often."

*crossbow*—short bow mounted "crosswise" on a wooden stock (see page 48). Its design meant that the string could be "braced" to a much higher tension than in the simple bow and the tension maintained until the projectile could be loaded before firing. Later improvements and modifications such as the *manivel and *cranequin enabled a still greater pull and tension. A remark by Margaret Paston of Norfolk, about a neighbor's preparations for a siege suggests that the crossbow was never fired from a prone position.

*culverin*—a long-barreled light cannon used in French field artillery from the mid-1450s.

*curtain-wall*—a non-structural wall of a castle intended purely as a defensive obstruction; to that end it could be punctuated by towers or turrets but it was also pierced by entry gates.

*donjon*—French term for the central tower or *keep of a castle. The fact that the English word "dungeon," presumably derived from it, denotes a subterranean prison cell, vividly reminds us that for the subject Anglo-Saxon population post-1066, the menacing Norman towers that sprang up across the English landscape, meant only one thing—the rat-infested torture chambers that were their cellars.

*drawbridge*—the French *pont-levis* (raise bridge) gives a perhaps more accurate description. The apparatus was more or less standard in any sizeable castle and was generally found in combination with a *portcullis. Raising mechanisms commonly used counterweights to assist the downpull required and so speed the lift. With this, the weight-driven mechanical clock and the counterweight trebuchet, medieval Europe may be said to have pioneered the use of gravity as applied energy.

*embrasure*—another word for a gun or *arrow loop, that is, a slit for firing through, with a widening opening behind that enables the marksman to vary his angle of fire. It also sometimes describes the gaps or crenels between the *merlons of a *battlement.

*enceinte*—the entire circuit of a *curtain-wall; and the area of a castle contained within it.

*fosse*—a defensive dry ditch to protect a castle or town wall.

*gabion*—a rubble- or earth-filled barrel or wicker basket, used to shore up an advancing sap in seventeenth- and eighteenth-century siege operations; but similar things are sometimes used in earlier periods.

*glacis*—a very pronounced and extensive outward-sloping masonry projection built out from the lower courses of a castle wall to protect from sappers and miners. An exaggerated version of the *batter.

*Greek fire*—the most famous of all medieval weapons using combustibles; according to tradition it was invented at Constantinople during the 674–8 Arab siege of the city by a Syrian Christian called Kallinikos. For a discussion of recipes and methods of deployment see pages 52–5.

*herald*—an official of the court of chivalry who carried messages between warring camps, issued the summons to surrender and discharged other "liaison" functions that could be dangerous. He usually wore a type of sleeveless tunic, embellished with highly colorful heraldic blazons of his employer's coat-of-arms, or of the particular office of arms in his employer's household military establishment. A kind of ambassador in the field in time of war, like that of an ambassador his person enjoyed immunity.

*joust*—a combat between two knights on horseback (*tourney).

*keep*—the central or the largest tower of a fortress, the last refuge of a garrison in time of siege. The French term *donjon* is also used.

*loop*—* arrow loop.

*machicolation*—a stone gallery-like projection from a castle wall. Generally floored with wooden planks, it had floor holes through which missiles could be dropped, typically on enemy sappers aiming to dislodge masonry from the lower courses of the wall.

*mangonel*—a mechanical sling hurling missiles on a low trajectory, possibly powered by torsion: in the early twenty-first century the very existence of such a device has been questioned.

*manivel*—a windlass mechanism for increasing the tension on a *crossbow string.

*mantelet*—a roofed shelter, usually mounted on a wheeled frame, to protect attackers approaching the walls of a castle—typically a battering-ram detail—from missiles. An unwheeled *mantelet might also be carried into place and, if possible, anchored to the wall so as to protect sappers dislodging masonry with picks.

*merlon*—the rising masonry element of a castellated battlement.

*meutrières*—French for "murder holes" or apertures, usually in the roof of an enclosed access passage along which the attackers were forced to travel to gain the entry gate; also such apertures in side walls.

*moat*—a water-filled ditch protecting, usually encircling, a fortress. It needed a river, stream or lake nearby from which it could be filled and kept replenished. Perversely it seems to derive from the French word *motte* the artificial mound on which stood the tower of a *motte and bailey castle. The French word for moat is *douve*. Another word from the French, *fosse* from Latin *fodere*, to dig up, is sometimes used to designate a dry moat guarding fortresses where no water is available to feed a moat proper— for example, the rock-hewn ravines at the crusader castle of Sayun in Palestine or at Château Gaillard, in Normandy.

*motte and bailey*—the name given to a type of castle widespread in Normandy and brought over to England after 1066. In its simplest form, it comprised a wooden fort on a mound of earth (the *motte*), thrown up so as to leave a ditch or moat round its base, surrounded by an open space or ward, the bailey guarded by a *palisade.

*murder hole*—*meutrières.

*palisade*—a defensive structure constructed of timber uprights rather than of masonry work.

*pavise*—a large heavy wooden standing shield, wedged firmly in the ground and secured with supports; its function was to provide shelter for *crossbow men while "bracing" their bowstrings and lodging the bolt in its channel in the stock for release against the enemy target.

*petrariae*—general term for stone-throwing war machines.

*portcullis*—literally a "sliding gate." The familiar grid of massive timber sliding in stone channels either side the main entrance to a castle that could be released to fall in an instant so as to bar any attempt to rush an entry, before the *drawbridge could be raised.

*postern*, or *postern gate*—literally "a back gate," the word deriving ultimately from the Latin *posterus* for "coming behind." In the terminology of fortification, a postern was any small gate or opening in the outer wall situated unobtrusively, possibly hidden by a fold in the terrain or giving on to a *fosse where a castle had such a dry *moat. If it was unobserved by the attackers it could be used by messengers from a relieving force; more usually it might be opened for a sortie to be made.

*rampart*—strictly an earthen embankment either surrounding a fortified place, or guarding a stretch of the defenses; often ramparts were topped with a *battlemented wall or wooden palisade.

*siege-tower*—fortified tower built by besiegers, typically to threaten or control an entry gate to the fortress under attack. A classic instance was the counter-castle erected opposite the great gates of that city at the crusaders siege of Antioch. The term can also sometimes designate a wooden tower structure on a wheeled frame base, more correctly called a *belfry, that could be moved up to the wall of a castle so that the attackers could fire down on the defenders. Commonly it had a swing platform: In the "up" position on the approach, so as to protect the soldiers from hostile missiles, this was dropped at the last moment to provide a bridge onto the top of the wall. All such structures were usually hung with soaked hides or matting to protect as far as possible from fire attack. Sometimes a battering ram, or even a cannon, was installed at the base of the tower.

*siphonophore*—(literally, siphon-carrier) a vessel of the Byzantines equipped with a kind of pressure pump flame-thrower for delivering *Greek or liquid fire.

*talus*—alternative term for a large *glacis.

*tortoise* (Latin, *testudo*)—in Roman terminology the *testudo* was an infantry formation in which the soldiers interlocked shields to the front and over their heads to create an armored protective covering when advancing against an opposing army or moving into an assault on a fortress. Medieval commanders and their advisers would be familiar with the term from Roman military handbooks, notably Vegetius, but chroniclers sometimes use the term of what are clearly *mantelet-like moveable structures, whether wheeled or carried, deployed to protect teams of sappers attacking the base of a wall.

*tourney*, or *tournament*—essentially a mock battle with its own rules of engagement in which often quite large bodies of knights fought in teams and in which prisoners and ransoms might be taken and even lives lost.

*trebuchet*—a mechanical sling, powered by a counterweight, hurling missiles on a high trajectory (see Chapter 4). It seems to have been invented in the twelfth century, being a European crusader development of a similar Chinese machine operated by manpower. The history of the weapon is still much debated.

*ward*—an open area or courtyard within a castle's defenses.

# Notes on the Sources

## Introduction

An incident from *Le Morte D'Arthur*, attributed by William Caxton, its first publisher (1485), to a "Sir Thomas Malory," opens the account; the sieges of Frederick Barbarossa are drawn from Peter Munz's biography of the emperor and those of his grandson, Emperor Frederick II, from the biography by Thomas Curtis Van Cleve. I am much indebted to these two authors in various later chapters. Events in the Holy Land, here and elsewhere in the book, draw on Sir Steven Runciman's classic account of the crusades in English. W. L. Warren's life of King John was the basis for my account of certain sieges and battles during that reign, and Richard Barber's *The Knight and Chivalry* provided some details for his brother's early career.

## Chapter 1

In this short chapter I drew again upon Van Cleve and, among other works, upon Thomas Hodgkin's epic, *Italy and her Invaders*. Mark Bartusis provided fascinating detail of events within the walls of Constantinople at a time of civil war.

## Chapter 2

Again, Runciman was useful but so also were my own early *Castles of Europe* and Alfred Duggan's lucid and fast-moving account of the Angevin family. The excellent HMSO guidebooks to Orford and Caernarvon (*sic*) were of great use, while Charles Ross's biography of Edward IV provided valuable detail and Arnold Taylor's important biography of James St. George in the *Oxford Dictionary of National Biography* provided authoritative updates on his career. Richard Barber's *The Pastons* provides an attractive access to that treasure trove of fifteenth-century social and political archive known as the "Paston Letters," edited by James Gairdner.

## Chapter 3

Anna Comnena, daughter of Byzantine emperor Alexius I, wrote a eulogizing biography of her father and so left a rich source for the late eleventh century in the Middle East. Mark Bartusis, in his book on the late Byzantine army, reminds us of the professionalism of that body, while for my comments on the siege of Rhodes and much else of the military knights I drew on Desmond Seward's *The Monks of War*.

## Chapter 4

Froissart provides us with the bulk of the narrative for the siege of Tournai. Here, Michael Prestwich's biography of Edward I sources much of the account of Welsh matters and Van Cleve's biography of Emperor Frederick II for the doings of the Brescians in the 1230s. The ingenious Arab sea captain is to be found in the second volume of Runciman's history of the Crusades, and the details of the site of Dolforwyn Castle in Wales in the pages of *Current Archaeology*.

## Chapter 5

The remarkable account of Greek fire burning underwater comes from John Julius Norwich; the travails of John of Gaunt in his Normandy campaign from his twentieth-century biographer Sidney Armitage-Smith, and the hazards of fire during the Damietta campaign from Joineville. I am indebted to an article by Jim Bradbury for the intriguing speculation that petroleum might have been one of the ingredients of Greek fire, while my observations on Vegetius are much indebted to Leo Stelten's translated edition of this classic work.

## Chapter 6

Professor Bert Hall's work on gunpowder was of basic importance to this chapter, including the detail of the events at St. Sauveur. Details of guns in London's Guild Hall come from the *Oxford English Dictionary*; the expenditure on men and artillery in France in the 1470s from P. S. Lewis; and of the Burgundian artillery establishment, its commanders and matériel from the ducal biographies by Richard Vaughan. The 1453 siege of Constantinople is covered in detail by Runciman in his book on the fall of the city, while I went to William Miller's *Latins in the Levant* for the siege of Corinth. The incident involving the French artillery man Jean Bureau and the fate of John Talbot, earl of Shrewsbury, is touched on in E. F. Jacob's classic, *The Fifteenth Century*, and the account of German and Italian mercenary artillerymen in Spain in the late 1400s is mentioned in Desmond Seward's *The Monks of War*.

## Chapter 7

Details of the siege of Bréteuil come from Froissart; the siege of Ascalon from volume two of Runciman's *Crusades*; and the account of Count Belisarius and the floating mills at the siege of Rome from Thomas Hodgkin's classic, *Italy and Her Invaders*. Inevitably, my account of the siege of Malta is indebted to Ernle Bradford's great book on the subject. As always, Richard Vaughan's biographies supply the foundation for my comments on matters Burgundian.

## Chapter 8

Professor Michael Prestwich's paper at the Medieval Warfare Day at the National Army Museum, Chelsea, in October 2006, provided a number of valuable points for this chapter. The land qualifications for knights at arms and much of the logistics of horse transport were found in Peter Reid's *By Fire and Sword*; Charles Wendell David's *The Capture of Lisbon* was the starting point for my account of the siege of Lisbon during the Second Crusade. For the Fourth Crusade I drew on translations of Villehardouin; and for the Damietta campaign volume two of Runciman's *Crusades*. The fate of Salerno under its own lord, Gisulf the Lombard, came from *The Normans in the South* of John Julius Norwich.

## Chapter 9

The story of the siege by trickery by the Bascot de Mauleon comes from Froissart, as does the account of the siege of La Rochelle. The maneuvers at Acre are found in Arabic sources in the anthology by Francesco Gabrieli; the account of the shepherd boys' game at the Ostrogoth siege of Rome is recorded in Thomas Hodgkin's account, while the episode of the Dover garrison during the barons' wars is recounted in Maurice Powicke's *Henry III and the Lord Edward*, with further detail from Jonathan Coad's *Dover Castle*. The campaigns of Villehardouin in Greece and the siege of Momenvasia come from Miller, and the siege of Damascus from the second volume of Runciman's *Crusades*.

## Chapter 10

Much here derives from the works of Arab historians, notably Imad ad Din, in Francesco Gabrieli's anthology. Valuable insights into the legal status of women in Outremer are to be gained from the articles of James A. Brundage. T. S. R. Boase on the crusaders provided further detail. I am also happy here to reciprocate a courtesy of the acknowledgment my friend the late Régine Pernoud in her *La femme au temps des Croisades* made to my biography of Saladin.

## Chapter 11

Perhaps not strictly related to my theme of the siege, though relevant in so far as King Henry V of England would not have campaigned in France had he not wished to vindicate his claim to the French throne, and, certainly remarkable, was the observation I cite by the French historian Jean-François Chiappe to the effect that that claim was probably the most secure in international law of any in history. However, more germane to this chapter is the work of Maurice Keen in his *Laws of War*. The account of the siege of Calais is filled out from the pages of Froissart and events in Gascony from the book by Margaret Labarge; Italian episodes from Allen's history of Verona and Orville Prescott's book on the Renaissance princes and that of the Scottish mercenaries at the siege of Melun from E. F. Jacob. For this chapter I also drew on Ian Mortimer's life of Henry IV, Armitage-Smith on John of Gaunt, and Kenneth Fowler, *The King's Lieutenant*.

## Chapter 12

Desmond Seward's *The Monks of War* outlines the siege of Marienburg, while the comments on the Burgundians at Granson come from Philippe de Commynes. The best account of the siege of Château Gaillard is still, I consider, that compiled from the French chronicles by Kate Norgate in her *England under the Angevin Kings*, and it was this that I used in my *Castles of Europe*, a somewhat more extended account than the one given here. The fate of the Brescians comes from Van Cleve's biography of Emperor Frederick II and that of the city of Piacenza from Prescott on the princes of the Renaissance. Finally, we revisit the great siege of Malta, courtesy of Ernle Bradford.

# Bibliography

Allen, A. M., *A History of Verona* (London, 1910)

Appleby, John T., *England without Richard, 1189–1199* (London, 1965)

Armitage-Smith, Sydney, *John of Gaunt* (London, 1964)

Ayton, Andrew, *History Today* (March 1992)

Barber, Richard, *The Knight and Chivalry* (London, 1970)

———, *The Pastons: A Family in the Wars of the Roses* (London, 1984)

Bartusis, Mark C., *The Late Byzantine Army: Arms and Society, 1204–1453* (Pennsylvania, 1992)

Boase, T. S. R., *Kingdoms and Strongholds of the Crusaders* (London, 1971)

Bradford, Ernle, *The Great Betrayal: Constantinople 1204* (London, 1967)

———, *The Great Siege: Malta 1565* (London, 1967)

Brereton, Geoffrey, ed. and trans., *Froissart Chronicles* (Harmondsworth, 1968)

Brundage, James A., *The Crusade, Holy War and Canon Law* (Aldershot, 1991)

Burne, Alfred H., *The Crécy War* (London, 1955)

Butler, Lawrence, *Current Archaeology* no. 120 (1990)

Chiappe, Jean-François, *La France et le roi de la restauration à nos jours* (Paris, 1994)

Cipolla, Carlo M. and Derek Birdsall, *The Technology of Man: A Visual History* (London, 1980)

Coad, Jonathan, *Dover Castle* (London, 2007)

Coles, Paul, *The Ottoman Impact on Europe* (London, 1968)

Commynes, Philippe de, *see* Michael Jones

Corrigan, Gordon, *Mud, Blood and Poppycock* (London, 2003)

Cowen, Janet, *Sir Thomas Malory Le Morte d'Arthur* (Harmondsworth, 1969)

David, Charles Wendell, *De expugnatione Lyxbonensis (The Capture of Lisbon)* (New York, 1936)

Davies, Norman, *Europe: A History* (London, 1997)

Duggan, Alfred, *Devil's Brood: The Angevin Family* (London, 1950)

DeVries, Kelly, *Medieval Military Technology* (Ontario, 1992)

Fowler, Kenneth, *The King's Lieutenant: Henry of Grosmont, First Duke of Lancaster, 1310–1361* (London, 1969)

France, John, *Victory in the East: A Military History of the First Crusade* (Cambridge, 1994)

Froissart, *see* Geoffrey Brereton

Gabrieli, Francesco, *Arab Historians of the Crusades*, trans. E J Costello (London, 1969)

Gairdner, James, *The Paston Letters 1422–1509*, 6 vols (London, 1901)

Hall, Bert, "European Gunpowder 1250–1600: From Oriental Curiosity to Critical War

Matériel," in *Proceedings of the Society for the History of Medieval Technology and Science* (Oxford, 8 June 2002) available online at http://www.shmts.org (accessed March 2008)

Heymann, Frederick G., *John Žižka and the Hussite Revolution* (Princeton, 1955)

Hindley, Geoffrey, *Castles of Europe* (London, 1968)

———, *Under Siege* (London, 1979)

———, *The Crusades* (London and New York, 2003)

———, *Saladin* (London, 1976; new rev. edn, London, 2007)

Hodgkin, Thomas, *Italy and her Invaders*, 2nd edn, 8 vols (Oxford, 1892–9)

Hooper, N. and M. Bennet, *The Cambridge Illustrated Atlas of Warfare: The Middle Ages 768–1487* (Cambridge, 1996)

Hutchinson, Harold F., *Edward II: The Pliant King* (London, 1971)

Jacob, E. F., *The Fifteenth Century 1399-1485* (Oxford, 1992)

James, Peter and Nick Thorpe, *Ancient Inventions* (London, 1995)

Jeffreys, Steven, *A Medieval Siege* (London, 1973)

Jones, Michael, trans., *Philippe de Commynes, Memoirs: The Reign of Louis XI 1461–83* (Harmondsworth, 1972)

Keen, M. H., *The Laws of War in the Late Middle Ages* (London 1965)

———, ed., *Medieval Warfare: A History* (Oxford, 1999)

Kendall, Paul Murray, *Louis XI* (London, 1971)

Labarge, Margaret Wade, *Gascony, England's First Colony* (London, 1980)

Lewis, P. S., *Later Medieval France: The Polity* (London, New York, 1968)

McKisack, May, *The Fourteenth Century*, 1307–1399 (Oxford, 1959)

Miller, William, *The Latins in the Levant* (London, 1908)

Mortimer, Ian, *The Fears of Henry IV* (London, 2007)

Munz, Peter, *Frederick Barbarossa: A Study in Medieval Politics* (London, 1969)

Nicolle, David, *The Routledge Medieval Warfare Source Book*, 2 vols (London, 1996)

Nohl, Johannes, *The Black Death* (London, 1961)

Norgate, Kate, *England under the Angevin Kings*, 2 vols (London, 1887)

Norris, John, *Medieval Siege Warfare* (Stroud, 2007)

Norwich, John Julius, *The Normans in the South* (London, 1967)

Pernoud, Régine, *La femme au temps des Croisades* (Paris, 1990)

Powicke, Maurice, *Henry III and the Lord Edward*, 2 vols (London, 1947)

Prescott, Orville, *Princes of the Renaissance* (London, 1969)

Prestwich, Michael, *The Three Edwards, War and State in England 1272–1377* (Methuen, 1980)

———, *Edward I* (Methuen, 1988)

———, National Army Museum Medieval Study Day, 28 October 2006

Reid, Peter, *By Fire and Sword* (London, 2007)

Ross, Charles, *Edward IV* (Berkeley, 1974)

Runciman, Steven, *A History of the Crusades*, 3 vols (Cambridge, 1951–4)

———, *Constantinople 1453* (Cambridge, 1965)

Scott, Martin, *Medieval Europe* (London, 1964)

Seward, Desmond, *The Monks of War* (London, 1995)

Taylor, Arnold, "James St. George," in the *Oxford Dictionary of National Biography* (Oxford, 2004)

Thompson, E. A., *A Roman Reformer and Inventor* (Oxford, 1952)

Van Cleve, Thomas Curtis, *The Emperor Frederick II of Hohenstaufen* (Oxford, 1972)

Vale, Malcolm, *War and Chivalry* (London, 1981)

Vaughan, Richard, *Philip the Bold: The Formation of the Burgundian State* (London, 1962)

———, *John the Fearless: The Growth of Burgundian Power* (London, 1966)

———, *Philip the Good, the Apogee of Burgundy* (London, 1970)

———, *Charles the Bold* (London, 1973)

Verbruggen, J. F., *The Art of Warfare in Western Europe during the Middle Ages*, 2nd edn (Woodbridge, 1997)

Warren, W. L., *King John* (London, 1961)

# Index

Page numbers in **bold** indicate illustrations or line drawings